THEORY AND POLICY IN POLITICAL ECONOMY

NEW DIRECTIONS IN MODERN ECONOMICS SERIES

Series Editor: Malcolm C. Sawyer, Professor of Economics, University of York.

New Directions in Modern Economics presents a challenge to orthodox economic thinking. It focuses on new ideas emanating from radical traditions including post-Keynesian, Kaleckian, neo-Ricardian and Marxian. The books in the series do not adhere rigidly to any single school of thought but share in common an attempt to present a positive alternative to the conventional wisdom.

The main emphasis of the series is on the development and application of new ideas to current problems in economic theory and economic policy. It will include new original contributions to theory, overviews of work in the radical tradition and the evaluation of alternative economic policies. Some books will be monographs whilst others will be suitable for adoption as texts. The series will highlight theoretical and policy issues common to all modern economies and is designed to appeal to economists throughout the world regardless of their country of origin.

Published titles:

Post-Keynesian Monetary Economics: New Approaches to Financial Modelling
Edited by Philip Arestis

Keynes's Principle of Effective Demand
Edward J. Amadeo

New Directions in Post-Keynesian Economics
Edited by John Pheby

THEORY AND POLICY IN POLITICAL ECONOMY

Essays in Pricing, Distribution and Growth

Edited by
PHILIP ARESTIS
and
YIANNIS KITROMILIDES

EDWARD ELGAR

Published by
Edward Elgar Publishing Limited
Gower House
Croft Road
Aldershot
Hants GU11 3HR
England

Gower Publishing Company
Old Post Road
Brookfield
Vermont 05036
USA

British Library Cataloguing in Publication Data

Theory and policy in political economy: essays in pricing, distribution and growth. – (Thames papers in political economy).
1. Economics
I. Arestis, P (Philip), *1941–* II. Kitromilides, Yiannis III. Series
330

Library of Congress Cataloging-in-Publication Data

Theory and policy in political economy : essays in pricing, distribution, and growth / edited by Philip Arestis and Yiannis Kitromilides.
p. cm.
Includes bibliographical references.
ISBN 1–85278–205–6
1. Prices—Government policy. 2. Distribution (Economic theory) 3. Economic development. I. Arestis, Philip, 1941– . II. Kitromilides, Yiannis.
HB236.A3T44 1989
330.15—dc20 89–23544
CIP

ISBN 1 85278 205 6

Contents

Contributors vii

Foreword ix
G.C. Harcourt, University of Cambridge

Introduction 1
Philip Arestis, Polytechnic of East London, and Yiannis Kitromilides, Thames Polytechnic

1 The Theoretical Significance of Keynes's General Theory 14
Athanasios Asimakopulos, McGill University

2 An Essay on Keynes and General Equilibrium Theory 43
Peter Skott, University of Aarhus

3 The Political Economy of the Phillips Curve 100
Malcolm Sawyer, University of York

4 Market Structure and Firm Behaviour: An Empty Box? 130
Paul Auerbach, Kingston Polytechnic

5 Competition, Monopoly Power and the Prices of Production 157
Amitava Krishna Dutt, University of Notre Dame

6 G.C. Means's Doctrine of Administered Prices 199
Frederic S. Lee, Roosevelt University

7 Kaleckian and Post-Keynesian Theories of Pricing: Some Extensions and Implications 229
Peter J. Reynolds, Staffordshire Polytechnic

8 Vicious Circles and Cumulative Causation 270
Peter Skott, University of Aarhus

Index 301

Contributors

Philip Arestis, Polytechnic of East London

Athanasios Asimakopulos, McGill University

Paul Auerbach, Kingston Polytechnic

Amitava Krishna Dutt, University of Notre Dame

G.C. Harcourt, University of Cambridge

Yiannis Kitromilides, Thames Polytechnic

Frederic S. Lee, Roosevelt University

Peter J. Reynolds, Staffordshire Polytechnic

Malcolm Sawyer, University of York

Peter Skott, University of Aarhus

To all contributors to the Thames Papers in Political Economy *series and in particular to Alfred S. Eichner, who was also in the past one of the editors of the series.*

Foreword

G.C. Harcourt

It is a pleasure to write a foreword to this, the third collection of *Thames Papers*. Until the *Cambridge Journal of Economics* and the *Journal of Post Keynesian Economics* were established there were few outlets for publication by maverick economists. The editors of the *Thames Papers in Political Economy* therefore provided an invaluable and courageous service by providing an alternative mode of publication for those scholars whose approaches came under the very broad heading of post-Keynesian economics. The present selection is, as I noted, the third to be put together, this time under the general rubric of pricing, distribution and growth, while the first section contains important reflective essays on theory and policy.

A characteristic feature – I would say *the* characteristic feature – of post-Keynesian economies is a preoccupation with the interrelationships between pricing, distribution and growth. Thus, it is no accident that our founding fathers and mothers put great emphasis on them, and, especially in the case of Kalecki, first explicitly built up their models of the operation of the economy as a whole over time by giving detailed treatment to each one of these aspects of economic life on the way, then integrated them together. This is true also of Keynes, except that he took his short-period pricing and distribution theory from Marshall (though he made some acute criticisms in his 'sundry observations on the nature of capital' on the way) and he left the aspects of growth to be developed by others.

Included in the present volume are essays by scholars who have made significant contributions to our understanding of these relationships. Lying behind them is their emphasis on the roles of time and uncertainty that initially comes from the work of Keynes, Kalecki and Kaldor. We are fortunate, therefore, to have as our guides here such clear-headed and experienced teachers as Tom Asimakopulos and Malcolm Sawyer. They have systematically and carefully written about Keynes and Kalecki, emphasizing the nature of their respective methods, and how their methods differ from those of mainstream economists. In this selection we get the fine fruits of their labours. Asimakopulos writes a thorough review of Keynes's theory in *The General Theory* and after, and Sawyer tackles the vexed problems of the Phillips Curve, its interpretation and misinterpretation, especially with regard to the canard that it is an essential part of Keynes's theoretical system and of the policy prescriptions that follow from his system. Very early on in his career Peter Skott saw the links between Keynes' work and the approaches of Nicholas Kaldor; he emphasizes how the latter made explicit what may be conjectured would have been Keynes's frustration at having his contributions confined within the boundaries of general equilibrium theory. For while Keynes would not have denied the existence of mutual determination within parts of his system, yet nevertheless wholly to concentrate on this would be seriously to distort what he was attempting to do, and to show us.

One of the virtues of the present selection is that we are taken back to our founders, e.g. by Fred Lee to G.C. Means and administered prices, and also taken forward into modern syntheses of various stands of post-Keynesian analysis by skilled practitioners, for example, Peter Reynolds, Paul Auerbach and Amitava Dutt. Finally, the important theme of cumulative causation which comes in modern times from the work of Kaldor's mentor Allyn Young, and from the works of Myrdal and Kaldor himself, is developed by Peter Skott.

The overall result is a pleasing set of highly readable papers, stimulating both in themselves and for the pointers which they give to further relevant developments under the broad rubric of post-Keynesian economics. Please read on.

Introduction

Philip Arestis and Yiannis Kitromilides

This is the third volume of a collection of articles drawn from *Thames Papers in Political Economy* (a series published jointly by Polytechnic of East London and Thames Polytechnic). The first volume, published in 1985, was entitled *Post-Keynesian Theory: A Challenge to Neo-Classical Economics* (edited by Philip Arestis and Thanos Skouras). The second, published in 1988, was more narrowly focused on monetary and credit phenomena as the title aptly suggests: *Post-Keynesian Monetary Economics: New Approaches to Financial Modelling* (edited by Philip Arestis).

There are *two* common threads running through the volume. The first is clearly spelt out by Geoff Harcourt in his *Foreword* to this volume: that the main characteristic of post-Keynesian economics is the preoccupation with the interrelationship between pricing, distribution and growth. Post-Keynesians emphasize the fact that modern capitalist economies are dominated by large corporations whose pricing behaviour is simply to add a mark-up on their costs of production. The mark-up is determined by the needs of these corporations to finance investment (there are, of course, post-Keynesian pricing theories which base the determination of the mark-up on Kalecki's 'degree of monopoly'). Consequently, there is a target rate of return required to facilitate the financial requirements of the corporations if the necessary investment is to be undertaken to meet *growth* objectives. Furthermore, a link is established between the mark-up and the wage share which implies that the wage share is determined by the needs of firms to raise finance for capital accumulation. Whilst it is clear from what follows in the volume that the first two features, pricing and distribution, are well covered, the growth element does not find as full a coverage as it might, although it certainly is accounted for in the papers included in the volume. The second common attitude shared by the essays in this collection is their critical appraisal of certain aspects of mainstream economics. We begin with two essays which concentrate on the treatment of time within Keynesian economics.

In Chapter 1 Athanasios Asimakopulos commences by assessing the theoretical significance of Keynes's *General Theory*. It is well known that Keynes was hoping to produce a revolutionary revision of 'classical' economists' 'fundamental theory'. For Keynes such a revision was far more important than acceptance of his policy recommendations. After all 'classical' economists, such as Pigou, had on occasions supported Keynesian policy measures without abandoning their 'fundamental theory'. Also the so-called 'Neoclassical Synthesis' produced Keynesian policy conclusions but with limited effect on the 'fundamental theory' that Keynes had wished to revise. Despite that limited impact, the *General Theory* was, nevertheless, theoretically significant and according to Asimakopulos its importance lies in the introduction of *historical time* as a major element in economic analysis.

Keynes' analysis is greatly indebted to Marshall but although it takes place in the Marshallian short-period, this period must be seen as an interval in an historical process. An important element of this historical process is the fact that short-period outcomes are influenced by expectations of future conditions, which by definition refer to some future time period. Thus, production and investment decisions, although in Keynesian analysis they take place in the short-period, what happens within that period is greatly influenced by events and conditions which occur in some future period of time.

Athanasios Asimakopulos points out that Keynes was not

always consistent in introducing historical time in his analysis. His treatment of the multiplier, for example, is 'ahistorical', in that he assumes that the full multiplier effects are completed within the short-period without reference to historical time or the possibility that such effects might not be completed within the short-period. Nevertheless, despite these limitations and inconsistencies, Athansios Asimakopulos stresses Keynes' great achievement and contribution to theory which was the reconciliation of the conflicting elements of historical time and 'equilibrium'. The conflict is between relevance on the one hand and precise results on the other. Historical time introduces more relevance in economic analysis but less precision, while the reverse is the case with 'equilibrium' analysis. Marshall had grappled with the same problem in his theory of the firm and individual industry. But whereas Marshall attempted to resolve the conflict by drawing a distinction between short-run and long-run equilibrium, Keynes extended Marshall's short-perod 'equilibrium' analysis to the economy as a whole, but he had no interest in long-period 'equilibrium' positions. Instead he concentrated on producing a short-period 'equilibrium' which, however, contained, admittedly only partially and at times inconsistently, historical time. According to Athanasios Asimakopulos it is this aspect of the *General Theory* which is theoretically significant and which constitutes a 'useful starting point for economic analysis that aims to be relevant.'

Peter Skott, in Chapter 2, is critical of the attempts to reinterpret Keynes' theory within the *General Equilibrium* framework. In doing so Skott directs a vigorous and rigorous attack on the thesis that *General Equilibrium* theory is essentially rooted in the *structural unities* of science. He argues that religious adherence to *General Equilibrium* theory certainly impedes progress and that all those attempts by economists to interpret Keynes within such framework illustrates vividly this point. His principal objection is that such interpretations are incompatible with the dynamic aspects of Keynes' analysis: *General Equilibrium* theory is primarily concerned with the properties of static equilibrium, whereas in Keynes' analysis sequential (dynamic) patterns play a crucial role.

Keynes, in Skott's view, attempted to analyse a sequence of temporary equilibrium rather than the properties of one temporary equilibrium configuration.

In this chapter, Peter Skott focuses attention on Keynes's theory of involuntary unemployment in which sequential patterns are of paramount importance. They are so important, in fact, that all *General Equilibrium* interpretations of Keynes' theory must be deficient since they completely ignore this fundamental 'sequential' premise.

What is meant here by sequential patterns is that decisions which need to be taken in a production economy are in practice separated in time. In the labour market, for example, workers' wages and employment levels are determined prior to the determination of prices and variations in stocks which are instrumental in clearing market output. In fact it was Keynes' insistence on the significance of these sequential patterns which led him to the theoretical conclusion of the possibility of 'market failures'. It would therefore be very misleading and contrary to the spirit of Keynesian analysis, which attempts to go beyond short-period equilibrium, to represent this theory within the Walrasian *General Equilibrium* framework, where input and output prices are determined simultaneously. Keynes's theory and *General Equilibrium* theory can be said to be on 'the same side of the fence' in that they are both *general* theories, not *partial* theories. But beyond that apparent and somehow unimportant similarity there is very little in common between the two theories.

Peter Skott argues that there are many objections to Keynes's economics which evolve around the many concessions Keynes made to neoclassicism: the nature of competition, the shape of marginal cost curves, the exogeneity of money supply are probably the most important objections in his view. When the assumptions of oligopolistic competition, of increasing returns and endogenous money are introduced into Keynesian economics, the relevant sequential patterns are bound to assume even greater prominence. This should provide a further firm impetus for the intellectual development of post-Keynesian theory.

In Chapter 3, Malcolm Sawyer offers not so much a critique of mainstream theory, but rather some reflections on the practices of orthodox economists who readily accept and persist with theories which are obviously weak in their theoretical and empirical foundations. Malcolm Sawyer concentrates on the Phillips curve and raises the question of the immense popularity of the Phillips curve explanation of inflation. Such popularity is particularly perplexing in view of the serious weaknesses, both theoretical and empirical, surrounding the Phillips curve. Malcolm Sawyer briefly reviews the strengths of the empirical support for the Phillips curve and notes that doubts were expressed about its empirical validity well before the breakdown of the relationship in the late sixties. He also establishes that there are four distinct and often conflicting measures attached to the term Phillips curve, each containing a different theoretical justification for the relationship. Such divergence of opinion is an indication of how weak the theoretical support is for this relationship and might also account for its wider acceptance, since it can mean different things to different people and still be called the Phillips curve!

The textbook treatment of the Phillips curve is a further illustration of the curious paradox, to which Malcolm Sawyer draws our attention: the relationship is widely and confidently presented as a well-established fact despite the equally widespread confusion over its precise meaning, theoretical derivation and policy implications. Malcolm Sawyer attempts to offer an explanation for this phenomenon. There are several suggestions, inevitably rather speculative, which might account for the Phillips curve's puzzling popularity. What these suggestions have in common is that they all help to explain the popularity of the Phillips curve in terms of the role that it played within the economics profession. For example, Keynesian economists felt uncomfortable with the charge that their conclusions depended on the assumption of wage–price rigidity. The Phillips curve by effectively integrating the labour market into the Keynesian macromodel made the assumption of wage rigidity unnecessary. Furthermore, the claim of discovering a stable long-term relationship is bound to be popular among economists and of course one which emphasizes the economic rather than the non-economic causes of inflation is bound to be even more popular. Another possible explanation is the fact that most economists have a strong faith in the importance of competitive market forces and the Phillips curve provided a reaffirmation in macro-economics of the importance of these forces. Yet another reason which might account for the Phillips curve's popularity is that it provided a very neat and appealing framework for policy debate in terms of the famous 'trade-off'. Finally, as already noted, the variety of meanings and interpretations associated with the Phillips curve may also explain its long-standing acceptance and popularity.

The next two chapters direct their critique of mainstream economics towards the issues of firm behaviour and distribution.

In Chapter 4 Paul Auerbach argues that orthodox micro-economic theory analyses the competitive process in a modern economy through the theoretical concepts of the 'market' and 'industry'. He expresses serious doubts whether such concepts can usefully form the basis of a research programme into firm behaviour. This is because of the impossibility of defining the boundaries, in a consistent and objective way, of the market. Without such delineation market analysis cannot be used to explain or predict firm behaviour. In other words, if the standard textbook proposition that market structure determines the behaviour of firms is to be sustained, it must be possible to define the extent and limits of this market structure without reference to the way firms actually behave. Paul Auerbach argues that such independent *ex ante* delineation is impossible and thus constitutes a serious failure of orthodox theory.

There have been, of course, several attempts to tackle this problem but none, according to Paul Auerbach, has succeeded in effectively delineating market boundaries. One possibility is to define a competitive market as one in which prices tend to uniformity. This procedure is unsatisfactory because, owing to a variety of 'market failures', identical products selling at different prices would have to be placed logically in different markets. Another possibility is to define a market as comprising of all those firms which are aware of each other's behaviour. However, this procedure also meets the objection that a market is defined in terms of the behaviour of its participants and therefore it cannot be simultaneously the determinant of such behaviour. A third possibility is to delineate a market by using the device of the cross-elasticity of demand. This procedure is also unsatisfactory because of the arbitrary nature of determining the 'cut-off' points between two classes of products.

Paul Auerbach's conclusion is that in the absence of any satisfactory method of defining a market or an industry such concepts cannot form the basis of a research programme into firm behaviour and into the nature of the competitive process.

Amitava Dutt's contribution in Chapter 5 deals with the question of the appropriate concept of competition for the analysis of modern economies with large firms. The concept plays contrasting roles in classical and neoclassical economics, but Amitava Dutt is particularly concerned with the debate between two divergent Marxist views on the nature of competition and he develops a model which attempts to reconcile these contrasting Marxist views.

Classical economists perceived competition as the tendency of the rate of profit to be equalized through the mobility of finance capital. Their conception did not rely on the assumption of large numbers of sellers. Neoclassical economics on the other hand developed the notion of perfect competition, which depended among other assumptions on the existence of many sellers, each reacting to a given price without being able individually to influence it. The two concepts are different in many ways, not least in the way they describe competition. Whereas for the classics competition was a process, for the neoclassicals competition refers to a state – an equilibrium state – without any attempt to describe how the economy gets to that state.

The rise of big business and the emergency of the twin phenomena of concentration and centralization of capital necessitated modification to the concept of competition both within neoclassical economics and Marxism. Within the neoclassical school the major modifications resulted from the work of Robinson and Chamberlain on monopoly and monopolistic competition. However, it is the developments which emanate from the work of economists that belong within the Marxist tradition that Amitava Dutt's paper is primarily concerned with.

One group of Marxist writers, the monopoly capital school, have argued that the changes in industrial structure have rendered the laws of competition obsolete and that in the age of monopoly capital it is the power relation between workers, capitalist firms and the state which is the prime regulating force of the capitalist system. For another group, however, these developments, far from removing the forces of competition, had the effect of actually intensifying them. Clearly, there is a sharp distinction between the neoclassical and classical concepts of competition. In the neoclassical sense, competition is perceived as the existence of a large number of price-taking firms. The group of classical Marxist economists considered here see competition as mobility of capital which is continuing and perhaps increasing, and not as price-taking behaviour.

A Sraffian type of model, which allows for the existence of long-run excess capacity despite the utilization of the classical notion of competition, is developed. The long-run equilibrium is determined through the theory of monopoly power and demand-determined output. Relative prices are thus determined by the balance of power relations among social groups. Consequently, the rise in monopoly power might very well increase competition in the classical sense, but would require a theory of prices different from the classical theory.

In the last two chapters, indeed in the whole post-Keynesian pricing theory, there is a tendency for the doctrine of administered prices, as epitomized in G.C. Means's contributions, to be ignored (with perhaps the exception of A.S. Eichner). Frederic Lee in Chapter 6 argues that Eichner's distinction between industrial pricing and commodity pricing, the concept of the megacorp as well as the industrial pricing model itself, and consequent analysis had been influenced by

G.C. Means' work. But that is just about all. Most of the other post-Keynesians hardly mention this work and, indeed, *none* of them discusses G.C. Means's work seriously at all. And yet this work is of paramount importance for post-Keynesian analysis, as is evident from Eichner's work. This chapter aims to elaborate on this proposition by concentrating on G.C. Means's doctrine of administered prices.

This doctrine is based on the notion that modern corporations are run by a common authority which controls and organizes economic resources and consequently co-ordinates economic activity. These large administrative units set the prices of the goods they sell, the wages for the labour they hire and the price of the securities they issue to finance economic activity. However, the degree of 'aggregate and market concentration' of economic activity defines two types of markets – the atomistic and the corporate. Absence of 'aggregrate and market concentration' defines the competitive corporate economy as defined above.

In the administrative sector the multi-plant modern industrial corporation is the typical form. Ownership is clearly separated from control and management. Controllers and high level managers are, therefore, at the wheel of the destiny of the corporate enterprise, not the owners. The large size of this corporation is in itself a barrier to entry. The objective is to maintain the corporate enterprise and to pay the necessary dividends. This growth strategy requires an *administered price policy* determined prior to transactions, not in the process of transaction as in the atomistic markets. These prices are held constant within pricing periods so that the flow of output is determined by demand conditions. Prices are changed, of course, within pricing periods; such changes are dictated by cost considerations. As for costs, they decline with increases in the flow of output (average variable costs are constant while average fixed costs decline with respect to increases in the flow of output). This led G.C. Means to argue that corporations utilize the notions of standard rate of flow of output and standard average total cost – which is, of course, independent of the actual costs of producing specific levels of output. Administered prices are, thus, insensitive to changes in aggregate demand. Consequently, inflation is a phenomenon caused by corporations' pricing policies and not by the prevailing demand conditions.

It would be illuminating at this juncture to consider the relationship between G.C. Means and Kalecki, given the apparent similarity of the two. It is in fact twofold: first, both made a dichotomy between sectors where prices respond to demand changes (Kalecki's demand-determined prices and G.C. Means's competitive corporate economy) and where prices respond to cost changes (Kalecki's cost-determined prices and Means' administered prices). Second, both paid most attention to the second sector, and argued that in this sector demand variations play virtually no role in the movement of prices.

It is because of these similarities with Kalecki's work that Frederic Lee concludes by urging post-Keynesians to pay more attention to the ideas of G.C. Means. Post-Keynesian price theory in particular will benefit enormously from such concern.

Chapter 7 concentrates crucially on the link referred to earlier on within post-Keynesian economics, that of pricing, distribution and capital accumulation. Peter Reynolds begins his contribution by outlining and comparing various approaches to pricing which may loosely be referred to as Kaleckian or post-Keynesian. The important consideration, which is common to all Kaleckian and post-Keynesian models, is that the prices of most finished goods – which Peter Reynolds is mainly concerned with in this chapter – are determined by a mark-up on some measure of unit costs.

As well as Kalecki's model, two models in the 'Kaleckian tradition', proposed by Asimakopulos and Cowling, are considered. In these models the institutional environment in which the firm operates, including particularly the effect of industrial concentration, has a direct and positive effect on firms' mark-ups. In this respect they capture an important feature of Kalecki's pricing analysis. Unfortunately, these models are far less true to Kalecki in their treatment of uncertainty.

The Kaleckian models are compared with the models

adopted by a group of post-Keynesian economists, whereby it is assumed that firms seek to maximize their rate of growth. The most important feature of these models is that a link is made between the pricing and investment decisions. Eichner's model is set out as illustrative of these and some of the standard objections to this model are discussed and dismissed. However, a potentially more serious problem is focused upon.

Eichner's model provides a determinate solution for price, whereby the level of planned investment, the sources of finance for that investment and the mark-up are all jointly determined by the marginal efficiency of investment funds relative to the marginal supply cost of those funds. However, in order to achieve this result, Eichner, too, has assumed away that very uncertainty which had led Kalecki to depart from a simple optimizing model.

By introducing roles for class struggle and uncertainty, an Eichnerian type mark-up model is shown to predict a relationship between the mark-up and the degree of monopoly in much the same way as Kalecki. Consequently, in conditions of a steady state, when expectations are fulfilled and uncertainty is assumed away, the determinate relationships predicted by Eichner would hold but the mark-up would none the less reflect the degree of monopoly factors identified by Kalecki.

Thus, it is argued that the objective of long-run profit or growth maximization need not be inconsistent with a Kaleckian approach to economics but that in the face of uncertainty this objective may come closest to being met by firms adopting a pricing strategy more in tune with Kalecki's own treatment, taking into account the various degrees of monopoly factors identified by him.

Peter Reynolds pursues then some of the implications of the pricing analysis. In the short- and medium-term, the return to higher levels of employment for Western countries as a whole requires not just the co-ordinated expansion of demand but if inflation is not to result, the necessity for a co-ordinated international programme of commodity price controls is highlighted.

By further considering the financing of investment in a modified Eichnerian model, Peter Reynolds shows how increases in the degree of monopoly, brought about, for example, by increases in industrial concentration, could have positive effects on both investment and output, indicating that some of the results of the monopoly capitalism literature may not be as robust as some had previously thought. Peter Reynolds also questions the way in which steady-state equations of the Kaldor–Pasinetti type are interpreted.

In the final chapter (8) Peter Skott returns to the critique of the *General Equilibrium* vision of the world. In this chapter, he contrasts this vision, so prominent in orthodox economic theory, with that of Kaldor–Myrdal, based on the principle of *cumulative causation*, with its twin emphasis on the dual characteristics of advanced and backward sectors in the economy and increasing returns.

The two visions can be distinguished with respect to *three* important respects.

First, in the Kaldor–Myrdal economy, unlike the *General Equilibrium* economy, sequential patterns play a crucial role in influencing the short-run effects of 'exogenous shocks' and producing short-run outcomes which have cumulative effects.

Second, the interplay between economic and non-economic factors is very predominant in the Kaldor–Myrdal model and almost completely absent from *General Equilibrium* view of the world. The model predicts uneven development and growth between regions and countries but also that these inequalities will produce socio-political tension and pressures. The final outcome will depend on economic factors but also on the relative strength of these socio-political forces.

Third, the two models differ fundamentally on the nature of the effective constraints on the economy. In neoclassical models the economy is constrained by exogeneous and real supply factors. In the Kaldor–Myrdal model the constraints come primarily from social and institutional factors which are themselves affected and modified by the inherent tendency of the system towards uneven development of regions and sectors.

Drawing on these differences Peter Skott argues that the fundamental message of the Kaldor–Myrdal cumulative causation approach is that economic theory must be based on socio-economic factors. The contribution here of Allyn Young is acknowledged, for as early as 1928 he was arguing that economic activity could not be constrained by exogenous resources. The operative constraint becomes then the socio-economic factors which determine the features of economic development and growth.

We would like to conclude this introduction by expressing our thanks to our respective institutions, Polytechnic of East London and Thames Polytechnic, for their continuous encouragement and support, financial and moral. Without this help, *Thames Papers in Political Economy* could not possibly manage to appear regularly. Sincere thanks are also due to Malcolm C. Sawyer and Edward Elgar for their comments and unfailing advice.

1. The Theoretical Significance of Keynes's General Theory

Athanasios Asimakopulos

INTRODUCTION

Government fiscal and monetary measures that are designed to affect the levels of output and employment are often labelled 'Keynesian' measures. This nomenclature is a reflection of the support for such measures to be found in Keynes's book, *The General Theory of Employment, Interest and Money*, and of the enormous 'Keynesian' literature that this book spawned. Keynes was never an academic economist in the usual sense of that term; he was always deeply involved with the world outside the university community, and events there affected the direction of his work on economic theory. In his *Treatise on Money*, Keynes was 'primarily concerned with what governs *prices*' (Keynes 1973a, p. 145; italics in original), and although output was not assumed to be constant, there was no systematic examination of the factors determining the levels of output and employment. The deepening world depression provided a strong impetus for Keynes to turn to the difficult task of bringing economic theory more in line with the world around him. He viewed his book and the General Theory[1] it developed, as presenting a fundamental challenge to the prevailing orthodoxy of his time, an orthodoxy – Keynes called it 'classical' – that assumed the existence of strong forces that tend to produce a situation of full employment equilibrium.

Keynes's complaint with 'classical' economists was not so

much over matters of economic policy, since they would often support *ad hoc* proposals to improve the position of the unemployed. For example, Pigou, whose theory of unemployment was sharply criticized in *The General Theory*, took the lead in 1932 in writing a letter to *The Times* of London, that Keynes signed, proposing expanded public works to increase employment (Keynes 1981, pp. 138–9). The problem, as Keynes saw it, was that these economists 'have not revised their fundamental theory' (Keynes 1936, p. 20), and often stepped outside it when making policy proposals. With the publication of *The General Theory,* Keynes hoped to bring about a drastic revision of 'fundamental theory', a change that would 'largely revolutionise . . . the way the world thinks about economic problems' (Keynes 1973a, p. 492). This book, as well as the supporting literature that quickly surrounded it, and wartime experience, certainly resulted in major changes in government economic policies designed to reduce unemployment in the post-war period. Its effect on 'fundamental theory' was, however, very limited as it quickly became absorbed into a slightly amended neoclassical theory that treated Keynes's results as the outcomes of 'special' cases.[2]

Keynes's theoretical apparatus became gutted, with essential elements of real-world economies being omitted and replaced by mechanical devices that produced policy conclusions that appeared to match those of Keynes. In some versions Keynes's theory was swallowed up in a 'neo-classical synthesis' (Samuelson 1955, p. vi) that assumed Keynesian policies would result in a world where pre-Keynesian theory would be applicable.[3] The title of this chapter is thus taken to refer to what is 'theoretically significant' in Keynes's General Theory, irrespective of its influence on the development of economic theory.

Keynes considered the 'orthodox theory' to be inadequate because it ignored essential aspects of historical time, it 'assumes that we have a knowledge of the future of a kind quite different from that which we actually possess. . . . The hypothesis of a calculable future leads to a wrong interpretation of the principles of behaviour which the need for action compels us to adopt, and to an underestimation of the concealed factors of utter doubt, precariousness, hope and fear. . . . It is therefore, incapable of dealing with the general case where employment is liable to 'fluctuate' (Keynes 1973b, pp. 122–3). Keynes drew a distinction between the scope of his theoretical analysis, and that of the policy suggestions for improving employment. He considered that this analysis (or 'diagnosis') 'of why output and employment are so liable to fluctuation. . . . [and] my main reasons for departing from the traditional theory. . . . are of a highly general character and are meant to be definitive' (*ibid*, pp. 121–2). In contrast, he emphasizes: 'But I consider that my suggestions for a cure, which, avowedly, are not worked out completely, are on a different plane from the diagnosis. They are not meant to be definitive; they are subject to all sorts of special assumptions and are necessarily related to the particular conditions of the time' (*ibid*, p. 122). This qualification to the economic policy suggestions contained in *The General Theory*, has often been ignored by some Keynesians. It will be argued here that, although Keynes's claim for the greater generality of his theory as opposed to orthodox theory, is valid, certain aspects of his analysis are also 'related to the particular conditions of the time' of writing of his book.

The General Theory is a complex, uneven, and incomplete book. In particular, historical time was only allowed to affect the analysis to a partial extent. Keynes was not a meticulous theorist, and he made a few slips in setting out his analysis, some of which will be pointed out below. They do not, however, affect the main thrust of his analysis or its conclusions. The focus of this paper will be on Keynes's methods of analysis. It should not be surprising to find that they owe a great deal to Marshall, whose approach to economic theory dominated Cambridge during Keynes's formative years. Marshall struggled with the very complex problem of how to bring time into economic models, and although he never dealt with it satisfactorily, a careful student of his writings could not but be aware of its importance for any theory that purports to shed light on the working of an actual economy.

THE SETTING OF THE ANALYSIS

Keynes's analysis takes place in Marshall's short-period, a period of time during which the changes in productive capacity that occur continuously in a dynamic economy can be legitimately ignored, because on average over this period they are small relative to the initial productive capacity. Marshall (1920, p. 379) provided an estimate of the length of his short-period – 'a few months or a year' – and Keynes's use of the short period is consistent with this time frame. Keynes's analysis is thus set, subject to the necessary abstractions of any theory, in an actual period of time, a 'present' that separates a 'past' that has provided the means for current production, attitudes, habits, etc., from a 'future', many of whose features cannot be known with any substantial degree of certainty. It was this setting, and the analysis of the complications thus introduced, that Robinson (1971, p. ix) saw as the most important element in Keynes's General Theory.

Even though Keynes's analysis is concentrated on the short-period, its significance can only be understood if this period is seen as an interval in an historical process. This was not always made clear by Keynes and, as we shall see below, some elements of his analysis were taken 'out of time'. Production decisions in this historical context could only be translated into final outputs, ready to be used or to be sold after the passage of some time. Because of this time lag, the competitive manufacturers in his model must base their production decisions on expectations of the prices for their products at the time when they are ready for sale, and he calls this type of expectation '*short-term expectation*' (*ibid*, p. 47, italics in original). Keynes observes that a production decision that has been put into effect can only be altered after some interval of time, and he notes: '*Daily* here stands for the shortest interval after which the firm is free to revise its decision as to how much employment to offer. It is, so to speak, the minimum effective unit of economic time' (*ibid*, p. 47n, italics in original). It is implicit in Keynes's treatment that his short-period contains many of these 'daily' intervals thus allowing short-term expectations and production decisions to be altered in the light of realized results. In fact, in spite of the formal recognition of the role and importance of short-term expectations,[4] express reference to them is usually omitted in *The General Theory* on the grounds that they can often be safely replaced by 'the most recently realised results' (*ibid*, p. 51), and attention is focused on situations where these expectations are borne out by events. With the realized prices, output and employment being endogenous (they are determined by the levels of investment and consumption expenditures), short-period expectations also take on the appearance of being endogenous.

Express reference to long-term expectations could not be avoided, because the realized results with which they can be compared will only occur over future periods of time. These expectations, on which investment decisions are based, are exogenous in Keynes's model and 'they are liable to sudden revision' (Keynes 1936, p. 51). Future conditions, or rather, expected future conditions, thus affect current output and employment by influencing investment decisions and expenditures. Although Keynes's analysis is concentrated on a particular short-period, this short-period is *not* 'self contained'.[5] Activity within the period cannot be explained without reference to plans and expectations concerning future periods of time, in which conditions can differ from current ones. Keynes saw that a critical feature of a monetary economy is that it 'is essentially one in which changing views about the future are capable of influencing the quantity of employment and not merely its direction.' (*ibid*, p. vii), and this was reflected in his model of such an economy. Keynes's analysis, in spite of its use of some static elements, was essentially dynamic because its short period outcomes were influenced by this important aspect of historical processes.

THE GENERAL THEORY OF EMPLOYMENT

Keynes used the adjective 'general' for his theory of employment to contrast it with the 'classical' theory, since equilibrium could occur in his model at many positions other than the one characterized by full employment (Keynes 1936, p. 3). By 'equilibrium' in this context Keynes means a position of 'rest' with respect to the level of employment (Asimakopulos 1973). Given the values of the parameters, there is no net tendency for the level of employment to change. Keynes is critical of the classical theory for making assumptions that 'happen not to be those of the economic society in which we actually live' (Keynes 1936, p. 3), and his theory incorporates important institutional features of this 'economic society'. One of these is that wage bargains are made in terms of money, with both real-wage rates and the level of employment being then determined by the prices that turn out to rule in product markets. From the Marshallian assumptions that underlie the short period of his analysis, Keynes infers that the real-wage rate is inversely related to the level of employment.[6] With given equipment and money-wage rates, and rising marginal cost curves, firms will only increase output and employment if prices are higher. Keynes develops his theory of employment with money-wage rates given, and then examines the possible effects on his conclusions if money-wage rates fall under the pressure of unemployment.[7]

In the segment of time for which Keynes's analysis considers the factors determining the 'equilibrium' level of employment, the decisions to produce, and thus to offer employment, are made by the entrepreneurs that control firms. These firms are assumed to be competitive, and their production decisions are based on the short-term expectations of prices. Each firm produces the output that equates expected price with its short-period marginal cost, and its employment of labour is determined in this way. In order to deal with the aggregate level of employment, Keynes assumes that labour can be 'homogenized' by using relative wage rates as weights to arrive at a measure of total employment in equivalent man-hours of unskilled labour (*ibid*, p. 41). To obtain an economy-wide representation of short-term expectations to use for analytical purposes, Keynes moved from prices that are product specific to proceeds – the product, less user costs, of prices and the corresponding quantities from the marginal cost curves – that are in the same value terms for all industries. These proceeds are used to define his aggregate supply function that shows the relationship between an amount of employment in the economy and 'the expectation' of proceeds which will just make it worth the while of the entrepreneurs to give that employment' (*ibid*, p. 24).[8] Employment is the dependent variable in this function, and the expectation of proceeds is the independent variable. This function is, of course, only an expository device. Employment is determined, given their marginal cost curves, by the individual firms' expectations of prices for their products.

Keynes then defines an aggregate demand function to be paired with the aggregate supply function: 'Similarly, let D be the proceeds which entrepreneurs expect to receive from the employment of N men . . . ' (*ibid*, p. 25), where D is the dependent variable. There is no basis in his competitive model for such an 'expectational' aggregate demand function. The expected prices of Keynes's entrepreneurs who sell in competitive markets, are independent of their individual output (and employment).[9] Keynes's theory subsequently makes use of an aggregate demand function that is consistent with its microfoundations. This function shows the relationship between the level of employment and the proceeds that will result. Keynes implicitly assumes that these proceeds are those that arise when actual investment is equal to planned investment, and consumption is in the desired relation to income. Effective demand is given by the value of proceeds at the point of intersection of the aggregate demand function and the aggregate supply function. This point also shows the equilibrium volume of employment for the short period. Its value 'depends on (i) the aggregate supply function . . . (ii) the propensity to consume . . . and (iii) the volume of investment . . . This is the essence of the General Theory of Employment' (*ibid*, p. 29).

This statement of Keynes's theory makes clear that he implicitly assumes that the full multiplier effects of any change in investment from its level in the previous period, have been completed within the short period. He has here taken liberties with historical time. There is no reason to believe that the short period, during which changes in productive capacity can be legitimately neglected, will be long enough to allow for the completion of the multiplier process (c.f. Hicks 1965, pp. 64–5). Keynes's treatment of the multiplier is thus 'ahistorical'. His presentation of it is also potentially misleading, because it can be confused with the 'logical' theory of the multiplier (Keynes 1936, p. 123) that makes use of a definitional 'marginal propensity to consume' (the ratio of the actual increase in consumption to the actual increase in income), over any arbitrary interval of time, rather than the economy's propensity to consume. But even with the 'standard' version of the multiplier, Keynes stated (without providing supporting empirical evidence) that where there is idle productive capacity in the consumption-goods industries 'there is no reason to suppose that more than a brief interval of time need elapse before employment in the consumption industries is advancing *pari passu* with employment in the capital-goods industries with the multiplier operating near its normal figure' (*ibid*, pp. 124–5).

Keynes used 'comparative statics' analysis with his equilibrium volume of employment to illustrate the effects of differences in the level of investment or in the propensity to consume This analysis could give no indication of the time required for a new equilibrium value to be reached after a change in one of these parameters, but Keynes did consider the stability of his equilibrium. He concluded that given the economy's propensity to consume and the level of investment, the equilibrium level of employment is stable. For example, if the firms' short-term expectations of proceeds are mistaken, and too high, then the level of employment they offer is greater than the equilibrium value. But forces will be set in motion, given an unchanging level of investment, to move employment back towards its equilibrium value, because the economy's marginal propensity to consume has a value less than one (*ibid*, p. 30). Keynes contrasted this with the classical theory that he saw as, in effect, assuming that the aggregate demand and supply functions coincide, so that any improvement in short-term expectations that increases employment will result in changes in demand that turn out to justify offering this higher level of employment.[10]

In considering the possible effects on his conclusions of changes in money-wage rates, Keynes went beyond comparative statics analysis.The later simply showed that lower money-wage rates would shift the aggregate supply curve to the right, and the aggregate demand curve downwards, with roughly the same volume of employment being shown by the intersections of the new and old pairs of curves. He looked at the possible effects of changing money-wage rates on the factors determining his equilibrium level of employment in a framework that dealt with the order of events as they occurred through time. In particular, the possible effects of current changes in money-wage rates on expectations of future values, were important determinants of the efficacity of a reduction of money-wages as a policy to increase the level of employment. Institutional factors, the existence of debts denominated in money terms and bankruptcy laws, were also introduced into the analysis. Keynes felt that 'if the fall of wages and prices goes far, the embarrassment of those entrepreneurs who are heavily indebted may soon reach the point of insolvency – with severely adverse effects on investment' (*ibid*, p. 264). Falling money-wage rates in depression would thus not tend to increase employment. In addition to its likely adverse effects on investment, the redistribution of income in favour of rentiers and against workers that would ensue, would lower the economy's propensity to consume. He concluded: 'There is, therefore, no ground for the belief that a flexible wage policy is capable of maintaining a state of continuous full employment. . . . The economic system cannot be made self-adjusting along these lines' (*ibid*, p. 267).

THE DETERMINATION OF INVESTMENT

The determination of investment in Keynes's model must, given that it is set in historical time, be 'open-ended'. Investment is based on long-term expectations that are rather tenuous in a world where 'our knowledge of the future is fluctuating, vague and uncertain' (Keynes 1973b, p. 113). The value of investment would then be determined by particular historical circumstances, institutional arrangements and attitudes that influence these expectations.[11] Recognition of this potential volatility of investment decisions was given prominence in chapter 12 of *The General Theory* and in Keynes's 1937 *Quarterly Journal of Economics* article, Keynes also developed in chapter 11 of his book, an 'investment-demand schedule – or, alternatively, the schedule of the marginal efficiency of capital' (Keynes 1936, p. 136) that gave the appearance of stability and precision to the factors determining investment. It was just a small step from Keynes's description of this schedule to its depiction as a downward-sloping 'demand' curve for investment activity, similar to a market demand curve for a good, with the rate of interest replacing the price of the good. In this form it became one of the bases for Hicks's IS curve in 'Mr. Keynes and the "Classics" ', and it could readily be absorbed into orthodox theory.

There are two main problems with Keynes's investment-demand schedule as a vehicle for his 'vision' of the working of a modern capitalist economy. By 'locking-up' long-term expectations in the form of the function is seems to make the future returns to investment expenditures 'calculable' in a way that readily permits comparison with the rate of interest. In order to derive, conceptually a downward-sloping marginal efficiency of capital schedule, Keynes takes his analysis out of historical time by mixing up *ex ante* and *ex post* elements. He also chooses only those elements that produce the result he wants.

In Keynes's short-period, the investment that takes place does not have an appreciable effect on the average amount of capital equipment in the economy in that period. The prospective yield on investment in that period can thus not be expected to be lower because of diminishig returns to capital equipment triggered by a higher level of investment. Keynes explains the lowering of prospective yields, in this case, as the result of higher supply prices of capital equipment when larger amounts are produced in the period. The rising short-period supply prices of output in Keynes's competitive model means that output increases require price increases. In this explanation, the mixing of *ex ante* (the prospective yields) and *ex post* features (the increase in capital equipment prices when investment is higher) in a single function, is illegitimate. The use of *ex post* elements is also selective, because he ignores the effect on prospective yields of higher current investment that increases current output and profits. The *ex ante* and *ex post* elements should be allowed for in separate functions, as is done by Kalecki in his double-sided relation between investment and profits.[12]

Keynes's analysis obscured the time pattern of the investment process. Investment decisions, which depend on long-term expectations and conditions in financial markets (including the rate of interest), are made, and lead to investment expenditures, which through their multiplier effects determine income and saving. With the investment demand schedule it is possible to set up a version of *The General Theory* (as did Hicks 1937, p. 134) that is based on 3 simultaneous equations. One shows the demand for money, which is set equal to the exogeneously-determined money supply, as a function of income and the rate of interest; another has investment as a function of the rate of interest; and the final one has saving as a function of income. Missing from this formulation is Keynes's vision of the order of things, with the primary role being accorded to investment,[13] which is liable 'to fluctuate for reasons quite distinct (a) from those which determine the propensity of the individual to *save* out of a given income and (b) from those physical conditions of technical capacity to aid production which have usually been supposed hitherto to be the chief influence governing the marginal efficiency of capital.' (Keynes 1973b, p. 118; italics in original). It is not surprising that Keynes felt the need to concentrate, in his reply to reviewers of his book, on the role of investment in his model as the '*causa causans*' (*ibid,* p. 121), and to emphasize that it was not a variable that could be captured by some stable function. The 'factors . . . which determine the rate of investment . . . are most unreliable, since it is they which are influenced by our views of the future about which we know so little' (*ibid*).[14]

MONEY AND FINANCE

Keynes was concerned with developing a rationale for government policies to improve employment in actual economies that had both unemployed labour and unutilized productive capacity. These economies were monetary production economies that moved through historical time, and these features had to be reflected in his theory. Money and the uncertainty over the outcomes of events that would only be completed in the future that is a characteristic of historical time, were thus essential elements in this theory. In fact, money as a store of wealth can potentially only have a role in a model that observes the rules of historical time. Keynes's fundamental criticism of classical theory is that it is 'out of time'. In such a theory there can be no role for money as a store of wealth in spite of its claims to the contrary.

With Keynes's model, in contrast, there are good reasons for holding part of one's wealth in money, or 'near-monies', that can be readily turned into money with negligible capital losses or difficulties. The ability to gain ready access to money is important because many contracts – not least of all wage contracts – are denominated in terms of money. When future conditions, and thus the money prices of other assets are uncertain, it is a sensible precaution to hold some amount of money (or 'near-monies').[15] Keynes views this action as an indication of awareness that the calculations on which commitments were made could be mistaken: '. . . our desire to hold money as a store of wealth is a barometer of the degree of our distrust of our own calculations and conventions concerning the future' (*ibid*, p. 116). Given this importance to holding part of wealth as a stock of money, it is not surprising that Keynes's explanation of the determination of the rate of interest on money is concerned with the terms at which the existing stock of money would be held 'voluntarily'. His liquidity preference function, as it concerns speculative balances, is designed to explain the demand for the holding of money that is additional to the demand for transactions and precautionary balances.[16]

The uncertainty over future conditions that exists in an

actual economy underlies both Keynes's liquidity preference function and the approach to the determination of investment emphasized in his 1937 *Quarterly Journal of Economics* article. Vicarelli (1984) has forcefully drawn attention to the basis for the two functions. 'There exists a . . fundamental link [between . . . the demand function for money and the demand function for investment]. . . . the presence of uncertainty. It is uncertainty which dominates investment decisions and displaces the classical identification of the capital accumulation process with the amassment of savings. Keynes substitutes a behavioral function in which "animal spirits" are the driving force. At the same time, however, uncertainty about the future compels individuals to seek a "liquid" shelter thereby underpinning a demand function for money' (p. 138).

The role of *The General Theory* can be seen as being twofold, the presentation of a theory that is applicable to actual capitalist economies, and an attack on the 'classical' theory that dominated economic thought. The latter was an essential part of the attempt 'to bring to an issue the deep divergences of opinion between fellow economists which have for the time being almost destroyed the practical influence of economic theory, and will, until they are resolved continue to do so' (Keynes 1936, p. vi). The logic of Keynes's opening-up of economic theory to admit historical time led, as we have seen, to the focus on the demand for money as a store of wealth – a demand for 'liquidity' – and thus to the view that the rate of interest 'is the "price" which equilibrates the desire to hold wealth in the form of cash with the available quantity of cash' (*ibid*, p. 167). This explanation also served the polemical purpose of helping to counter Say's Law, by leaving no room for the view that the rate of interest adjusted so as to equate investment and saving. He thus emphasized that '[T]he rate of interest is not the "price" which brings into equilibrium the demand for resources to invest with the readiness to abstain from present consumption' (*ibid*).

Keynes explicitly introduced in *The General Theory* only those aspects of money, and the financial system generally, that he considered essential for his theory. His detailed analysis of money and financial institutions is to be found in the earlier, two volume, *Treatise on Money*. The only financial assets that figure prominently in *The General Theory* are money and fixed-interest securities (or 'debts'). Given the high degree of substitutability between money and shorter-term securities, the dividing line between money and debts must be somewhat arbitrary. Keynes recognized this problem, but he adopted a very restrictive assumption 'that money is co-extensive with bank deposits' (*ibid*, p. 167n). Similarly, there was extreme simplification in his derivation of an investment demand function, which incorporates the marginal efficiency of capital, that gave undue emphasis to the rate of interest as a regulator of investment. The risk and uncertainty involved in investment projects are covered by an apparently calculable 'rate of return', and the cost of funds borrowed for investment is identified with the rate of interest. This identification might be a reasonable representation of the opportunity cost of retained earnings used for this purpose, but funds borrowed through fixed-interest securities, because they entail the risk of loss of managerial control in case of default, have a cost higher than the rate of interest. The cost of equity financing, in a world with taxes on profits and partial payouts of earnings, is also substantially above the rate of interest.

Chapter 17 in *The General Theory* entitled 'The Essential Properties of Interest and Money', that Robinson (1965, p. 132) calls 'mysterious', does not fit with the historical time perspective in which he embedded his theory of money. It is introduced with reference to the investment demand schedule, developed in chapter 11, that gives a prominent role to the rate of interest as a regulator of investment activity. This schedule, as argued in section 4 above, does not observe the rules of historical time because it mixes *ex ante* and *ex post* elements at the same point of time in a single function. 'It seems, then, that the *rate of interest on money* plays a peculiar part in setting a limit to the level of employment, since it sets a standard to which the marginal efficiency of a capital-asset must attain if it is to be newly produced . . . It is natural to enquire wherein the peculiarity of money lies as distinct from other assets . . . ' (Keynes 1936, p. 222; italics in original).

This 'peculiarity' is found to lie in money's liquidity premium – the potential convenience or security that the holding of money bestows – and its negligible carrying costs. Other capital assets tend to have neglible liquidity premiums and substantial carrying costs, with yields that are assumed to be negatively related to the amounts of these assets. Keynes points to two characteristics of money as an explanation for why its 'own rate of interest' tends not to fall in the same way as the rates of other assets. Their combined effect is to make money 'a bottomless sink for purchasing power, when the demand for it increases' (*ibid*, p. 231). They are: (i) '. . . money has, both in the long and in the short period, a zero, or at any rate a very small, elasticity of production, so far as the power of private enterprise is concerned, as distinct from the monetary authority' (*ibid*, p. 230); and (ii) '. . . money . . . has an elasticity of substitution equal, or nearly equal, to zero; which means that as the exchange value of money rises there is no tendency to substitute some other factor for it' (*Ibid*, p. 231). The first characteristic means that if the price of money rises relatively to prices of other goods, increased labour is not employed to produce it.

Both of these characteristics are dependent on the definition of money, and on the dividing line used to separate money from other financial assets. The proliferation of financial innovations – the introduction of 'new monies' – at times of high interest rates and credit constraints, certainly increases the amount of finance available, while possibly adding some employment in financial institutions. Keynes's statement of the second characteristic can be interpreted to refer only to the substitutability between money and physical assets because of the high substitutability between money and many types of financial assets.[17]

Keynes treated the money supply in *The General Theory* as being under the complete control of the monetary authority. It was only in his articles on finance (Keynes 1937a, 1937b, and 1938) that the money supply was assumed to respond to the demand for bank loans by investing firms, and a step was taken towards making the supply of money endogenous.[18]

Keynes was reaffirming his liquidity-preference theory of the rate of interest, in those articles, in response to Ohlin (1937), Hicks, (1936) and Robertson (1936). These economists claimed that Keynes's approach was just an alternative way of expressing the dependence of the rate of interest on the demand and supply for credit, or 'loanable funds'. Keynes did not accept this. He resisted fiercely anything that could be construed as re-introducing the notion that the rate of interest is a 'price' that brings saving and investment into equality. Investment was the *causa causans* of his theory, a factor that he maintained was independent of saving. In order to maintain this position, it was necessary to provide within his model a source of funds for entrepreneurs out of which they could *increase* investment. (Retained earnings finance only a part, even though a significant part, of total investment.) Keynes pointed to the banking system, or rather to the financial system generally, as this source. 'It is, to an important extent, the "financial" facilities which regulate the *pace* of new investment' (Keynes 1973b, p. 210; italics in the original). In the December 1937 article, Keynes returned to this theme and acknowledged that his theory required an explicit statement on how firms could be in a position to increase investment. The accommodation by the banking system of the increased demand for bank credit in order to increase investment (in working, as well as in fixed, capital), increases the money supply. If this increase in planned investment and its accompanying multiplier effects are completed, then 'the banks cannot keep the previous amount of cash outstanding at the same rate of interest, unless a new activity is coming along to replace the old activity or there is an increase in the inactive demand' *(ibid*, pp. 230–1). These considerations can be seen as a step towards the introduction of an important element of endogeneity in the money supply.

Keynes's writings on finance were polemical as well as expository, and some of his statements did not take seriously the passage of time required in order to reach the short-period equilibrium positions, on which his theory was based, after an increase in investment.[19] In trying to steer clear of any implication that saving could influence investment, he denied that saving, or expected saving, had any effect on finance.

> . . . the finance required during the interregnum between the intention to invest and its achievement is mainly supplied by specialists, in particular by the banks, which organise and manage a revolving fund of liquid finance.
>
> For 'finance' is essentially a revolving fund. It employs no savings. It is, for the community as a whole, only a book-keeping transaction. As soon as it is 'used' in the sense of being expended, the lack of liquidity is automatically made good and the readiness to become temporarily unliquid is available to be used over again. Finance covering the interregnum is, to use a phrase employed by bankers in a more limited context, necessarily 'self-liquidating' for the community taken as a whole at the end of the interim period *(ibid*, p. 219).

The 'lack of liquidity' mentioned in the above quotation, appears to refer to the position of the banking system, although Keynes confuses matters by not always making clear whose position is being considered.

For the banking system, the 'lack of liquidity' is *not* 'automatically made good' as soon as the loans made to investing firms are 'expended'. The initial position of the banking system's balance sheet will only be restored after bank loans, equal to those provided to the investing firms, are repaid as a result of the increased saving that is a consequence of the higher level of investment. For such loans to be repaid, this saving must be desired saving (saving that is in the equilibrium relation to income) and not simply *ex post* saving that results from the necessary (definitional) equality between saving and investment at all points in time. Keynes, with his frequent disregard of the time required for the multiplier process, falls into the trap of identifying *ex post* saving with equilibrium saving. '. . . there will always be *exactly* enough *ex post* saving to take up the *ex post* investment and so release the finance which the latter had been previously employing. The investment market can become congested through shortage of cash. It can never become congested through shortage of saving. This is the most fundamental of my conclusions within this field' (*ibid*, p. 222; italics in original).[20]

The lack of attention by Keynes to the details of his analysis is a likely reason for his neglect of the time lag before desired saving catches up with an increase in investment. He first introduced the concept of a 'revolving fund' of finance in a situation where 'investment is proceeding at a steady rate' (*ibid*, p. 209). At each point in time, in this special case, short-period equilibrium can be assumed to hold, and saving that is in the desired relation to income, as well as *ex post* saving, is equal to investment. But this assumption cannot safely be made when investment has been increased. Time must pass before the increase in equilibrium saving catches up with the increase in investment.

Keynes begins his December 1937 article by explicitly recognizing that an increase in investment decisions requires some confidence about the availability, at reasonable terms, of both short- and long-term finance. 'The entrepreneur when he decides to invest has to be satisfied on two points: firstly, that he can obtain sufficient short-term finance during the period of producing the investment; and secondly, that he can eventually fund his short-term obligations by a long-term issue on satisfactory conditions' (*ibid*, p. 217). The role of long-term finance then tends to be ignored in the rest of the paper, and it ends up with the strong conclusion, quoted above, that it is only the 'shortage of cash' that can result in a 'congested' investment market. Kaldor (1939) saw that this conclusion, although it may hold in many cases, does not hold in all. The term structure of interest rates may be altered in a manner that increases long-term rates of interest, even though the banking system expands the money supply to keep short-term rates at low levels. The 'speculators' (Kaldor's term) or intermediaries, facilitate the financing of investment (before desired saving can increase in response to the higher investment). They take a position by borrowing short to provide the long-term financing required by firms who are increasing investment. At certain times they may only be willing to perform this function at sharply increased premiums, because of concern over possible increases in long-term interest rates. These higher rates might have a negative impact on investment even though there is no 'shortage of cash'. Kaldor pointed out that Keynes's implicit assumption about the stability of the term structure of interest rates might *not* be valid in an *open* economy when investment is being increased (Kaldor 1939, pp. 49–52). Asimakopulos (1983) noted that the same problem could arise where there is heightened concern about inflation, or where the government deficit is expected to absorb a substantial portion of private saving. Keynes's analysis of the factors required to make an increase in investment possible is thus to some extent subject 'to the particular conditions of the time' (Keynes 1973b, p. 122). He had considered that only his 'suggestions for a cure [for unemployment]' *(ibid)* were subject to this restriction.

TIME AND EQUILIBRIUM IN THE GENERAL THEORY

Historical time and equilibrium – two elements that do not readily mix – both find roles in the General Theory. Introduction of the former can make an economic analysis exceedingly complex with a bewildering array of possible outcomes, while concentration on the latter might give definite results, but results that can provide few or no insights into the problems of actual economies. Events in these economies always take place in historical contexts that cannot be characterized by anything that resembles equilibrium. It was the genius of Keynes that made possible a start in the analysis of the aggregate behaviour of actual economies. He combined critical features of long-term decisions made in historical time with the minimum of equilibrium conditions needed in order to arrive at conclusions that may be of assistance in the formulation of economic policy.

Keynes was helped in his endeavours by having been trained in the Marshallian tradition. There is an awareness in it of the need to try to incorporate some aspects of the passage of time. Marshall's short-period, with given productive capacity, is anchored, conceptually at least, in a definite interval of time, 'of a few months or a year'. His short-period equilibrium is an equilibrium position *only for firms*, as they produce the outputs which are appropriate to the demand they face at this point in time. Keynes kept this short-period framework, with its equilibrium for firms, but since his analysis was concerned with the operation of the economy as a whole, he had to deal with the relation between aggregate employment and aggregate demand. Effective demand in his model makes use of (in addition to all the potential positions of short-period equilibrium for firms that make up the aggregate supply function) another equilibrium concept that is implicit in Keynes's aggregate demand function. The investment expenditure included in this function is what has been intended by firms for this particular short period, while the consumption expenditure is in the desired (or equilibrium) relation to income. The point of effective demand thus indicates a position where, given the values of the parameters, firms are in short-period equilibrium, according to the 'chosen' position definition of that term.[21] They are making the best of the situation facing them; they are on their short-period supply curves. This is not the case for workers who are not, in general, on their labour supply curves in Keynes's model. The labour market can be said to be in 'equilibrium' if another definition of this term – one that was implicitly employed by Keynes (1936, p. 3) in this connection – is used. Given the values of the parameters and the short-period equilibrium of firms, there are no net forces at work tending to change the level of employment.[22]

Keynes's use of short-period equilibrium for the economy can be seen as an extension to the economy of Marshall's short-period equilibrium analysis for a particular industry. But it does *not* lead, as did Marshall's, to a consideration of long-period equilibrium. There is no place in Keynes's vision of the operation of actual economies for movement to anything approximating long-period equilibrium situations. These economies are subject to a variety of shocks whose nature and timing can only be determined after the event. The stable conditions for long intervals of time, which are required to give credence to long-period equilibrium analysis, were remote from Keynes's view of the world. In abstaining from long-period equilibrium analysis, Keynes was observing the limitations imposed by historical time. Long-period equilibrium, in the latter context, can only be a *very* special case that is explored only for purposes of illustration and completeness. It cannot be the focus of the analysis.

Keynes (1936, pp. 48–50) does make passing reference to 'long-period employment' in *The General Theory,* but this has nothing to do with long-period equilibrium (Asimakopulos, 1984–85). This term refers to a very special situation where all the employment in a particular situation – which, as always in his analysis, is short-period equilibrium employment – flows directly, or indirectly, from the same 'state of long-term expectation that has been supposed to continue for a sufficient length of time' (Keynes 1936, p. 58). All investment currently taking place is the result of this state of expectations.[23]

Keynes can be faulted, as noted above, for concentrating only on positions of short-period equilibrium and thus taking part of his analysis 'out of time'. This is not to deny that these equilibrium positions have a role to play in his analysis, especially for the critical comparisons Keynes wanted to make between his theory and classical theory. He should, however, have been more careful in his treatment of the time required for the full operation of the multiplier. It would have been useful, as he himself recognized (Keynes 1973b, p. 181), to have given explicit recognition to the possibility of disappointed short-term expectations, and to have traced out their consequences. This would, perhaps, have saved him from some of the errors arising from his neglect of the time lags in the working of the multiplier.

Keynes had the genius to see that it was possible – and necessary – to begin the analysis of the determination of output and employment in a model that reflects important elements of actual economies at a point in time where the changes in productive capacity can be legitimately ignored, while recognizing the factors that make investment so liable to fluctuation. An important dynamic element – the change in productive capacity that is a result of investment – was thus not dealt with by his analysis. This could only be handled, within his theoretical framework, by linking adjacent short periods. The effects of investment on productive capacity would, in this way, enter the analysis. Harrod (1939, 1948) and Robinson (1956) developed their theories of accumulation along these lines. Keynes's short periods can thus be linked, at least in principle, to investigate capital accumulation over time.[24] The time path traced by outputs in these periods is unlikely to be a smooth one. Needless to say, it is much more difficult to get clear-cut results in this case – if Keynes's historical time framework is maintained – than it is for the outcomes in a particular short period.

CONCLUSION

The theoretical significance of Keynes's General Theory lies in its introduction of historical time as a key element in economic analysis, even though this is done only partially, and in some instances inconsistently. This movement of economic theory towards increased relevance is not without its costs. It makes economic theory less 'self-contained', or more 'open-ended', with its recogition that many of the factors that affect important economic variables lie outside the purview of this theory. The values for these variables must be taken to be, in large part, exogenous. Historical, social, and political factors are critical influences here, and they cannot be included in an economic model in a form that will allow economic theorists to derive the clear-cut equilibrium results to which they are accustomed.

Keynes had the necessary self-confidence along with a keen sense of the 'real world', required to attempt to change the nature of economic theory, so that it could deal sensibly with the serious economic problems of the early '30s. His lack of concern about the necessary absence of precision of an analysis that relies heavily on expectations, whose genesis lies largely outside the scope of economics, is shown by his advice to Shove. The latter had noted, in writing to Keynes on the publication of *The General Theory*, that he had been trying to develop an analysis of the behaviour of firms that relied heavily on expectations, but felt defeated because 'I can't make it precise' (Keynes 1973b, p. 1). Keynes replied: 'But you ought not to feel inhibited by a difficulty in making the solution precise. It may be that a part of the error in the classical analysis is due to that attempt. As soon as one is dealing with the influence of expectations and of transitory experience, one is, in the nature of things, outside the realm of the formally exact' (*ibid*, p. 2).

Keynes's introduction of historical time into his analysis is, as shown in the preceding sections, incomplete. It has a prominent role in his treatment of the determination of investment in chapter 12, and in his 1937 *Quarterly Journal of Economics* article, as well as in many of his discussions of the theory of money, but it is left out in his comparative statics analysis of short-period equilibrium positions. It is the latter that provides the definite results on which Keynes's (and subsequent Keynesian) economic policy suggestions are based. These equilibrium results, plus Keynes's investment demand schedule, whose derivation is flawed, helped make it possible for his theory to be treated as a special case of neoclassical analysis. The General Theory has thus not led to the revolution in economic theory that Keynes had hoped to initiate. The challenge that Keynes's general approach poses to orthodox economic theory is, however, still present. It is a useful starting point for economic analysis that aims to be relevant. It is rooted in an actual period of historical time, with some attention being paid to institutional arrangements, and it recognizes the unreliability of the factors affecting investment. Many of these factors depend on the social, historical and institutional features of particular economies. Keynes's approach requires economic theorists to be more humble about the possibilities for precise results in their work, but at the same time it opens up vistas of economic analyses that are relevant to the operations of actual economies.

NOTES

This paper was written while I was on a sabbatical leave that was financed, in part, by the Social Sciences and Humanities Research Council. An earlier version was the basis for seminars given at Glendon College, the

Catholic University of Milan, and the Universities of Messina, Siena and Venice.

1. The convention followed here will be to use the term the General Theory, non-italicized, to stand for the theory developed in Keynes's book, *The General Theory*, and in his 1937 articles.
2. This was, for example, the conclusion of Hicks (1937) in his extremely influential 'Mr Keynes and the Classics', where it is stated that 'the General Theory of Employment is the Economics of Depression' (p. 155). It should be noted that Keynes, in this instance, did not rise to the defence of the generality of his theory. He wrote to Hicks about this paper that 'I found it very interesting and really have next to nothing to say by way of criticism' (Keynes 1973b, p. 79).
3. Robinson (1971, p. ix) felt that 'Keynes himself began the reconstruction of the orthodox scheme that he had shattered', because of his statement that once government controls had succeeded in maintaining full employment 'the classical theory comes into its own again from this point onwards' (Keynes 1936, p. 378).
4. See, for example, in the surviving rough notes for his 1937 lectures: 'The *expected* results are not on a par with the *realised* results in a theory of employment. The *realised* results are only relevant in so far as they influence the ensuing expectations in the next production period' (Keynes 1973b, p. 179; italics in original).
5. The adjective 'self-contained' is used by Hicks (1985) for a single period in a static analysis where the equilibrium values in that period are determined solely by the values of the parameters in that period, values that will be repeated in subsequent periods.
6. Keynes first explains this relation as due 'to decreasing returns in the short period during which equipment is constant' (Keynes 1936, p. 17) even though labour of equal efficiency to that already employed is available. He later also notes that the need to resort to 'less suitable labour involves a higher labour cost per unit of output' *(ibid*, p. 42) thus requiring the prospect of higher prices if this labour is to be employed.
7. If money-wage rates rise as employment increases, then prices increase for this reason as well as for the rising supply curve of output.
8. For a consideration of the ways in which the aggregate supply function can be derived from industry short-period supply curves, see Asimakopulos (1982).
9. The lack of microfoundations for Keynes's first statement of his aggregate demand function was pointed out, independently, by Parrinello (1980), Casarosa (1981), and Asimakopulos (1982).
10. Robertson (1936), in his review of *The General Theory*, raised the possibility that the expectations that led to an increase in output, which would appear to be mistaken when an aggregate demand function with a given volume of investment is compared with an aggregate supply function, may turn out to be justified when allowance is made for induced investment.

11. Hodgson (1985) argued that Keynes paid insufficient attention to the social and institutional factors that condition expectations in the type of world he tried to model.
12. Kalecki's use of this double-sided relation that observes the historical time pattern of the investment process, in his 1933 business-cycle paper (Kalecki 1971, pp. 1–14), placed him in a position to see immediately where Keynes went wrong. In Kalecki's 1936 review article of *The General Theory*, he judged the investment-demand function to be unsatisfactory because it is based on 'an approach which is basically static to a matter which is by its nature dynamic' (Targetti and Kinda-Haas, 1982, p. 252).
13. Pasinetti (1974) has observed that the methodological procedures of Keynes and Ricardo are similar in making use 'of a system of equations of the "causal type".' He adds that '[A]s against the attitude – so common to marginal economics theorists – that "everything depends on everything else," Keynes (as Ricardo) takes the opposite attitude that it is one of the tasks of the economic theorist himself also to specify which variables are sufficiently interdependent as to be best represented by simultaneous relations, and which variables exhibit such an overwhelming dependence in one direction (and such a small dependence in the opposite direction) as to be best represented by one-way-direction relations' (p. 44).
14. Coddington (1983) labels as 'fundamental Keynesianism' the approach that tries to base its theory on these statements by Keynes on investment.
15. Economists who can be labelled 'Post Keynesians' have emphasized this point. See for example, Minsky (1975) and Rousseas (1986).
16. The distinction between the precautionary and speculative motives is not always clear, as Kahn (1972) has emphasized, since both are related to possible changes in the rate of interest.
17. This is the way it is interpreted by Davidson (1978) who emphasizes the importance of these properties of money. He then refers to 'the high substitutability between money and securities, and the resultant low substitutability between financial assets and real capital' *(ibid*, p. 196). Kahn (1984) is more critical of Keynes's second characteristic of money. 'There is an appreciable elasticity of substitution between money and equities; and also between money and houses, and between money and commodities which are dealt with in organised produce markets' (p. 140).
18. For the importance placed by Post-Keynesians on the endogeneity of the money supply, see Rousseas (1986, pp. 62–98).
19. See Asimakopulos (1983, 1985b) for a discussion of some of the problems with Keynes's statements about finance.
20. Robertson quickly spotted Keynes's error, and wrote to him in a 31 December, 1937, letter: 'I cannot see that any revolving fund is released, any willingness to undergo illiquidity set free for further employment, by the act of the borrowing entrepreneur in spending his

loan. The bank has become a debtor to other entrepreneurs, work-people etc. instead of to the borrowing entrepreneur, that is all. The borrowing entrepreneur remains a debtor to the bank: and the bank's assets have not been altered either in amount or in liquidity' (Keynes 1973b, pp. 228–9). This point was repeated in Robertson (1938).

21. Hicks (1965) has provided such a definition: '. . . equilibrium when all the "individuals" in it are choosing those quantities which, out of the alternatives available to them, they prefer to produce and to consume' (p. 15).
22. A definition of equilibrium along these lines is provided by Hansen (1970): '. . . if we have an economic model that explains certain variables, and if there is no tendency for these variables to change, given the data of the model, then the system of variables is in equilibrium' (p. 4).
23. Eatwell (1979) and Milgate (1982) have claimed to have found a theory of the long-period level of output in *The General Theory*. For a criticism of this position see Asimakopulos (1985a).
24. In contrast to this position, Hicks (1985) has argued that Keynes's theory 'cannot be used as the "single-period" theory of a dynamic analysis, to which a theory of continuation, into subsequent periods, is to be joined. For a theory of continuation, the things that are carried over, at the end of the period, must be of major importance' (p. 60). But the period-to-period changes in productive capacity can be carried over, and they are of 'major importance'. It might also be possible to allow the multiplier effects of changes in investment to spill over into adjacent periods, but this is less crucial for a theory of accumulation.

REFERENCES

Asimakopulos, A. (1973), 'Keynes, Patinkin, Historical Time and Equilibrium Analysis', *Canadian Journal of Economics* (May).

Asimakopulos, A. (1982), 'Keynes' Theory of Effective Demand Revisited', *Australian Economic Papers* (June).

Asimakopulos, A. (1983), 'Kalecki and Keynes on Finance, Investment and Saving', *Cambridge Journal of Economics* (September–December).

Asimakopulos, A. (1984–85). ' "Long-period employment" in *The General Theory*', *Journal of Post Keynesian Economics* (Winter).

Asimakopulos, A. (1985a), 'Keynes and Sraffa: Visions and Perspectives', *Political Economy: Studies in the Surplus Approach* (No. 2).

Asimakopulos, A. (1985b), 'The Role of Finance in Keynes's General Theory', *Economic Notes* (No. 3).

Casarosa, C. (1981), 'The Microfoundations of Keynes's Aggregate Supply and Aggregate Demand Analysis', *Economic Journal* (March).

Coddington, A. (1983), *Keynesian Economics: The Search for First Principles* (Allen and Unwin: London).

Davidson, P. (1978), *Money and the Real World*, 2nd edition (Macmillan: London).

Eatwell, J. (1979), 'Theories of Value, Output and Employment', *Thames Papers in Political Economy* (Summer).

Hansen, B. (1970), *A Survey of General Equilibrium Systems* (McGraw-Hill: New York).

Harrod, R.F. (1939), 'An Essay in Dynamic Theory', *Economic Journal* (March).

Harrod, R.F. (1948), *Towards a Dynamic Economics* (Macmillan: London).

Hicks, J.R. (1936), 'Mr. Keynes's Theory of Employment', *Economic Journal* (June).

Hicks, J.R. (1937), 'Mr. Keynes and the Classics', *Econometrica* (April). (All page references in this paper are to its reprinting in Hicks, 1967.)

Hicks, J.R. (1965), *Capital and Growth*, (Clarendon Press: Oxford).

Hicks, J.R. (1967), *Critical Essays in Monetary Theory* (Clarendon Press: Oxford).

Hicks, J.R. (1985), *Methods of Dynamic Economics* (Clarendon Press: Oxford).

Hodgson, G. (1985), 'Persuasion, Expectations and the Limits to Keynes', in Lawson and Pesaran (1985).

Kahn, R. (1972), *Selected Essays on Employment and Growth* (Cambridge University Press: Cambridge).

Kahn, R. (1984), *The Making of Keynes' General Theory* (Cambridge University Press: Cambridge).

Kaldor, N. (1939), 'Speculation and Economic Stability', *Review of Economic Studies* (October). (All page references in the text are to its reprinting in Kaldor, 1960.)

Kaldor, N. (1960), *Essays in Economic Stability and Growth* (Duckworth: London).

Kalecki, M. (1971), *Selected Essays on the Dynamics of the Capitalist Economy: 1933–1970* (Cambridge University Press: Cambridge).

Keynes, J.M. (1936), *The General Theory of Employment, Interest and Money* (Macmillan: London).

Keynes, J.M. (1937a), 'Alternative Theories of the Rate of Interest', *Economic Journal* (June). (All page references in the text are to the reprinting in Keynes, 1973b.)

Keynes, J.M. (1937b), 'The Ex-Ante Theory of the Rate of Interest', *Economic Journal* (December). (All page references in the text are to the reprinting in Keynes, 1973b.)

Keynes, J.M. (1938), 'Mr Keynes on "Finance" ', *Economic Journal* (June). (All page references in the text are to the reprinting in Keynes, 1973b.)

Keynes, J.M. (1973a), *The General Theory and After: Part I Preparation.* Edited by Donald Moggridge, Vol. XIII of the Collected Writings (Macmillan for the Royal Economic Society: London).

Keynes, J.M. (1973b), *The General Theory and After: Part II Defence and Development.* Edited by Donald Moggridge. Vol. XIV of the Collected Writings (Macmillan for the Royal Economic Society: London).

Keynes, J.M. (1981), *Rethinking Employment and Unemployment Policies, 1929–1931.* Edited by Donald Moggridge. Vol. XX of the Collected Writings (Macmillan for the Royal Economic Society: London).

Lawson, T. and Pesaran, H. (1985), *Keynes' Economics: Methodological Issues* (Croom Helm: London).

Marshall, A. (1920), *Principles of Economics*, 8th edition (Macmillan: London).

Milgate, M. (1982), *Capital and Employment: A Study of Keynes's Economics* (Academic Press: London).

Minsky, H. (1975), *John Maynard Keynes* (Columbia University Press: New York).

Ohlin, B. (1937), 'Some Notes on the Stockholm Theory of Saving and Investment', *Economic Journal* (March and June).

Parrinello, S. (1980), 'The Price Level in Keynes's Effective Demand', *Journal of Post Keynesian Economics* (Fall).

Pasinetti, L. (1974), *Growth and Income Distribution: Essays in Economic Theory* (Cambridge University Press: Cambridge).

Robertson, D.H. (1936), 'Some Notes on Mr. Keynes' General Theory of Employment', *Quarterly Journal of Economics* (November).

Robertson, D.H. (1938), 'Mr Keynes and "Finance" ' *Economic Journal* (June).

Robinson, J. (1956), *The Accumulation of Capital* (Macmillan: London).

Robinson, J. (1965), *Collected Economic Papers, Vol. III* (Basil Blackwell: Oxford).

Robinson, J. (1971), *Economic Heresies* (Basic Books: New York).

Rousseas, S. (1986), *Post Keynesian Monetary Economics* (M.E. Sharpe: Armonk, New York).

Samuelson, P. (1955), *Economics: An Introductory Analysis*, 3rd edition (McGraw-Hill: New York).

Targetti, F. and Kinda-Hass, B. (1982), 'Kalecki's Review of Keynes' *General Theory*', *Australian Economic Papers* (December).

Vicarelli, F. (1984), *Keynes: The Instability of Capitalism* (University of Pennsylvania Press: Philadelphia).

2. An Essay on Keynes and General Equilibrium Theory

Peter Skott

INTRODUCTION

At one level this chapter deals with the question of whether Keynes's theory of employment can be understood within a general equilibrium framework. This is hardly a novel and unexplored question so a few words by way of introduction may be called for to motivate the reader.

My main reasons for writing the chapter are perhaps best expressed with reference to the following quotations from Weintraub (1979): General equilibrium theory 'is a meta-theory, or an investigative logic, which . . . is used to construct all economic theories' (p. 73) and it is 'rooted . . . in the very structural unities of science itself. To attack general equilibrium in economics as a legitimate model of reasoning is to *simultaneously* deny homeostatic reasoning to psychologists and morphogenic analysis to the biologist' (p. 72).

It is unusual to see the faith in general equilibrium theory professed in such an explicit and extreme fashion, but the GE paradigm still seems to dominate most theoretical work in economics and has done so for several decades.

Unless one defines GE theory so broadly as to make the concept almost void of content, I find Weintraub's statements absolutely false. If one wants to analyse dynamic questions – and what economic questions of interest are not inherently dynamic? – then strict adherence to a GE framework will inevitably impede progress.[1] The many attempts to interpret

Keynes within a general equilibrium framework illustrate this. I shall argue that sequential (or dynamic) patterns play a fundamental role in Keynes's theory of involuntary unemployment and that GE interpretations of Keynes's theory are deficient because the sequential patterns are ignored.

The main purpose of the chapter is, thus, not to give yet another version of what Keynes really, really meant. I do hope, of course, that my presentation of (a small part of) Keynes's analysis will be acceptable from an exegetical point of view. But the underlying argument of the paper concerns the crucial importance of sequential patterns; dynamic complications should not just be added to static theories as a belated afterthought when (if) the theories reach the stage of empirical application. Theories which do not take the dynamic complications into account from the very beginning are likely to be misleading at best.

The argument of the chapter can be summarized as follows: Keynes's theory of employment is a general theory in the sense that it pertains to the economy as a whole. In this respect Keynes's theory and GE theories are on the same side of the fence; they are both 'general' as opposed to 'partial', Keynes, however, was a Marshallian economist, and one feature of Marshallian economics is the tripartite analysis of ultra short run equilibrium, short run equilibrium and long run equilibrium. In the General Theory Keynes focused on the short run. A short run equilibrium configuration can be described in static or simultaneous terms, but Keynes did more than describe a short run equilibrium with unemployment. He also argued forcefully that endogenous market forces will not tend to eliminate involuntary unemployment and his argument was based on ultra short run sequential patterns. Keynes thus went beyond static equilibrium analysis. His short run unemployment equilibrium was backed up with an explicit analysis of the likely properties of a sequence of ultra short run equilibria and this sequential analysis provides a fundamental theoretical reason for the possibility of involuntary unemployment.

Theories of GE – including simple Arrow-Debreu models,

fix-price models with quantity constraints and Hahn's conjectural equilibrium models – which concentrate on the properties of simultaneous or static equilibria cannot accommodate the crucial dynamic aspects of Keynes' analysis. In GE terminology, Keynes attempted to analyse a sequence of temporary equilibria and not just the properties of one temporary equilibrium configuration.

Keynes never developed the long run implications of his theory in any detail and – in spite of the dynamic aspects of the analysis – the Marshallian notion of short run equilibrium remained at the centre of the stage. The usefulness of the notion of short run equilibrium, in particular when dealing with medium to long term issues, is questionable. It may be preferable to build up a dynamic long run theory as a sequence of ultra short run equilibria. These questions are explored briefly at the end of the paper in connection with Kaldor's growth and distribution theory.

The conclusion of the chapter is not that the specific dynamic structure analysed by Keynes (or the sequential structure of Kaldor's models) is 'correct' and should be incorporated into all post-Keynesian models. The aim of the paper is to emphasize the importance of sequential patterns, and the analysis of Keynes and Kaldor may, I think, be a fruitful source of inspiration in the develoment of the dynamic aspects in post-Keynesian theory.

The chapter is structured in seven sections. Section 1 discusses some GE-inspired interpretations of Keynes' General Theory (GT). In section 2, two origins of GE-Keynesianism in Hicks' early work are examined briefly. The following two sections deal with the Marshallian roots of Keynes's analysis and the Keynesian short run unemployment equilibrium. Section 5 takes up the question of the effects of changes in money wages. Section 6 contains a discussion of the usefulness of the concept of short run equilibrium and of the extension of Keynes's theory to cover long run developments. The final section presents a few concluding remarks.

GE-KEYNESIANISM

'Keynes was concerned with what we have called temporary equilibrium'. This is how Arrow and Hahn open their discussion of 'The Keynesian Model' in the final chapter of their authoritative survey of general equilibrium theories (Arrow and Hahn 1971, p. 347). Indeed, until quite recently this was the almost unanimous view among economists and it probably still has the support of a great majority.

Having specified the theoretical framework, Arrow and Hahn go on to suggest two possible interpretations of Keynes's analysis in GT: on the first interpretation Keynes denied the existence of temporary equilibrium (TE) in his model while on the second he merely argued that the price mechanism could not be relied upon to bring about equilibrium.

They conclude the examination of the first interpretation by suggesting that Keynes has actually presented powerful arguments for the possible non-existence of equilibrium in a TE model. It is well known that it is difficult to establish rigorously the existence of equilibrium in TE models under reasonable assumptions. Some of the main problems arise because of the existence of commitments in money terms which agents carry with them from the past. Because of these commitments, contracts negotiated in money terms, variations in (nominal) prices may cause bankruptcies and hence discontinuities in excess demand correspondences, discontinuities which threaten the existence of equilibrium. In other words, the fact that money forms 'a link between the present and the future' and that contracts are made in terms of money gives us some good and very Keynesian reasons why a temporary equilibrium may not exist.

The question of stability in GE models has never been satisfactorily resolved. The basic reason for this is simply that the stability issue by definition involves the question of what happens outside equilibrium; a 'disequilibrium' theory is needed.[2] The familiar Walrasian tatonnement process cannot qualify as a serious disequilibrium theory. It describes a purely notional process with no disequilibrium activities ever taking place. It is therefore difficult to attach any meaning to tatonnement based stability results (in the form of, for instance, gross substitutability criteria). Since there is no agreement on any alternative disequilibrium theory and the stability question has been investigated only for a very small number of exceedingly simple disequilibrium hypotheses, GE/TE theories are wide open to stability type criticism.[3] Predictably, therefore, Arrow and Hahn find that they cannot dismiss arguments based on their second interpretation either.

One implication of both interpretations is that Keynes's theory deals with 'disequilibrium' phenomena (that is, disequilibrium from the point of view of TE/GE theory). How is this reconcilable with Arrow and Hahn's opening statement, that Keynes was concerned with TE? It is not logically possible to claim simultaneously that Keynes uses a TE framework and that he denies the existence and/or relevance of equilibrium in the TE model. The TE model is silent on non-equilibrium phenomena and thereby useless for a theorist who wants to discuss disequilibrium behaviour. There is another problem with a disequilibrium interpretation of Keynes: it so blatantly contradicts Keynes's own claim that the unemployment states which he analysed in GT were equilibrium states.

The traditional resolution of these problems has been to argue that a sticky – or even completely rigid – money wage rate prevents the economy from attaining its full employment equilibrium. The Keynesian 'unemployment equilibrium' in effect becomes a TE with a reverse L-shaped labour supply curve. Or in other words, from a theoretical point of view Keynes has not contributed much; he has 'merely' focused attention on relevant special cases. If wages – or prices in general – are sticky then the flex-price TE becomes inappropriate and a fix-price TE is needed to replace it. Notice that this is perfectly compatible with the view that Keynes has also presented powerful arguments against the existence of flex-price equilibria but that the relevance of a 'Keynesian' fix-price TE is obviously predicated on assumptions of both existence and stability of this fix-price TE.

The overall conclusion of Arrow and Hahn fits this pattern. They seem to suggest that Keynes:

- may or may not have denied the existence of flex-price TE
- denied the stability of flex-price TE (assuming its existence)
- replaced the notion of full employment flex-price TE with a fix-price unemployment TE, which he assumed to be stable.

With minor variations in emphasis this has been the conclusion of most economists. It is part of the neoclassical synthesis; textbook versions have tended to focus on the third point and the arguments offered to substantiate the first point have often been rather vague or even flawed.[4] The reinterpretation of Keynes initiated in the late 60s by Clower (1965) and Leijonhufvud (1968) did not break with this interpretation either. Leijonhufvud, for instance, claimed that

> *In the Keynesian macrosystem the Marshallian ranking of price- and quantity-adjustment speeds is reversed:* In the shortest period flow quantities are freely variable, but one or more prices are given, and the admissable range of variation for the rest of the prices is thereby limited. The revolutionary element in the *General Theory* can perhaps not be stated in simpler terms.
> *(Leijonhufvud, 1968, p. 52.)*

Hence in this particular respect the contribution of Clower and Leijonhufvud[5] was to clear up some theoretical and terminological puzzles associated with a fix-price Walrasian interpretation of Keynes; 'effective demand' vs 'notional demand', Walras' Law vs 'Say's Principle', 'spillover effects'. A new terminology was suggested to clarify the choice theoretic foundations of Keynesian macrotheory.[6]

If all prices or a subset of prices are fixed – at non-equilibrium levels – then, by definition, it becomes impossible for all agents to carry out the trades which were optimal in relation to the standard budget constraints. The macroeconomic identity between realized demand and realized supply implies that some agents must encounter quantity constraints on their trading; and of course the failure of a consumer to acquire cigarettes may diminish his interest in matches just as the failure of a worker to sell his labour power may influence his total consumption demand. In other words, the existence of macroeconomic trading identities implies 'quantity constraints' on the choice of set of at least some individual agents and the quantity constraints of any one agent are likely to produce reactions which will in turn affect other agents' trading possibilities. The quantity constraints of one agent depend upon the actions of all other agents, whose choices, however, depend on *their* quantity constraints. Perceived quantity constraints and the specification of rationing schemes must be introduced to solve the puzzle and cut off an infinite regress. Barro and Grossman (1976), Drèze (1975), Benassy (1975) and Malinvaud (1977) (among others) have presented fix-price models along these lines and with various different specifications of the perceived quantity constraints and the rationing schemes.[7]

In spite of its obvious technical qualities, this literature has not really progressed much beyond the simple (neo)classical idea that fixity of nominal wage rates may cause unemployment.[8] And since the fixity of wages and prices is simply postulated at the outset, it seems difficult to take seriously the claim to have provided sound choice-theoretic foundations; why should prices remain fixed if it is in the interest of some agents to change them? The obvious questions of why agents are unable or unwilling to change prices when they face quantity constraints is not even posed. Furthermore, in most of the models the quantity constrained fix-price equilibria are obtained as the result of a process of quantity tatonnement. The Walrasian auctioneer has not been made redundant; instead of conducting a price tatonnement he now dictates a fixed price vector and then proceeds to cry out quantity sinals in the quantity tatonnement.

Hahn's notion of 'conjectural equilibrium' was devised to overcome these problems.[9] Let all agents form conjectures concerning the relationship between changes in their offer prices and the associated changes in the quantity constraints which they face. In Hahn's formulation a pure Walrasian equilibrium without quantity constraints would qualify as a special case of conjectural equilibrium but the existence of 'non-Walrasian' quantity constrained equilibria cannot be ruled out.[10] The relative advantage of this formulation is obvious: equilibrium prices and quantities are determined jointly (as in the traditional Arrow–Debreu model) by the optimizing behaviour of individual agents in an interrelated system. Prices are not arbitrarily fixed nor is the full market clearing price vector found by the intervention of fictitious auctioneer directed tatonnement processes. Equilibrium is a state where agents do not perceive of any actions which would make them better off, and therefore choose to trade at the ruling prices and quantity constraints.[11]

The conjectual equilibrium construction constitutes a genuine generalization of both the flex-price and the fix-price equilibrium. Flex-price equilibrium emerges as one limiting case by assuming that agents conjecture atomistic market conditions, i.e. when agents believe that arbitrarily small changes in their offer prices will cause infinite changes in quantity constraints. The fix-price case follows on the opposite extreme assumption of conjectural demand and supply curves that are reverse L-shaped. The generality of the construction does not however settle the questions of whether the notion of conjectural equilibrium provides a promising theoretical framework and whether Keynes's theory can be represented/interpreted within this theoretical framework. The second question is – in itself – perhaps not terribly interesting. As Coddington (1976) noted, economists have started to read 'not so much between the lines as off the page' (p. 1268) in their attempts to understand and interpret Keynes. Nevertheless, a discussion of differences and similarities between a theory of conjectural equilibrium and Keynes's theory may help to shed light on substantive issues concerning the usefulness of different theoretical approaches in economics.

HICKS AND KEYNES – TWO ORIGINS OF GE-KEYNESIANISM

On the exegetical question, Hahn himself seems to be in no doubt; conjectural equilibrium is not an adequate representation of Keynes:

> the Keynesian spirit of the thing, namely that there is something for government to do, receives confirmation even before any dynamic processes have been studied. But I think that is all the Keynesian juice there is and I do not think it useful to call each and every departure from Walras, Keynesian.
>
> (Hahn, 1977b, p. 35)

I agree with this rather negative judgement, but before presenting my reasons for it, I should like to emphasize that Hahn's notion of conjectural equilibrium provides an excellent theoretical representation of at least one strand of 'Keynesian' theory. As noted by Clower.

> 'Keynesian Economics' owes as much or more to the author of *Value and Capital* and 'Mr. Keynes and the Classics' as to the author of the *General Theory of Employment, Interest and Money*.
>
> (Clower, 1975, p. 7)

The strand of Keynesianism emanating from *Value and Capital* (Hicks, 1946) – and *Capital and Growth* (Hicks, 1965) – has found its culmination in the notion of conjectural equilibrium. To be sure, there is still plenty of scope for technical exercises and the whole issue of conjecture formation may also invite further discussion. But on a conceptual level I think the Value and Capital-inspired Keynesian research programme has been completed.

In *Value and Capital* Hicks presented the TE framework. He suggested that a proof of the existence of equilibrium in the TE model could follow the same lines as existence proofs for full GE models but he also pointed to the Keynesian factors – expectations, uncertainty, money contracts and bankruptcies – which may destabilize the system or even jeopardize the existence of equilibrium. He furthermore argued that price rigidities and in particular wage rigidities may help to stabilize the system at what is in effect a fix-price TE (although the terms fix-price and flex-price were not to be introduced until *Capital and Growth* which also contains a fuller discussion of the hypotheses about the behaviour of prices and wages and their implications). The treatment of Keynes by Arrow and Hahn more than thirty years later echoes Hicks' position in *Value and Capital;* all the main ingredients in Arrow and Hahn's discussion were present already in *Value and Capital*. The technical investigation of GE systems in the hands of Arrow, Debreu and others during three decades by and large confirmed Hicks' hunches concerning the properties of TE systems and the GE school is therefore in a position to pronounce Hicks's suggested Keynes interpretation logically sound.[12]

The distinction between fix-price and flex-price markets in *Capital and Growth* is backed up by a discussion of factors that determine the price behaviour likely to be found in any particular market. Hicks's basic contention is that stocks and middlemen are of paramount importance in decentralized economic systems and that the existence of independent middlemen – independent of both producers and consumers – tends to be associated with flex-price markets whereas the fix-price behaviour is likely to be found in markets where the role of stock-carrying middlemen has been taken over by producers themselves. Personally I do not find this argument very convincing but for present purposes the main point to note is that the existence of price flexibility or rigidity is explicitly related to the actions of optimizing agents facing a set of perceived constraints and that Hahn's notion of conjectural equilibrium provides a formal and unified representation of fix- and flex-price equilibria as well as of intermediate cases.[13]

The distinction between Value and Capital Keynesianism and 'Mr. Keynes and the Classics Keynesianism' (Hicks, 1937) is sometimes made with reference to an alleged difference in operationality. The Value and Capital branch is held to be purely theoretical and concerned with questions of existence and stability in GE type model whereas 'Mr. Keynes economists' are guided in their work by immediate and practical issues and therefore seek tractable aggregate models which will be useful in applied work.[14] The distinction between theoretical and operational branches may of course be highly appropriate for some purposes but there are also, I think, on a purely theoretical level important differences between the Value and Capital formulation and 'Mr. Keynes and the Classics'; 'Mr. Keynes' is not just an aggregative and/or incomplete version of the Value and Capital model and it is very likely, I think, that Keynes may have accepted the theoretical skeleton of 'Mr. Keynes and the Classics' and objected to the Value and Capital formulation precisely because of these theoretical differences.[15]

The IS-LL (or IS-LM) model which Hicks introduced in 'Mr. Keynes and the Classics' explicitly deals with three aggregate economic goods, a consumption good, an investment good and money. The (money) prices of investment and consumption goods are determined by standard marginal cost conditions derived from given short run production functions in labour input, the money wage rate being given exogenously. Any given nominal demand for investment (consumption) goods may thus readily be transformed into real demand which is in turn – in equilibrium with demand being equal to supply – related to the (sectoral) demand for labour.[16]

The model is set out in two simple equations

$$(1)\ M = L(Y,i)$$
$$(2)\ I(i) = S(Y)$$

where S, I, Y, M, i denote savings, investment, income, the money supply and the rate of interest respectively.[17] From (1) one gets the LM curve and from (2) the IS curve.

The IS-LM apparatus provides a neat two-dimensional method illustrating the simultaneous equilibrium in these three markets, investment goods, consumption goods and money. Implicitly, however, Hicks's model contains another two aggregates, labour services and bonds. The complete model has five goods and four relative prices.[18] Now, in a GE system with n goods, equality between the supply and demand for n-1 goods ensures that also the last good will have zero excess demand, but if just n-2 excess demands are known to be zero then Walras' Law only enables one to conclude that the values of the excess demands in the two remaining markets sum to zero. From a GE point of view, the IS-LM framework is therefore incomplete.

The incompleteness, is, I think, indicative of the most important difference between the Value and Capital model and 'Mr. Keynes and the Classics'.[19] It may seem only a small difference and the IS-LM may even appear to be obviously inferior to the full Value and Capital model, albeit an inferiority which is easily remedied: simply introduce a labour supply function which by the assumption of fixed money wages becomes reverse L-shaped.[20] The labour market is now seen to be in equilibrium, provided the labour demand, derived from the IS-LM apparatus, does not exceed the maximum labour supply.[21] Since four out of five markets are now in equilibrium the fifth will be likewise; the supply and demand functions for bonds are given implicitly by the specification of other behavioural relations. By virtue of Walras' Law, the bond market will also be in equilibrium.

I think the above gives a fairly accurate account of the way the IS-LM model is usually interpreted. It is seen as a convenient but strictly speaking incomplete exposition of a GE system, an exposition which is perfectly legitimate as long as the supply of labour is perfectly elastic at the given money wage rate[22] and total employment is therefore determined by demand in the product markets and the form of the short run production functions. On this interpretation the IS-LM framework is merely a clever way of dealing with certain Value and Capital type TE systems which happen to decompose in a particular way. The Value and Capital strand of Keynesianism has swallowed up 'Mr. Keynes and the Classics.'

There is an alternative interpretation of the IS-LM model. But before presenting it (pp. 73–4) some preparation is needed.

KEYNES AND MARSHALL

It has become a commonplace that Keynes's approach was Marshallian and not Walrasian in character. The Cambridge (UK) Keynesians have maintained this all along (e.g. Robinson, 1969) and after Clower and Leijonhufvud had been converted and renounced their earlier neo-Walrasian disequilibrium interpretation of Keynes the view has gained general acceptance. Unfortunately, it is not always quite clear what are the implications of the Marshallian character. 'Marshallian' sometimes seems to be defined only negatively – and very vaguely – as 'non-Walrasian'.

In their recent work Clower and Leijonhufvud emphasize mainly the differences between Marshallian and Walrasian theories regarding transactions technologies. In the Marshallian tradition the middlemen, the professional traders, are at the centre of the exchange process whereas Walrasian theory has relied on fictional tatonnement processes. These differences between the two traditions are undoubtedly extremely important and the actual functioning of markets and the role of professional traders are issues which have certainly been neglected by mainstream (theoretical, Walrasian) economics and which deserve careful investigations.[23] But I am not sure that these differences between the Marshallian and the Walrasian approach are the most important for an understanding of GT. The problems of an economy with production and long term investment are at the heart of Keynes's analysis in GT (and in the *Treatise*) and an analysis of Marshallian vs Walrasian pure exchange systems is by itself not likely to throw much light on these problems.

The Marshallian clue to GT – and a possible clue to Keynes's acceptance of the IS-LM representation of GT – is to be found in another aspect of the Marshallian approach, probably the best known aspect, the period analysis. Marshall adopted a tripartite division of the analysis of single industries. In the ultra-short period (the market day) supply is given and the market price, the ultra-short period equilibrium price, is determined by demand.[24] In the short period at least one factor of production is variable and in equilibrium producers have adapted the variable inputs and output to the levels which are optimal given the combination of fixed and variable factors that constrain their choice set. Finally, in the long run all factors are freely variable and in equilibrium firms have chosen input and output levels which are optimal when there are no inherited constraints on factor inputs.

The terminology sounds more dynamic than is really warranted. The notions of short and long period equilibrium are basically static concepts; a long period equilibrium is a 'full equilibrium' in the sense that all factors are variable whereas a short period equilibrium is a 'restricted equilibrium', the equilibrium is conditional on an historically given set of fixed capital equipment. The 'full' long period equilibrium is also of course conditional on certain 'givens' for example technical knowledge. The distinction between full and restricted equilibria is one of degree; in the long period equilibrium less has been locked up in the Marshallian 'pound of ceteris paribus' (Hicks, 1965, p. 49), but the price for this increased generality is more stringent equilibrium conditions and a more stationary equilibrium concept.[25] There is no analysis of a process which could generate long period equilibrium as the (asymptotic) result of a sequence of short period equilibria, just as the short period equilibrium is not explicitly constructed as the outcome of output adjustments in a sequence of ultra-short period equilibria. A long period equilibrium may be conceived of as a (trivial) sequence of identical short period equilibria and a short period equilibrium as a sequence of identical ultra-short period equilibria. There is no question of getting into equilibrium, but merely a set of static equilibrium concepts which are ordered hierarchically according to their 'restrictiveness', the number of influences which are frozen with a ceteris paribus clause.[26] The Marshallian scheme does not solve the problem of stringing together ultra-short period equilibria in a genuine process analysis. The problem is ingeniously sidestepped by the use of ceteris paribus clauses in a nested set of equilibrium concepts. In Hicks's (1965) words although 'the method of Marshall can be regarded . . . as a last stage in the evolution of static method, it gets very near to dynamics' (p. 57).

Keynes obviously was not dealing with an isolated industry. If he used the Marshallian apparatus then it was an apparatus which had been amended so as to deal with the whole economy instead of just an industry. The principal problem with an adaptation of Marshallian categories to the macrolevel[27] concerns the determination of demand and supply schedules for output as a whole. In the partial analysis of single industries which are small relative to the size of the economy it may be admissible to regard wage rates, interest rates, the prices of raw materials, intermediate deliveries and fixed capital inputs as well as total real income in the economy as given independently of what happens in the industry.[28] These assumptions – when combined with stipulations concerning firms' decision criteria and consumer tastes and preferences – enable one to draw well-defined and strictly independent demand and supply functions for the inputs and outputs of the industry. If one looks at output as a whole, however, then matters become more complicated; independent demand and supply curves for output as a whole can hardly be constructed on the assumption of 'given incomes'. (Nominal) wage incomes are generated by the labour market effects of firms' production decisions and profit incomes arise as the result of demand pressures working on a given level of output. Neither wage nor profit incomes will therefore be independent of supply decisions and aggregate demand will presumably depend on income.[29] In other words, the Marshallian apparatus needs considerable amendment if it is to be used to analyse the demand and supply of output as a whole. It was Keynes' contention that Marshallian partial equilibrium analysis had illegitimately been applied to the economic system as a whole and the main purpose of GT was to develop appropriate concepts of aggregate demand and aggregate supply functions as well as their intersection at the point of 'effective demand'. Thus, after the first presentation of the aggregate demand and supply functions at the beginning of chapter 3, the first constructive chapter of GT, Keynes (1936) states:

Since this (the determination of the level of employment by the principle of effective demand, PS) is the substance of the General Theory of Employment, which it will be our object to expound, the succeeding chapters will be largely occupied with examining the various factors upon which these two functions depend. (p. 25)[30]

The 'classical' advocacy of flexible money wages as a remedy against unemployment was, Keynes suggested, based on an analysis which ignored the economy-wide interdependencies between supply and demand functions. The 'classical' argument according to Keynes relies on partial equilibrium tools that are inapplicable to the question of the general level of unemployment[31]:

The demand schedules for particular industries can only be constructed on some fixed assumption as to the nature of the demand and supply schedules of other industries and as to the amount of aggregate effective demand. It is invalid, therefore, to transfer the argument to industry as a whole unless we also transfer our assumption that the aggregate effective demand is fixed. Yet this assumption reduces the argument to an *ignoratio elenchi.* For, whilst no one would wish to deny the proposition that a reduction in money-wages *accompanied by the same aggregate effective demand as before* will be associated with an increase in employment, the precise question at issue is whether the reduction in money-wages will or will not be accompanied by the same aggregate effective demand as before measured in money, or, at any rate, by an aggregate effective demand which, is not reduced in full proportion to the reduction in money-wages (i.e. which is somewhat greater measured in wage-units). But if the classical theory is not allowed to extend by analogy its conclusions in respect of a particular industry to industry as a whole, it is wholly unable to answer the question what effect on employment a reduction in money wages will have. For it has no method wherewith to tackle the problem.

(Keynes, 1936, pp. 259–60; italics in original)

In fact, the term *general* theory is, according to Keynes himself, used to signify that his theory is valid for the system as a whole and is not restricted to the partial analysis of individual industries. In the preface to the French edition, written three years after the English publication, Keynes (1936) explains:

I have called my theory a *general* theory. I mean by this that I am chiefly concerned with the behaviour of the economic system as a whole, – with aggregate incomes, aggregate profits, aggregate output, aggregate employment, aggregate investment, aggregate saving rather than with the incomes, profits, outputs, employment, investment and saving of particular

industries, firms and individuals. And I argue that important mistakes have been made through extending to the system as a whole conclusions which have been correctly arrived at in respect of a part of it taken in isolation.
(p. xxxii; italics in original)

THE SHORT RUN UNEMPLOYMENT EQUILIBRIUM

Within the tripartite division of Marshallian period analysis the focus of attention in GT is primarily on the short-period. The major part of GT is devoted to the exposition of a theory of short-period equilibrium for output and employment as a whole. The stock of fixed capital is taken as given and constant and throughout most of the book it is assumed that 'short-period expectations' are fulfilled. The problems which arise if short-term expectations are disappointed (i.e. if the demand for output turns out to be less than expected by entrepreneurs at the beginning of the production process) are mentioned at several points in GT but not dealt with in any detail.[32] In this sense Keynes remained within the static Marshallian methodology.[33] Indeed, in his 1937 lecture notes on 'Ex Post and Ex Ante', Keynes suggested that it would have been preferable to set out the General Theory on the assumption that short-term expectations are always fulfilled before even raising the difficulties implied by disappointed expectations:

I now feel that if I were writing the book again I should begin by setting forth my theory on the assumption that short-period expectations were always fulfilled; and then have a subsequent chapter showing what difference it makes when short-period expectations are disappointed.

For other economists, I find, lay, the whole emphasis, and find the whole explanation in the *differences* between effective demand and income; and they are so convinced that this is the right course that they do not notice that in my treatment this is *not* so.
(Keynes, 1973, p. 181; italics in original)

Keynes is not primarily concerned with the *process* whereby a short-period equilibrium with fulfilled short-term expectations might be reached. It was his contention that involuntary unemployment could appear even if short term expectations were fulfilled; the cause of unemployment was not to be found in the disequilibrium phenomena associated with disappointed short period expectations. Because of this and because most Western countries were in the depth of depression, it seemed far more important to describe the factors influencing the position of short-period equilibrium – in particular unemployment equilibrium – than to analyse the 'method of trial and error', the 'higgling of the market' by which entrepreneurs groped for and approximated the equilibrium position.

> The main point is to distinguish the forces determining the position of equilibrium from the technique of trial and error by means of which the entrepreneur discovers where the position is.
>
> (Keynes, 1973, no. 182)

And, as a comment on the Swedish distinction between ex ante and ex post

> I'm more classical than the Swedes, for I am still discussing the conditions of short-period equilibrium.
>
> (Keynes, 1973, p. 183)

The heavy emphasis on short period *equilibrium* emerged during the actual writing of GT. The *Treatise* (TM), finished six years before GT (see Keynes, 1930), had concentrated almost exclusively on the Marshallian ultra-short period. Output was taken as given and

> My so-called 'fundamental equations' were an instantaneous picture taken on the assumption of a given output. They attempted to show how, assuming the given output, forces could develop which involved a profit-disequilibrium, and thus required a change in the level of output. But the dynamic development, as distinct from the instanteous picture, was left incomplete and extremely confused.
>
> (Keynes, 1936, p. xxii)

The transition from TM to GT was not immediate. The first drafts of what was to become GT attempted to string together a sequence of (TM like) ultra-short period equilibria:

I reached the conception of effective demand comparatively late on. Those who are old enough and attended in 1931–1932 may remember a contraption of formulas of process of all sorts of lengths depending on technical factors with income emerging at a given date corresponding to input at an earlier date. My distinction then was between input and output. I would lecture on this at considerable length and at one time it occupied several chapters in my book. But I discarded it partly because it was frightfully complicated and really no sense in it, but mainly because there was no determinate time unit. I found I could get all that was required by the conceptions of effective demand and income which were identical for factors but income of entrepreneurs at any time depended on outcome of prediction undertaken at various previous periods under influence of effective demand.

When one is dealing with *aggregates*, aggregate effective demand at time A has no corresponding aggregate income at time B. All one can compare is the expected and actual income resulting to an entrepreneur from a particular decision. Actual investment may differ through unintended stock changes, price changes, alteration of decision. The difference, if any, is due to a mistake in the short-period expectation and the importance of the difference lies in the fact that this difference will be one of the relevant factors in determining subsequent effective demand.

I began, as I have said, by regarding this difference as important. But eventually I felt it to be of secondary importance, emphasis on it obscuring the real argument. For the theory of effective demand is substantially the same if we assume that short-period expectations are always fulfilled.

(Keynes, 1973, pp. 180–1)

Keynes, in other words, wanted to examine the possibility of equilibrium with involuntary unemployment. This to many economists – both past and present – has sounded like a contradiction in terms;[34] if there is unemployment then some prices – and in particular the money wage rates – should change, and if they do not, then unemployment must be voluntary in the sense that workers – individually or as a group – have not taken steps to ameliorate the alleged unemployment. It is certainly correct that the coexistence of persistant unemployment and rigid money wage rates would require an explanation.[35] But leaving aside for the moment this question, assuming that some satisfactory explanation for sticky wage rates can be found,[36] one could go on and ask (i) what are the determinants of equilibrium if the money wage rate is given and (ii) what would be the likely effects on the equilibrium thus determined of changes in the money wage rate?

This is Keynes' procedure. The first question is dealt with in Books I–IV of GT. By focusing on an aggregate version of Marshall's short-period equilibrium[37] where employment is fully adjusted to the level which entrepreneurs consider optimal in the light of existing fixed capital equipment and of their perceptions of the demand conditions facing them, Keynes is able to disregard production, information and decision lags. The sequential structure *within* the short period can be neglected and for analytical purposes all events within the period may be telescoped into a static simultaneous framework.[38]

But having established the principle of effective demand, i.e. having developed a *general* Marshallian framework of short-period equilibrium with given money wages, Keynes had to face the second question and the answer to that question was crucial for his theory.

If a drop in money wages would serve to increase the level of employment then high wages would be a cause of unemployment; unemployment would be 'voluntary'. In this case there would be no need for government intervention to relieve unemployment, except possibly for measures to remove institutional obtacles to wage flexibility or policies to reduce frictional unemployment.

If, on the other hand, cuts in money wages have no effect on employment (or perhaps even increase the rate of unemployment) then high and sticky money wages cannot be held responsible for unemployment. The normal price mechanism does not work in the labour market; excess supply in the labour market is invariant with respect to (or perversely affected by) changes in money wages. Workers may be rationed in the labour market and unable to relax the quantity constraint they face by adjusting the price of the commodity, labour power, which they would like to sell.[39] Or in Keynesian terminology, unemployment may be involuntary even if observed money wages are rigid. A different test for 'volition' is needed. Keynes' 'contrived' definition of 'involuntary unemployment'[40] as well as his decision to measure values in terms of wage units must be understood in this light; the results of his analysis of changes in money wages was anticipated in the choice of units of measure and in the definition of involuntary unemployment.

What is at stake here is obviously not just the selection of suitable names for different 'types of unemployment'; the voluntary/involuntary distinction does not at all concern the possibility of classifying individual workers into one or the other of the two categories as Lucas (1978) suggests.[41] It concerns the causes of the aggregate level of unemployment. Involuntary unemployment is caused by market failures. It is the manifestation of an inability of the economic system to generate price movements which could eliminate excess supply in the labour market.

CHANGES IN MONEY WAGES

Consider the question of changing money wages. If a fixed wage short period unemployment equilibrium has been established what will be the likely effects of changes in the wage rate? Notice the restricted character of the question. The general dynamic question has been tamed by assuming that a fix-wage equilibrium has been attained before any change in the wage rate is contemplated. The question in fact concerns the stability of the fix-wage equilibrium. The equilibrium whose stability is being investigated is an unemployment equilibrium but that does not change the fact that it is the disequilibrium repurcussions of a particular and judiciously chosen disturbance that are being traced out. It is therefore somewhat surprising that Clower in his celebrated 1965 appraisal of Keynes's contribution completely dismissed the stability issue; discussing Keynes's insistence on the importance of the fact that the wage bargain is conducted in terms of money wages, Clower suggested that

> the burden of his argument seems to be that if labour is ever forced to move 'off its supply curve' it may be unable to get back again. If this is an accurate interpretation, we may say immediately that Keynes' criticisms are not of

fundamental theoretical significance, for there is no reason to suppose that Keynes was more expert at stability analysis than his orthodox predecessors.

(Clower, 1965, p. 109)

Well, why not??? Is there any reason to suppose that he was *not* more expert than his predecessors? Stability issues are at the heart of Keynes's theory and it is only because of this that it becomes so important to insist on a Marshallian approach.[42]

Based as it is on timeless tatonnement processes, the orthodox Walrasian stability analysis is a curious affair. The more recent neo-Walrasian fix-price theories of TE present a slightly more complicated picture. The introduction of quantity constraints and spillover effects imply that prices can no longer plausibly be expected to respond to aggregate notional excess demands. The fix-price theories specify possible outcomes outside the full Walrasian equilibrium and suggest that price changes should reflect the 'effective excess demands' characterizing these 'disequilibrium' states. The stability question in Walrasian and Neo-Walrasian models is by no means fully resolved but for present purposes this does not really matter.[43] The important point is simply that both Walrasian and Neo-Walrasian approaches assume that all current prices – as well as selected forward prices – are given simultaneously. In the context of an exchange economy where given endowments are bestowed upon agents at the beginning of each period, the assumption of a given current price vector is unequivocal. When one turns to production economies this is no longer so and production is at the centre of the stage in the economy that Keynes attempted to analyse. Keynes's stability analysis therefore bears little resemblance with the familiar Walrasian exercises.

Production takes time and inputs are contracted before outputs can appear. Furthermore, there are usually costs involved in changing the scale of production, partly for technical reasons but the more important reasons are likely to be economic in most cases. Inputs, and in particular labour power, are bought on forward contracts which make the input costs downward inflexible in the very short run and the costs associated with the hiring and training of new workers give firms a powerful incentive to reduce fluctuations in the size of the labour force. Decisions at time t_o about the size of the labour force will therefore be governed by expected output prices (demand conditions) over some period in the future, say, the period from $t_o + \mu + \delta$ to $t_o + \mu + \delta + \rho$ where μ, ρ and δ can be loosely interpreted as the period between employment decision and implementation, as the shortest interval after which it will be feasible/economical for the firm to revise its employment level and as the production period respectively.[44] From the point of view of production decisions of firms the 'current' prices that matter are the prices of inputs during the interval $(t_o + \mu, t_o + \mu + \rho)$ and the prices of output during $(t_o + \mu + \delta, t_o + \mu + \delta + \rho)$.[45]

I shall assume that firms know the path of input prices over the interval $(t_o + \mu, t_o + \mu + \rho)$ at time t_o.[46] Firms will usually possess sufficient knowledge to estimate their 'short run labour supply function'; this is likely to be the case particularly in times of substantial involuntary unemployment. The fact that labour contracts are usually negotiated for considerable time periods imparts a certain stability and predictability on labour costs; it insulates the firm against sudden surprises on the cost side in a near future.

On the demand side, however, things are different.[47] The demand estimate for the period from $t_o + \mu + \delta$ to $t_o + \mu + \delta + \rho$ will usually be impaired by considerable uncertainty. There will not usually be organized forward markets and demand will be subject to stochastic fluctuations making it difficult to ascertain even short run trend elements to form a reliable basis for predictions of future demand. When investigating the implications of a change in nominal wage rates it therefore seems singularly inappropriate to use a framework which takes the (relevant) sets of input and output prices to be contemporaneous and assumes that they are known – or estimated – with equal confidence. The effect on employment of a fall, say, in the wage rate when the demand function for future output, produced by labour currently employed, is known, is likely to be very different from the effect if future demand is uncertain. This difference is likely to be enhanced if demand is known to fluctuate stochastically and firms therefore keep buffers in the form of stocks.

This is not the main point, though. The crucial issue concerns the likely consequences of a decision to expand employment following a decline in the money wage rate. If producers are induced to increase production and employment in the expectation that demand functions have not shifted downwards in proportion to the drop in wage rates, will their judgement then be vindicated by subsequent market experience? This, of course, is the central question of chapter 19 in GT. Keynes first makes the – today obvious – observation that the question must be answered by analysing the effects on the determinants of the major demand categories, consumption and investment:

> the reduction in money-wages will have no lasting tendency to increase employment except by virtue of its repurcussion either on the propensity to consume for the community as a whole, or on the schedule of marginal efficiencies of capital, or on the rate of interest. There is no method of analysing the effect of a reduction in money-wages, except by following up its possible effects on these three factors.
>
> (Keynes, 1936, p. 262)

Unfortunately, the ensuing analysis is – as noted by Leijonhufvud (1968) – 'less than thorough'; Keynes, for instance, ignored the Pigou-effect which was later to cause so much furore. The main problem with the analysis, however, arises in a different direction. The examination of dynamic issues is never an easy matter but it is not likely to become easier if one is committed to a static conceptual framework. An example: Keynes's consumption function is defined as the relation between the aggregate supply price of output measured in wage units and aggregate consumption which is also measured in terms of supply prices deflated by the wage unit. Even if one completely disregards the problems which stem from the possible maladjustment of the composition of consumption supply to the composition of demand (at supply prices) as well as the variations in income distribution, total employment and sectoral output levels which may be compatible with the same aggregate supply price of output, even if one disregards these aggregation problems, the consumption function still remains tied to the notion of short-period equilibrium. If a new short-period equilibrium is not established at the higher level of employment, i.e. if firms did not correctly anticipate demand conditions, then there is no reason why prices should be kept equal to supply prices. This particular objection obviously loses its force if firms act as price-makers and choose to set prices equal to supply prices.[48] But even if one accepted this assumption concerning price behaviour, the consumption function would not be rescued from its status of short-period equilibrium tool. Consumption will in general depend on a weighted average of past and (expected) future incomes as well as on the distribution of income. The weighting, the relative importance of past, present and expected future income in influencing current consumption, will differ between groups of income receivers. For workers the weighting is likely to exhibit a high degree of concentration on incomes in the recent past whereas rentiers and capitalist – the recipients of residual incomes – will probably on average be influenced much more in their consumption decisions by perceptions of 'normal' income which depend less strongly in recent experience. Strictly speaking, a functional relation between consumption at time t_o and the entrepreneurial expectations at time $t_o - \mu - \delta$ concerning aggregate demand at time t_o therefore only makes sense in the stationary conditions of short-period equilibrium. Furthermore, outside short-period equilibrium the (expected) profit component of the aggregate supply price which supposedly influences consumption demand cannot be distributed to ultimate income recipients (consumers) until after the consumption plans have been executed. And it does not seem plausible that firms/managers should actually wish and be able to communicate *their* profit expectations (and expected dividend payments and capital gains) with such conviction and persuasive power that shareholders will act as if the profits had already materialized.[49]

The terminological framework of GT, thus, was not well-suited for dynamic analysis. In spite of this Keynes did make the crucial point. It can be stated quite simply.[50] Entrepreneurial optimism in expanding production is not likely to be vindicated unless aggregate investment demand is also increased. When it appears on the market, the increased production of output must be matched in part by an increased investment demand.[51] An important bootstrap element is hereby introduced. If firms are thoroughly optimistic and believe that good times are there to stay and if they therefore increase their long-term commitments by expanding investment programmes – and if they do so sufficiently swiftly – then their optimism will prove justified. Should they, on the other hand, adopt a more cautious attitude and stick to the previously planned investment programme until the apparent improvements had proved themselves in the form of increased profit margins and/or (real) sales, then they will be disappointed. This latter possibility is all the more likely in depressions with considerable margins of excess capacity.

There are, of course, exceptions to this statement. If, for instance, consumption expenditure in nominal terms is fairly inflexible, then firms may experience increased profit margins.[52] The Pigou-effect is one possible – but hardly important – factor making for some stability in nominal consumption expenditure. Lags between the receipt of income and expenditure is another possible source; whether these lags are justified by reference to money illusion, relative income theories or permanent income/life cycle hypotheses makes little difference. As a first approximation, it seems reasonable to assume, though, that workers' consumption expenditure is constrained by and closely related to current (very recent) incomes; the average wage-earner does not exactly have access to perfect credit markets and experience has even shown that saving propensities will often be raised in times of uncertainty as a precautionary measure. Workers' consumption is therefore unlikely to hold up for very long in the face of variations in nominal wage incomes. Consumption expenditure which is not constrained by current incomes i.e. the consumption of capitalist, rentiers and upper middle class salary earners or self-employed, on the other hand is likely to exhibit a considerable degree of stability in real terms. Overall, therefore, there seems little prospect that inflexible nominal consumption expenditure will provide sufficient demand to vindicate increased production levels. The groups of income receivers who will be the main benefactors of an increase in 'real wealth' associated with the existence of outside assets of fixed nominal value will typically have relatively inflexible levels of *real* consumption and the redistribution of wealth from debtors to creditors does not promise much of a stimulus to demand either. Workers' nominal consumption expenditure, finally, will be affected by the decline in money wages and is therefore highly unlikely to justify an expansion of output.[53]

Even without any consideration of possible negative effects of a drop in money wages it therefore seems unlikely that significant improvement in employment and production should be warranted. As a result, downward pressures on money wages in conditions of unemployment would tend to produce not just a single decline in money wages which quickly reestablished labour market equilibrium but a continuous fall in money wages and output prices. This, however, would bring into play strong negative influences; depressive expectations of further falls in wages and prices will be generated and bankruptcies of vulnerable firms with large commitments in nominal terms may cause severe disruptions to both financial and industrial systems. The weak and unreliable positive impact effects of a decline in money wages combine with potentially devastating effects of prolonged periods of falling money wages to make wage-flexibility undesirable.[54] An intensified class struggle and possibly political instability caused by the predictable resistance to wage reductions from at least some sections of the working class would provide additional reasons – also mentioned by Keynes – why a policy of increasing money wage flexibility may destabilize the system.

The preceding discussion may be summed up as follows: Keynes discusses the stability of an already established short-period unemployment equilibrium with respect to a particular disturbance, a decline in money wages. The disturbance is chosen with care. Since, by assumption, all other markets are in equilibrium, the initial endogenous impetus for change can only come from the labour market. It is only the money wage rate, the relative price between labour services and money, which is subject to pressures of (negative) excess demand. The stability issue is dealt with by considering two questions; whether the drop in money wages will induce firms to expand employment and whether an expansion of production and employment – if undertaken – will subsequently turn out to be warranted by demand conditions. In order to answer these questions it is necessary to look first at the decision problem facing firms. The crucial point to notice in this respect is that employment and production decisions will be influenced by expectations concerning future demand conditions and that this influence of expectations will be even more pronounced in the case of decisions concerning investment in long-lived fixed capital. In other words, the immediate response of firms to a drop in money wages is dependent on their assessment of future demand conditions.[55] The response will also be influenced and constrained by the adjustment costs associated with different reaction patterns and reaction speeds. The existence of adjustment costs – combined with the imperfect nature of virtually all markets – implies that firms find it optimal to maintain buffers in the form of unused capacity – of both equipment and labour power – and of stocks of finished goods. These buffers enable firms to smooth out the time path of employment and investment levels without losses of incomes or market shares. The increased supply flexibility means that the influence of changes in demand or supply conditions on employment and investment decisions will be slower than in the absence of buffers. The buffers make it optimal for firms to gather more information than would otherwise have been the case before making potentially very costly decisions to increase productive capacity. In particular, it seems highly unlikely that a drop in money wages should cause a significant immediate change in (fixed) investment plans for the near future. This means that the increase in demand (in wage units) which is required to validate an expansion of production must come from consumption expenditure.[56] The expansionary influence from consumption does not, however, look promising either. Real wealth effects – including redistributional effects between debtors and creditors – are likely to benefit groups with inflexible levels of real consumption. Workers are the main group with a consumption level that is strongly influenced by current (very recent) levels of income, but nominal wage rates have declined and consequently workers' consumption demand can only absorb the increased output if prices fall proportionately more than wages thus disappointing the expectations of a less than proportionate decline in prices which prompted firms to expand output.

So far I have neglected the possibility of increases in the desired level of stocks. This, however, is a highly implausible source of demand in the stated circumstances: stocks are kept as buffers and when firms are optimistic, the existence of adjustment costs – which is the very rationale for keeping buffers – implies that the desired (real) level of stocks should decrease; the only exceptions arising in cases where the optimistic expectations are frustrated. Increases in stocks would more likely to be a sign of disappointed expectations rather than a possible source of demand vindicating optimistic expectations.

The impact effect of a fall in money wages on the warranted level of production is therefore likely to be limited with the further implication that second round accelerator effects on fixed investment will be absent. The only positive second round effect derives from the possibility of a fall in interest rates following a decrease in the demand for money balances. If the long-term interest rates fall, then the optimal techniques of production may change and – barring instances of capital reversing or reswitching which are probably of minor practical importance[57] – investment in fixed capital will increase while firms adapt to the new situation with a higher optimal capital–labour ratio.[58] Against these possible expansionary effects must be set the contractionary influence emanating from expectations of a further decline in prices and wages and from increased debtor burdens. The strength and importance of the negative effects, however, depends crucially on the weakness of the positive impact effects. The negative effects will only gather momentum in so far as employment does not improve rapidly and the downward movement of wages therefore continues. In this sense, the crucial part of the analysis centres on the weakness of the positive impact effects and this weakness is intimately linked with the sequential order of events.

Workers' ability to effect a change in real wages and in employment levels hinges on the response of firms to a change in money wages. This response in turn is determined by firms' expectations concerning future events. And because firms know the future to be uncertain and therefore maintain buffers, the events that would warrant increases in employment and capital capacity may never materialize. Keynes's argument not only

> *seems to be* that if labour is ever forced to move 'off its supply curve' it may be unable to get back on again.
>
> (Clower, 1965, p. 109: italics added)

This *is* the argument. Keynes is quite explicit that this is in fact the case:

> there may be *no* method available to labour as a whole whereby it can bring the wage-goods equivalent of the general level of money wages into conformity with the marginal disutility of the current volume of employment. There may exist no expedient by which labour as a whole can reduce its *real* wage to a given figure by making revised *money* bargains with the entrepreneurs. This will be our contention.
>
> (Keynes, 1936, p. 13)

The argument which backs up this contention is based on explicit sequential assumption. If all the relevant 'current prices' were given simultaneously, if firms could somehow be provided with definite information concerning the demand conditions for new production initiated after a fall in money wages and if this information promised a very favourable state of demand then the likelihood of a swift expansion of employment and of investment would increase tremendously. A swift expansion of investment, in turn, would itself generate the favourable demand conditions that had been promised. Walrasian models which take all 'current' prices and quantities to be simultaneously determined are therefore grossly misleading as soon as one goes beyond the short-period equilibrium. At the very least it should be recognized that labour market events – the determination of money wages and employment levels – take place prior to the determination of the prices and/or changes in stocks which serve to clear the market for output. The hiring of workers and the marketing of the output produced by those workers are separated in time.

By taking nominal wage rates as given and leaving out completely the labour market, the IS-LM analysis at least does not violate this principle. It is true that Hicks in 'Mr. Keynes and the Classics' considered only short-perod equilibria where firms' short term expectations are fulfilled – as did Keynes in most of GT. And as argued above, the sequential assumptions only assume importance when stationarity is abandoned. If one were concerned with nothing more than the description of short-period equilibria, no great harm would be done by adding a labour market to the IS-LM system and thus making it formally equivalent to a Value and Capital type TE model. But Keynes did more than just describe short-period (fix-wage) equilibria. He also presented reasons why a fix-wage equilibrium may be relevant. The reasons were two-fold. The fundamental theoretical reason was that the effects on employment of a change in money wages are uncertain and may go either way. This argument was developed in chapter 19 and relied on the Marshallian sequential patterns associated with a production economy. Given the ambiguity of the employment effect, the appropriate benchmark assumption would be that employment is invariant with respect to (moderate) changes in money wages and that, consequently, the employment predictions of the fix-wage model would hold true even if money wages were not in fact rigid. The second reason was empirical in character; the actual attitude and behaviour of workers meant that money wages were relatively sticky. The two arguments reinforced each other. The empirical observation that money wages are sticky strengthened the case for the fix-wage model and ambiguous (possibly perverse) effects of money wage changes provided a rationale for workers' resistance to money wage cuts.

The apparently incomplete IS-LM model is compatible with the sequential patterns which are at the heart of Keynes's theoretical argument for the occurrence of market failure. A full TE representation of Keynes's analysis, on the other hand, would be misleading since it would obscure the sequential patterns of a production economy. Or more accurately, the standard textbook representation where input and output prices are determined simultaneously would obscure the sequential patterns.[59] The very generality (and vacuity) of the general TE framework means that Keynes's theory can be expressed in TE terms – provided that one includes as part of the TE framework the problem of stringing together a sequence of TE. Keynes's analysis of the effects of changing money wages can be seen as an attempt to derive the properties of the new TE configuration which would result if an initial unemployment equilibrium – a particular TE – were disturbed by a decline in money wages.[60]

KEYNES AND KALDOR – IS THE FOCUS ON SHORT RUN EQUILIBRIUM USEFUL?

As argued in the previous section, Keynes first developed a theory of short run Marshallian fix-wage equilibrium. He then went on to demonstrate that changes in money wages could not be relied upon to eliminate unemployment. This demonstration constituted the fundamental theoretical argument for the relevance of conclusions based on the model of fix-wage equilibrium: as long as changes in wage rates are moderate,[61] the equilibrium level of output and employment will not be affected and as firms adjust their short term expectations in the light of realized results, output and employment will move towards the levels predicted by the fix-wage model. And if the movement towards equilibrium is 'sufficiently rapid' then the error introduced into the analysis by assuming that the economy is always in short-period equilibrium will be negligible. This sort of assumption, of course, underlies all Keynesian short period models.

Is there in fact any reason to expect that the economy will

ever attain (or come very near to) short-period equilibrium? The short-period equilibrium will itself shift over time under the influence of changes in the capital stock and in long period expectations.[62] Changes in long-period expectations will to some extent be due to political, sociological and psychological factors which influence what Joan Robinson (and Keynes) called 'animal spirits' and it seems highly unlikely that these factors could be made endogenous in economic models. But for given 'animal spirits', the long-run expectations will hardly be invariant with respect to variations in actual outcomes and associated changes in short-period expectations.

The question arises, whether it is useful to give pride of place to the short-period equilibrium. Is it not possible instead to analyse movements over time directly as a sequence of ultra-short equilibria? As Joan Robinson and Kalecki have always insisted, a 'long-period' is nothing but a sequence of 'short-periods', it has no independent existence. And it does not seem obvious that the appropriate choice of basic 'short-period' for the analysis should be a Keynesian/Marshallian short-period with satisfied short-period expectations. With given animal spirits, i.e. assuming that there are no exogenous shifts in long-term expectations, an economy where short-period expectations are always fulfilled must in fact almost by necessity evolve along a time path which is consistent with the initial long-period expectations; i.e. the economy will effectively be in long-run equilibrium. The reason is simple: if firms are in any way rational in their formation of expectations then long- and short-period expectations must be mutually consistent. Since animal spirits are assumed constant, firms will revise their initial long-term expectations concerning the optimal time path of production and investment if and only if initial expectations are proved wrong in actual events. Given the consistency between short and long expectations, this can only happen if short-term expectations are disappointed at some point along the path. Phrasing it differently, since the long-period is no independent entity but merely a succession of short-periods, erroneous long-term expectations must involve a divergence between expected and actual outcomes in some short-period.

The implications of the above are straightforward. Even when dealing with short-term economic problems, it may be misleading to use a model of Keynesian/Marshallian short run equilibrium since the position of the equilibrium will itself be shifting. Furthermore, the notion of short-period equilibrium will almost certainly be of little use in an extension of Keynesian theory to cover long run developments. The possibility of disappointed expectations must be allowed for. Indeed, disappointed short-term expectations are probably – via their immediate effects on production and employment levels and the cumulative effects on long-term expectations and hence investment – among the most important factors driving the economy. A theory is needed which draws on Keynes' analysis of ultra-short run equilibria in TM and on his analysis of the effects of changes in money wages in GT.[63] It is the purpose of this section to give a brief discussion of one of the most interesting attempts to develop Keynesian theory in this direction, namely Kaldor's work on growth and distribution.

It is impossible to discuss here all the novel ideas which Kaldor presented in his papers on growth and income distribution.[64] I shall more or less ignore all issues related to the endogenous determination of technical progress, the appropriate specification of the investment function, the justification of the Kaldorian savings function and the problem of stability in the models.[65] The focus of attention will be on the sequential patterns in Kaldor's theory.

The basic Kaldorian model contains two aggregate agents (firms and households) and three commodities (money, labour power and output). Output is homogeneous and can be used for consumption or investment. All transactions involve money; labour power is exchanged against money and produced goods are exchanged against money but there is no direct trade of labour power for produced goods. There are thus two markets, a labour market and a goods market, and two associated relative prices, the money wage rate and the money price of output. The monetary transactions structure – and thus the existence of money in the system – is crucial. An explicit treatment of money in the model would therefore be preferable but for the sake of simplicity all other aspects of money than the monetary transactions structure will be ignored. All financial issues are dodged too.[66] In keeping with the assumption of homogeneous output it is assumed that firms are fully vertically integrated. There are no intermediate inputs; output is produced by labour and fixed capital equipment.

The movement of the economy over time can be described as a series of overlapping production cycles. At the beginning of each cycle the stock of fixed capital is given. Firms form expectations concerning the optimal level of employment and production. After an implementation lag, μ, the new level of employment has been attained and following a production lag, δ, the revised volume of output starts appearing on the goods market. The lengths of the two lags are assumed fixed and their combined length may serve as the unit of time.[67] Let us consider first the market for produced goods over a given short time interval. The total available supply of goods will be predetermined by past production decisions and the inherited stocks of finished goods at the beginning of the interval. Against this predetermined supply is set a demand coming from two different sources; a household demand for consumption goods and an investment demand from firms.

Consumption demand (in money terms) will be determined by past levels of (distributed) money incomes and in accordance with the discussion in the previous section it seems reasonable to assume that the average time lag between the receipt of wage income and consumption expenditure is shorter than – but of the same order of magnitude as – the lag between the formation of production and employment decisions and the appearance of the associated output. Owing to both the greater short run volatility of distributed profits and to the time lag between the receipt of profits in firms and subsequent distribution of dividends, the average lag between profits and consumption expenditure is likely to be longer.[68]

Fixed investment will usually be subject to significant gestation lags. Demand from this source will therefore largely depend on capacity and profitability conditions which prevailed when – or before – current output was planned. Fixed investment demand, furthermore, is likely to be inflexible in real terms and, if anything, the effect of high current (very recent) prices (booming demand conditions) will probably be positive as firms speed up their investment plans under the influence of boosted expectations.[69]

Given the overall supply of goods and these two demand components – one fixed (inflexible) in money terms and one in real terms – the equilibrium in the goods market is brought about by some combination of price and stock adjustments, the exact outcome depending on firms' pricing policies (which will, of course, be influenced by expectations concerning the permanence/transience of current demand conditions). In a fix-price economy the burden of adjustment will fall entirely on stocks and in a pure flex-price economy price variations – and the associated variations in real consumption demand – will be the equilibrating factor. The important point, however, is that the market signals which firms receive regarding the optimal future production and investment plans are unaffected by their chosen mix of price and stock adjustments. Or, more precisely, their reaction pattern may be an indication of how they perceive the market signal and as such may yield indirect information on their future production and investment response. If, say, a high level of demand is considered to be a temporary aberration then stock adjustments will probably be preferred to price adjustments and the effect on fixed investment plans will be minimal, whereas unanticipated demand conditions which are perceived as more permanent will cause price adjustments and a larger immediate effect on investment plans. The basic current signal, however, is the same and no matter how firms perceive it, the direction of the optimal production and investment response will be the same. Within the given framework, the possible variations in response could be dealt with by relating the response and thereby the effects on future production and investment plans to a distributed lag function of several past 'basic signals'; i.e. to past levels of consumption and fixed investment demand relative to past levels of supply and capacity. But for present purposes no great harm is done by ignoring these complications[70] and assuming – with Kaldor –

that the price of output adjusts so as to equate flow demand to (predetermined) flow supply. Since money wages are predetermined the share of profits in income is now determined. This realized share of profits gives rise to a demand schedule for labour (in terms of money wages) and influences the volume of fixed investment (in real terms) which is to be carried out after a gestation lag. The supply of labour – also a function of money wage rates – and the firms' demand function for labour determine the new level of employment which is implemented after a short time lag. The new level of employment implies a certain utilization rate for fixed capital equipment and thereby constitutes the other factor which together with profitability – determines fixed investment. As a (plausible) simplification it may be assumed that the lag between the formation of firm, irreversible investment plans and their execution is approximately equal to the production lag.

Finally, in order to analyse the model within a discrete time framework and avoid the complexities of differential systems with discrete lags, it is assumed that the level of employment, fixed investment and output as well as the money wage rate are so inflexible in the short run that the movements of each variable can be approximated by a primitive step function where the length of each step is equal to the combined length of the implementation lag and the production lag. In other words, it is assumed that the levels of employment, fixed investment, output and wage rates are changed only at discrete points in time and that, for each variable, the distance between two adjacent points is given by the time 'normally' required before a signal to change production levels has been transformed into actual changes in the flow of output.[71]

The sequential characteristics described above are illustrated schematically in Figure 2.1. At time $t_0 - \mu$ the flow of (real) output, real investment demand, money wages and nominal consumption demand are all predetermined and the price of output adjusts so as to clear the product market. The price (and the associated share of profits in income) and the size of the capital stock determine firms' demand curve for labour as a function of nominal wages. This demand curve

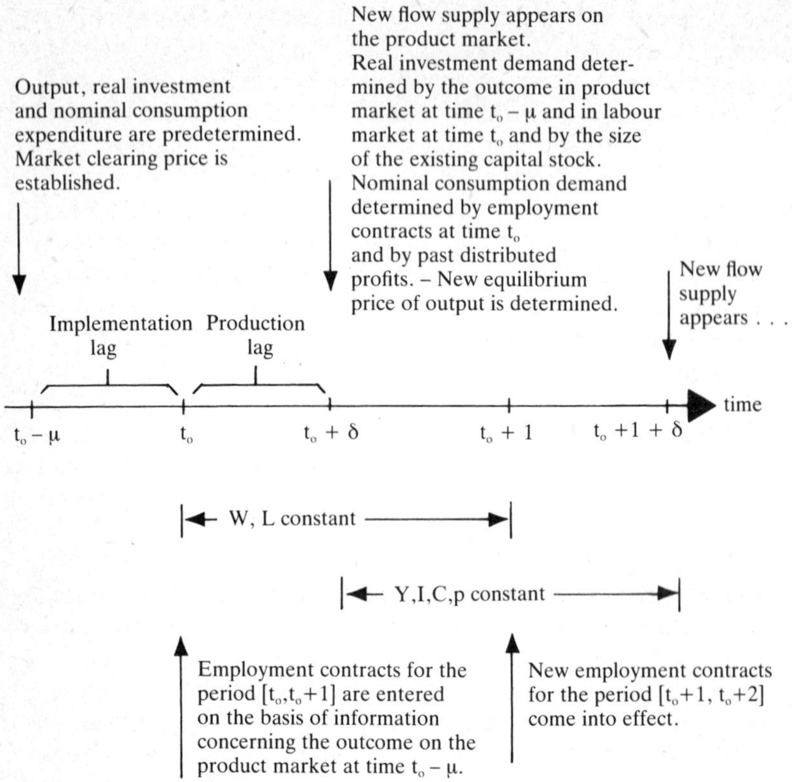

Figure 2.1

together with the supply curve of labour determine the new employment contracts which are implemented at time t_o. At time $t_o + \delta$ the flow of output associated with this level of employment appears on the market. Consumption demand in nominal terms at time $t_o + \delta$ is determined by the employment and wage contracts which were drawn up at time t_o and by past levels of distributed profits. Real investment demand is determined by firms' long term expectations[72] at time t_o and by the size of the capital stock. A new price of output to clear the product market at time $t_o + \delta$ is then determined. This in turn influences the labour supply and demand curves and hence the outcome on the labour market at time $t_0 + 1$; and so so and so forth.

The Kaldorian model discussed in this section obviously gives a highly schematic and simplified picture of the real world. There can be no pretentions of full descriptive 'realism'. Nor can it be claimed that the model – and in particular the sequential pattern – scores highly on 'generality'. This, however, is not in itself a weakness. Generality is not always to be strived for. The notion of TE is almost vacuous precisely because of its generality; nothing is said about linkages between subperiods and the nature of sequential patterns. The significance of the Kaldorian model hinges on the appropriateness of the particular assumptions underlying it; on whether the model – despite its simplicity and because of its particularity – gives a representation of the real world which is both non-vacuous and adequate with respect to some questions of interest.

This is not the place to attempt a more detailed evaluation of Kaldor's model and of the sequential assumptions embodied in it.[73] The important point here is merely that the sequential pattern of the model is of paramount importance[74] and that the pattern is firmly rooted in a Marshall-Keynes tradition. Abstracting from the more detailed assumptions which are introduced primarily for technical reasons in order to make the model analytically tractable, the main assumptions can be stated briefly in four points.

- There are no instantaneous feedbacks from current demand to current wages (and other distributed incomes) or from the current price of output to current wages.
- The adjustment of production to a new desired level takes time.
- The level of employment – although not perfectly flexible – is more flexible than the capital stock.
- The demand for consumption goods is constrained by past levels of distributed incomes whereas firms' demand for fixed investment is not similarly constrained in the short run.

Having noticed the Marshallian roots of Kaldor's theory, one should not, however, overlook the fact that it also diverges from Keynes–Marshall in some respects. It is a more genuinely dynamic analysis. A long run development is built up as a sequence of interlinked subperiods. Furthermore, although the basic, unit-length period is defined in Marshallian terms as the period over which firms are free to alter their production levels through a change in labour-inputs but where changes in the stock of fixed capital equipment can be ignored, the basic period is not characterized by the attainment of short-period equilibrium. When firms try to adapt their employment and production levels to perceived demand conditions they will probably also alter the level of fixed investment and the demand for consumption goods certainly will have shifted as a consequence of the change in production and employment. There is no reason to expect that a short-period equilibrium will ever be reached. At each point in time, production and employment are determined by Keynesian effective demand: production will be pushed to the point where *expected* proceeds (aggregate demand in GT terminology) equal supply price. But there is no assumption that short-period expectations will be fulfilled; actual proceeds will in general differ from expected proceeds. The outcome is a sequence of short-period disequilibria which can be analysed by a modified Marshallian ultra short-period equilibrium method. Or phrasing it differently, Kaldor's theory can be seen as an extension of traditional partial cobweb analysis. Kaldor recognizes the interdependence between supply and demand at an aggregate level and derives a generalized[75] Keynesian cobweb analysis with endogenously shifting demand curves.

In Kaldor's original papers the sequential characteristics are not discussed explicitly. One reason for this is that Kaldor assumed full employment[76]. This implies that the feedback from the product market to the labour market can be neglected; the full employment assumption – and an inelastic labour supply – provides the necessary information on labour market outcomes and also serves to determine the supply of produced goods[77]. This means that attention can be focused almost exclusively on the goods market and the determination of aggregate demand. The dynamic interaction between the labour market and the goods market is relegated to a shadowy position in the background. It is therefore perhaps not surprising that many later commentators have failed to pay sufficient attention to the sequential structure of the model. It has gone largely unnoticed that Kaldor's theory constitutes a further development of Keynes' first attempt to analyse the movement of an economy by filling in the gaps in the Marshallian tripartite period analysis – or, in the terminology of GE theory, by stringing together a sequence of interrelated temporary equilibria.

CONCLUDING REMARKS

The purpose of this paper has been to point out the crucial importance of sequential (or dynamic) patterns. In the real world there are no auctioneers and no instantaneous feedbacks, and economic theories which are cast in the form of simultaneous equilibrium conditions may be terribly misleading. Sequential patterns do not just influence the 'disequilibrium traverse towards equilibrium'. Explicit attention to sequential patterns is required in order to determine the properties of the 'equilibrium' itself.

This may sound a trivial point (and indeed it ought to be trivial). Unfortunately, it is often overlooked. This paper has focused on the attempts to interpret Keynes within the framework of simultaneous GE models, but numerous other examples could be found[78]. I have tried to argue that sequential patterns play a fundamental role in Keynes's theory of involuntary unemployment and that all GE interpretations of Keynes's theory are deficient because the sequential patterns are ignored.

Keynes's theory is open to many objections not dealt with in this paper. He made, I think, far too many concessions to neoclassical orthodoxy – for instance as regards the nature of competition, the shape of marginal cost curves and the exogeneity of the money supply. Assumptions of oligopolistic competition, increasing returns and an elastic supply of inside money may seem more approptiate. If these assumptions were introduced then the influence of 'real factors' and 'real constraints' on the economy would diminish and sequential patterns would probably assume even greater importance. The relevant sequential patterns, however, might also change; a time lag between A and B may be extremely important for the working of an economy under some assumptions and irrelevant under other assumptions. It is not therefore the 'constructive conclusion' of this paper that the sequential structure of the Kaldor model (described in the last section) is 'correct' and should be incorporated into all models of capitalistic economies. I do think, though, that the Keynes example illustrates the importance of sequential patterns and that the analyses of Keynes and Kaldor may serve as a fruitful source of inspiration in the further development of post-Keynesian theory.

NOTES

I would like to thank Philip Arestis, Paul Auerbach, George Bulkley, Victoria Chick, Meghnad Desai, Seren Bo Nielsen, Thanos Skouras and Peter Swann for helpful comments on an earlier draft of this paper.

1. Given the absence of a precise definition of the central terms 'dynamic' and 'GE theory', this of course is rather a fatuous claim, Skott (1986) develops the argument in greater detail.
2. The terms 'equilibrium' and 'disequilibrium' being used here with reference to the orthodox Walrasian notion of equilibrium. If equilibrium is taken in the wider sense, as a term for the theoretical representation of the regularity in the subject-matter which makes scientific inquiry possible, then obviously, the term 'disequilibrium theory' involves a contradiction in terms; if something can be theorized about then it possesses regularities and these regularities are described by the equilibria of the theory. In this terminology the question of 'stability' of a given equilibrium really concerns the possibility of detecting more detailed regularities, of developing a more general theory with a more general equilibrium, and of showing that if one were to accept the general theory then the old and more special theory would constitute a good approximation at least in most situations.

3. Cf. Hahn's comment in Hahn (1973b): 'GE is strong on equilibrium and very weak on how it comes about' (p. 327).
4. A 'liquidity trap', for instance, would not affect the existence of flex-price TE (cf. Hahn, 1977b, p. 26).
5. Both Clower and Leijonhufvud have since changed their views and now advocate a 'Marshallian' interpretation of Keynes (cf. Clower, 1975, and Clower & Leijonhufvud, 1975). I shall return to the Marshallian interpretation below.
6. In the process of cleaning up, new confusions unfortunately crept in. Walras' Law and Say's principle were originally seen as sharply contrasting and incompatible, whereas later it was admitted that the distinction might be fastidious (cf. Clower and Leijonhufvud, 1973). The term 'effective demand' in Clower's scheme, furthermore has little to do with Keynes' usage of the term; Arrow and Hahn's use of 'active demand' in place of 'effective demand' in Clower's sense therefore seems far preferable. Finally, there has, as pointed out by Hahn (1977b), been considerable confusion concerning the importance of a money-based transactions technology; Clower has not always been careful to distinguish between the effects of 'money' and the effects of 'fixed prices'.
7. Muus (1981) gives a useful survey of the fix-price models and also relates the models to both Walrasian flex-price theory and Marshallian theory.
8. In Hahn's words, 'all that has been achieved is the formulation of a proper concept of short period unemployment equilibrium with a given money wage. Indeed all one has done is to make explicit the micro-theory which underlies the budget identities and behavioural postulates of generations of macroeconomists. It is easy to replace the postulate of a given money wage with the assumption that it is positively and arbitrarily bounded below and one is then tempted to say that the sum total of Keynesian theory is in this 'price rigidity'. Many textbooks say just that. It is true that, until recently, it was not understood that the set of signals to which agents respond must now include quantities if a proper notion of equilibrium with some fixed prices is to be formulated. But once this is done there is not much left of the 'revolution'. For Keynes' contemporaries were all agreed that lack of 'price flexibility' was responsible for the trouble. I believe there is a good deal more to Keynesian economics than that' (Hahn, 1977b, p. 32).
9. See, for example, Hahn (1973a; 1977a; and 1978).
10. It is also possible to make imperfect competition an intrinsic property of the model and thus rule out orthodox Walrasian equilibria (cf. Negishi, 1960).
11. The crucial question of how a conjectural equilibrium may come to be established is unsettled. The notion of conjectural equilibrium was suggested as the answer to a question concerning the properties of hypothetical 'terminal states' of an economy.

12. One of the major lacunae in *Value and Capital* and *Capital Growth* is the neglect of spillover effects. This defect was remedied by the Clower-Leijonhufvud inspired reexamination of fix-price models.
13. As indicated above, Clower and Leijonhufvud's present emphasis on the Marshallian character of Keynes' theory and the importance of middlemen and stocks is also anticipated in Hicks' earlier work; see e.g. *Capital and Growth* chapter V–VIII. Clower and Leijonhufvud present their argument in Clower (1975), Clower and Leijonhufvud (1975), Leijonhufvud (1973). It has been common to label different Keynesian schools by reference to the chapters to GT where they pick up their cue. A taxonomy based on *Value and Capital, Capital and Growth* and 'Mr. Keynes and the Classics' may be equally, or more, appropriate for the large majority of economists who have absorbed their Keynes through Hicks' mediation.
14. This is the distinction adopted by Clower (1975).
15. Keynes's acceptance of the 'Mr. Keynes and the Classics' formulation is documented in Hicks (1973) – reprinted in Hicks (1977) – and in Keynes (1973). Keynes never commented on *Value and Capital* itself and what he would have thought of more recent developments of the Value of Capital inspired Keynesianism is anybody's guess.
16. In later textbook versions of the model output is often taken to be homogeneous, whereas Hicks's original version retains and formalizes GT's two-sector disaggregation into consumption and investment goods. Hicks's version is therefore not open to Leijinhufvud's criticisms of the standard income-expenditure model regarding 'aggregation structures'. (Leijonhufvud, 1968, p. 130 ff.)
17. S, I and Y are in nominal terms but the money wage is taken as given and the functions are conditional on the given money wage rate. In this respect the model is therefore in full agreement with the wage unit measurement used by Keynes in GT.
18. There is no problem in 'Mr. Keynes and the Classics' of a missing relative price; Leijonhufvud's (1968) aggregation discussion therefore is not pertinent. Notice that although apparently the system (1)–(2) contains only one relative price – the rate of interest – the remaining three prices are implicitly present; money wages were given and the money price of investment goods is determined by the level of investment in conjunction with the production function for the investment goods sector; income is the sum of the value of investment output and the value of consumption output and thus depends inter alia on the price of consumption goods which is determined by the consumption function – given by (2) – and the production function for the consumption goods sector.
19. The difference which has attracted most attention, namely the appearance of quantities in demand functions in 'Mr. Keynes and the Classics', is I think of relatively minor importance. Chick (1978), an extremely interesting paper, discusses this in some detail. As will be apparent, I agree with her also on the crucial character of sequential patterns in Keynes' theory.

20. The rigidity assumption can obviously be replaced by an assumption of downward inflexiblity. Notice that the argument in the labour supply function here is nominal wage rates and not real wage rates. With decreasing marginal productivity of labour – and the assumption that firms are on their supply and demand schedules – this implies that a drop in real wages is associated with an increase in the supply of labour. From a strict neo-classical perspective the implication would seem to be that Keynes assumed leisure to be an inferior good – but strict neoclassical perspectives are unfortunately sometimes misleading. Solow (1979) and Hicks (1974) (plus of course Keynes himself in GT) have given good reasons why money wages may have a certain stickiness. Keynes' rather roundabout definition of involuntary unemployment was not just an eccentric way of phrasing something simple.
21. If the labour demand function does not cut the supply function along the horizontal stretch then nominal wages cannot be assumed exogenous and the IS–LM subsystem cannot be solved separately.
22. Textbook versions usually take labour supply to be a function of real wages. This is revealing – an indication of the GE framework at the back of the author's mind – but the interpretation does not depend on it and Hicks certainly did not make it and neither did Keynes. A real wage labour supply function makes it easy to solve the system from the supply side whereas a labour function in money wages makes a solution algorithm starting at the demand side more attractive.
23. Recently this has been emphasized also by, for example, Hicks (1974) and Kaldor (1972).
24. Except in extreme cases involving non-storable commodities, the ultra-short run demand will include the reservation demand of producers and independent speculators. This implies that expectations and other intertemporal factors will play a part in the determination of ultra-short run equilibrium.
25. My discussion here relies heavily on chapter V, 'The Method of Marshall', in Hicks (1965).
26. Clower (and Leijonhufvud) have suggested that the term 'process analysis' 'is more accurately descriptive of Marshall's method than the more familiar term, "equilibrium analysis" ' (Clower, 1975, p. 4). This may be a slightly misleading terminology; equilibrium analysis however is not preferable to process analysis since the former has come to be completely identified with Walrasian equilibrium analysis. I agree fully with Clower's more substantive point, that Keynes should not be interpreted in Walrasian but in Marshallian terms; the question is, what do we mean by 'Marshallian terms'?
27. Or for that matter to an interrelated simultaneous system. With respect to the distinction between 'partial' and 'general', Keynes and GE theory are on the same side of the fence.
28. Marshall's ceteris paribus assumption has been interpreted either to mean that other prices are adjusted so as to maintain real income – giving a sort of compensated demand function – or to mean that all

prices and incomes remain fixed with (minor) changes in real income concomitant on variations in the output prices of the industry (cf. Friedman, 1949). For present purposes the exact interpretation of the ceteris paribus clause is not important.

29. In orthodox Walrasian GE theory (notional) demand and supply are functions of prices only; the interdependence between supply and demand functions vanish because of the assumption that agents draw up plans without regard to anything but the budget constraints – and since this is impossible except when prices are general equilibrium prices, orthodox GE theory in effect has no room for demand and supply schedules but only for equilibrium levels of demand and supply. In the Walrasian fix-price disequilibrium theory the interdependencies between supply and demand schedules reappear as the celebrated spillover effects and quantity constraints.
30. See also Keynes's letter to Harrod of 30th August 1936 (reprinted in Keynes, 1973, pp. 84–86).
31. Whether Keynes's reconstruction of the 'classical' argument is in fact fair I am not in a position to judge. For present purposes this is also irrelevant.
32. Disappointed short-term expectations would not invalidate the determination of employment by effective demand; the point of effective demand is defined as the intersection between the aggregate supply curve and the aggregate demand curve and Keynes defined the aggregate demand curve as the relation between employment and *expected* proceeds. The problem of disappointed short-term expectation relates to changes in effective demand as firms adjust their short-term expectations in the light of realized results.
33. Some qualifications are required here. Intertemporal considerations (e.g. long-term expectations) which go beyond the short-period play an important part in the determination of user cost, investment demand and the speculative demand for money. This is analogous to the influence of reservation demand on the formulation of ultra-short run equilibrium.
34. Cf. the currently fashionable views of the 'New Macroeconomics' school Lucas (1978) states their position in this issue particularly sharply.
35. It is therefore not quite correct when Keynes suggests that his discussion of 'the actual behaviour of labour' – the resistance to wage cuts – 'is not theoretically fundamental' (cf. Leijonhufvud, 1968, p. 95).
36. Keynes (1936), Hicks (1974) and Solow (1979) – among others – have actually provided important elements in an explanation of (downwards) inflexibility of money wages. – A 'rational expectations' explanation, which should appeal to the 'New Macroeconomists', can also be constructed; an explanation of this kind is even given in GT. (Cf. note 39 below.)
37. Disregarding here the occasional references to unfulfilled short-term expectations, which Keynes later suggested should have been kept separate from the exposition of the principle of effective demand.

38. The Walrasian fix-price theory is not misleading as an interpretation of some aspects of this first part of Keynes's inquiry. Keynes, of course, did not assume fixed prices of output; Keynes's case is located on the border between the 'classical regime' and the 'Keynesian regime' in Malinvaud's terminology. As long as one does not consider dynamics but only the short run equilibrium position, the Walrasian and Marshallian apporoaches are indistinguishable.
39. Notice that this would provide a 'rational expectations' explanation of rigid wages. Not all economists may have realized that market failures exist but, luckily, workers are wiser:

    It is fortunate that the workers, though unconsciously, are instinctively more reasonable economists than the classical school inasmuch as they resist reductions of money-wages . . . even though the existing real equivalent of these wages exceeds the marginal disutility of the existing employment; whereas they do not resist reductions of real wages, which are associated with increases in aggregate employment and leave relative money-wage unchanged, unless the reduction proceeds so far as to threaten a reduction of the real wage below the marginal disutility of the existing volume of employment (Keynes, 1936, pp. 14–15).
40. The definition is:

    Men are involuntarily employed if, in the event of a small rise in the price of wage-goods relatively to the money-wage, both the aggregate supply of labour willing to work for the current money-wage and the aggregate demand for it at that wage would be greater than the existing volume of employment (Keynes, 1936, p. 15).
41. Even individuals who become unemployed because of frictional factors will not usually have 'chosen' to become unemployed. From an individual choice perspective, they are involuntarily unemployed, yet they are not involuntarily unemployed in the sense of Keynes.

    'Technological unemployment' is perhaps an even clearer example. If some workers are unemployed because the available stock of capital goods sets an upper limit to employment, these workers would not be involuntarily unemployed in Keynes's sense.
42. Leijonhufvud (1968, pp. 319–353) has given an account of Keynes's argument which emphasizes the stability aspects. He suggests, however, that the full equilibrium price vector and the unemployment equilibrium price vector deviate primarily with respect to the price of fixed capital goods.

    although the most eye-catching symptom of maladjustment is that of great excess supply in labor markets, money wage rates may very well be 'correct', i.e. roughly equal to the money wages that the system would have in equilibrium (Leijonhufvud, 1968, p. 336; italics in original).

    Unless Leijonhufvud implicitly relies on very unusual behavioural assumptions, this interpretation is not very convincing. A higher level of employment and an unchanged money wage rate implies higher consumption demand in both nominal and real terms and Leijonhufvud assumed that both output and price of the investment good would be higher in equilibrium; the demand price of investment goods is – with given long period expectations – inversely related to the rate of interest which must therefore be lower; the money market is supposedly in equilibrium both before and after the change in fixed capital prices/interest rates but with a lower interest rate and a higher volume of transactions the demand for money in the new full equilibrium should be higher – equilibrium in the money market can only be maintained if the money supply (the credit policy of the central bank) is relaxed and/or if the preferences, perceptions and expectations of producers and consumers have shifted.

43. Arrow and Hahn (1971) contains a useful survey of the Walrasian and neo-Walrasian stability literature.
44. μ, δ and ρ obviously are not technically given or in any way exogenous. Productions processes can usually be speeded up, employment decisions can be revised almost any time and the lag between decisions and implementation can be shortened, provided the firm is willing to accept the costs involved; not even at the level of the individual firm is the time relation between decisions and outcomes 'capable of being made precise'.
45. Input and output prices further ahead in the future – or rather firms' expectations of these prices – do also of course play some part in the production decisions of firms since they influence, for example, the imputation of user cost.
46. The length of the implementation lag will depend on the firm's pay and work conditions – relative to the conditions offered by other firms and relative to minimum or standard conditions as negotiated by unions or imposed by legislation and on the general state of the labour market.
47. There are, of course, exceptions, e.g shipbuilding and aero-space industries, where forward contracts for output play a very important role and where these contracts tend to extend further into the future and be firmer than contracts related to inputs. The exceptions relate almost exclusively to producers of fixed capital goods and the main implication is simply that the burden of risk is shifted from the producer, say, the shipyard, to the buyer, the shipping company, who will be entering a commitment on the basis of expected demand in an even further future. The volume of orders from the buyers will therefore tend to be inelastic in the short term with respect to variations in current prices.
48. Indeed Hicks (1965) suggested that this was Keynes's implicit assumption in GT. Hicks labelled it the fix-price method and he argued that there is a transition from (almost) pure flex-price analysis in TM to (almost) pure fix-price theory in GT. I am not convinced that there is this transition between TM and GT; I know of no conclusive evidence indicating a transition. Anyway, the distinction between fix- and flex-

price analysis is not, I shall argue below, as important as is commonly believed. Far more important are the assumptions concerning timing and sequentiality.

49. There are indications that Keynes was aware of the problems. In the lecture notes on 'Ex Ante and Ex Post', for instance, he wrote

> Propensity to consume is determined *solely* by a psychological composite of actual and expected income and is determined neither by effective demand at a date nor by income at a definite date.
>
> (Keynes, 1973, p. 180)

It is difficult to reconcile this with his conclusion in GT,

> We are left therefore, with the conclusion that in a given situation the propensity to consume may be considered a fairly stable function, provided that we have eliminated changes in the wage-unit in terms of money.
>
> (Keynes, 1936, p. 95)

50. The analysis here is obviously based on the assumption of a closed system. I have also chosen to disregard the possible disproportionality complications which have figured prominently in the writings of so diverse economists as Marx (1954) and Hayek (1935) and which, according to Leijonhufvud, were also at the forefront of Keynes's analysis. The disproportionality questions are obviously very important but they do not have much bearing on the issues dealt with in the text – or rather, abstracting from the disproportionality questions should not prejudice the conclusions of this particular inquiry.

51. Cf. the following quote from Keynes (1936) p. 261,

> Thus the proceeds realized from the increased output will disappoint the entrepreneurs and employment will fall back again to its previous figure, unless the marginal propensity to consume is equal to unity or the reduction in money-wages has had the effect of increasing the schedule of the marginal efficiencies of capital relatively to the rate of interest and hence the amount of investment.

52. Whether or not they do will depend on both the extent to which output has been increased and the strength of the demand effects arising from stickiness in the level of nominal consumption expenditure.

53. The marginal propensity to consume (MPC) out of wage income – measured in terms of wage units – would need to exceed unity. Assuming atomistic competition and standard profit maximizing firm behaviour, the exact value of the required MPC will depend on the form of the short run production function.

54. A closed economy has been assumed throughout. In an open economy, a decline in domestic wages relative to foreign wages (assuming fixed foreign exchange rates) will obviously be more likely to stimulate production and employment; a beggar-thy-neighbour policy may be successful for some countries but as a generalized policy prescription for all countries disaster becomes a more likely outcome.

55. As well as on expected future time paths of the prices of inputs.
56. It is irrelevant here whether the expansion is accompanied by increased employment levels or whether it is brought about by using existing internal labour reserves; e.g. by intensifying the work process, by shifting workers from low productivity, 'therapeutic' activities to main-line production activities or by extending overtime work.
57. The absence of a significant scope for changes in the capital output ratio seems to me a far more important reservation regarding this effect.
58. The higher level of investment will then have multiplier effects on total demand which may in turn induce further investment via accelerator mechanisms.
59. Chick (1978) expresses very similar views. I disagree with her on some minor points only. She argues, for instance, that the sequential patterns invalidate Walras' law. This, I think, is incorrect.
60. Kalecki's name has not been mentioned yet and it is high time that this defect is remedied. It is well-known that the principle of effective demand was developed independently by Kalecki who came to economics from a very different tradition. But of course sequential patterns also played a crucial part in Kalecki's work and his writing, furthermore, is characterized by an admirable clarity which is sometimes lacking in Keynes's work (the costs of this clarity being perhaps a less sophisticated analysis of for instance financial aspects). The following extended quote from Kalecki (1935) on the issue of money wage reductions as a means of stimulating employment illustrates the power of Kalecki's approach and also sums up the essential ingredients in Keynes' argument.

    Let us assume that wages have in fact been generally reduced, and likewise taxes as a counterpart of cuts in civil servants' salaries. Now the entrepreneurs owing to the 'improved' price-wage relation utilize their equipment to capacity and in consequence unemployment vanishes. Has depression been thus overcome? By no means, as the goods produced have still to be sold. Now, production has risen considerably and as a result of an increase in the price-wage relation the part of production equivalent to profits (including depreciation) of the capitalists (entrepreneurs and rentiers) has grown even more. A pre-condition for an equilibrium at this new higher level is that this part of production which is not consumed by workers or by civil servants should be acquired by capitalists for their increased profits; in other words, the capitalists must spend immediately all their additional profits on consumption or investment. It is, however, most unlikely that this should in fact happen. Capitalists' consumption changes in general but little in the course of the business cycle. It is true that increased profitability stimulates investment but this stimulus will not work right away since the entrepreneurs will temporize until they are convinced that the higher profitability is going to last. Therefore the immediate effect of increased profit will be an accumulation of money reserves in the hands of entrepreneurs and in the banks. Then, however, the goods which are the equivalent of the increased profits will remain unsold. The accumulating stocks will sound the alarm for a new price reduction of goods which do not find an outlet. Thus the effect of the cost reduction will be cancelled. On balance only a price reduction will have occurred, offsetting the advantage of the cost reduction to the entrepreneurs since unemployment going hand in hand with under-utilization of equipment will reappear.

In fact wage reduction does not, as a rule, result even in the temporary increase in production described above. Indeed, not only investment but even utilization of existing equipment will not respond immediately to an improvement in profitability. For immediately after the reduction of wages and before the entrepreneurs manage to increase production within the existing capital equipment a fall in prices makes its appearance. As the entrepreneurs do not at once make use of the means taken away from the workers for buying consumption or investment goods, the revenue of industry is reduce *pro tanto*. What the entrepreneurs gain on wage reductions is soon dissipated through price declines. All this could be noticed in all countries during the world depression in the period 1931–2, when the wave of wage reductions brought about a rapid fall in prices rather than an increase in production.

(Kalecki, 1935; quoted from Kalecki, 1971, pp. 26–28.)

61. And if they are not moderate, the stability of the whole system would be called into question:

The chief result of this policy (of money wage flexibility, PS) would be to cause a great instability of prices, so violent perhaps as to make business calculations futile in an economic society functioning after the manner of that in which we live.

(Keynes, 1936, p. 269)

62. Keynes, of course, was fully aware of this:

the state of expectation is liable to constant change, a new expectation being superimposed long before the previous change has fully worked itself out. (Keynes, 1936, p. 50)

63. In his discussion of the effects of changing money wages, Keynes assumed that the economy started out from a position of short run equilibrium. If one assumes – not unreasonably – that the effects on the actual demand schedule of changing money wages is 'additive', the argument would also be applicable to situations where the economy is not initially in short run equilibrium.

64. The most important papers are Kaldor (1956, 1957 and 1966). Kaldor (1961) and Kaldor & Mirrless (1962) are often referred to as more fully developed and advanced statements of the basic Kaldorian ideas. This, however, is not correct. Both papers are flawed in a number of ways and basically represent an unintentional return to neoclassical orthodoxy; cf. Skott (1989a).

65. These issues are discussed at length in Skott (1981a, 1989a). See also Skott (1989b) for a synthesis of Keynesian and Marxian theories of cycles and growth.

66. Kaldor 'justified' this – in Kaldor (1957) – by assuming 'that monetary policy plays a purely passive role – which means that interest rates, subject to differences due to borrowers' risk, etc., follow in the long run, the standard set by the rate of profit obtainable on investments'. But this assumption, leaving apart its vagueness and questions regarding its appropriateness, does not really suffice. The conditions of finance are one of the determinants of investment and in Kaldor's theory, accumulation rates exert influence on profitability. To assert that monetary policy is passive and that finance conditions adapt to the standard set by the profitability of fixed investment therefore leaves the whole issue suspended in mid-air. Furthermore, ignoring the stock demand for money and financial assets from the household sector, implies that also capital gains/losses and their impact on consumption decisions are left out. In a long run theory this seems dubious. Finally, households are the ultimate owners of firms; or, in other words, the model implicitly contains another financial asset, securities issued by firms. Even in this simplified model it therefore becomes difficult to ignore the problem of households' portfolio choice. The individual household can hold its wealth in the form of securities or money and depending on the precise assumptions of the model maybe also in the form of interest bearing time deposits with banks or other financial intermediaries. Analogously, firms have access to at least two different sources of finance (apart from retained profits). They can issue new securities or take up loans through banks – or financial intermediaries – at the interest rates determined by the 'passive monetary policy'. Leaving out the financial sector of the economy therefore severs the interactions between firm and household decisions at an important point and it is not satisfying to replace these interactions with a blanket assumption of (ill-defined) 'passive monetary policies'. These issues are dealt with more fully in Skott (1981, 1989a, 1989b).
67. Readers familiar with Marxian theory will notice the similarity of this approach with Marx's analysis of the circuits of capital in vol. II of Capital (see Marx, 1954).
68. For simplicitly it is assumed here that consumption out of non-wage income is fixed in nominal terms. As argued in the previous section, this is probably not a reasonable assumption; it is adopted here merely for reasons of expositional simplicity. The effects of capital gains on consumption, which are probably subjected to time lags of a similar or longer duration, are also neglected.
69. In the original 1957-model Kaldor assumed that investment was strongly influenced by current demand conditions. But in an exchange with Encarnacion (1962) he suggested that a time lag should be introduced (Kaldor, 1962).
70. Notice that this question of the optimal variations in response according to perceptions of demand is unrelated to whether firms are in general inclined to adopt fix-price policies. The overall behavioural

characteristics of firms and the variations in the optimal response within a given behavioural regime are two different issues and if a solution to the problems arising from the latter has been formed then the former issue poses no special difficulties. Differences in overall behavioural regimes would be reflected merely in differences in the form of functional relations and in the value of certain parameters.

71. A similar sort of assumption is, of course, implicit in all discrete time analysis.
72. These expectations were probably revised in the light of the actual outcome in the product market at time $t_0 - \mu$ and in the labour market at time t_0.
73. To my mind the sequential pattern does seem to capture some essential features of real world timing.
74. In this respect Kaldor's theory stands out in stark contrast to Pasinetti's work. Pasinetti merely describes some properties of logically conceivable ultra long run equilibrium configurations. Questions of causality and sequentiality are completely absent from Pasinetti's analysis. His analysis is perfectly compatible with traditional neoclassical theory; cf. Pasinetti (1962, 1966) and Samuelson and Modigliani (1966).
75. As discussed above it was because of the inclusion of the economy-wide interrelations between supply and demand that Keynes considered his theory general.
76. Keynesian growth theory, as developed by, e.g. Harrod (1973) and Joan Robinson (1962), suggested that full employment growth in capitalist economies would be virtually inconceivable. The development of actual economies – at least after 1945 – appeared to contradict the Keynesian vision. Most Western countries seemed to enjoy fast rates of growth with only minor fluctuations and low levels of unemployment. (It could be argued that this fortunate state of affairs was caused by the active pursuit of Keynesian demand management by governments. Matthews (1968), however, examined this argument and concluded that in Britain government policies had not been a major factor behind full employment growth.)

    Kaldor's growth and income distribution models were devised to explain and remove the apparent anomaly in Keynesian thought. Kaldor tried to build a model on strictly Keynesian principles which could accommodate full employment growth and elucidate the mechanisms behind it. There was a need to demonstrate 'that neo-classical theory is, at the very least, not indispensible – it is possible to build an equilibrium model using entirely different bricks' (Kaldor, 1980, p. XXV).
77. From a theoretical Keynesian perspective, this is somewhat puzzling. From the account given above it follows that variations in nominal wage rates is the only factor in Kaldor's model which could serve to maintain full employment. And that money wages should be capable of performing this function is a very un-Keynesian idea. The (lack of

explicit) treatment of the labour market and – related to this – the discussion of stability of the full employment growth path are two of the major weaknesses of Kaldor's growth and distribution theory.

78. And it is not only neoclassical economists who are sometimes guilty in this respect. It is quite common for instance to see post-Keynesians discuss the effects of changes in real wage rates on the basis of the comparative statics of a simultaneous equilibrium model. – Rowthorn's (1981) stimulating paper could be criticized on these grounds.

REFERENCES

Arrow, K.J. and Hahn, F.H. (1971), *General Competitive Analysis* (North-Holland: Amsterdam).

Barro, R.J. and Grossman, H.E. (1976), *Money, Employment and Inflation* (Cambridge University Press: Cambridge).

Benassy, J.P. (1975), 'Neo-Keynesian Disequilibrium Theory in a Monetary Economy', *Review of Economic Studies* (October).

Chick, V. (1978), 'The Nature of the Keynesian Revolution: A Reassessment', *Australian Economic Papers* (June).

Clower, R.W. (1965), 'The Keynesian Counterrevolution: A Theoretical Appraisal', in F.H. Hahn and F. Brechling (eds), *The Theory of Interest Rates*, (Macmillan: London and Basingstoke).

Clower, R.W. (1975), 'Reflections on the Keynesian Perplex', *Zeitschrift für Nationalökonomie* (Vol. 35–1).

Clower, R.W. and Leijonhufvud, A. (1973), 'Say's Principle, What it Means and Doesn't Mean: Part I' *Intermountain Economic Review* (Fall).

Clower, R.W. and Leijonhufvud, A. (1975), 'The Coordination of Economic Activities: A Keynesian Perspective', *American Economic Review* (May).

Coddington, A. (1976), 'Keynesian Economics: The Search for First Principles', *Journal of Ecónomic Literature* (December).

Dreze, J. (1975), 'Existence of an Exchange Equilibrium Under Price Rigidities', *International Economic Review* (June).

Encarnacion, J. (1962), 'Overdeterminateness in Kaldor's Growth Model', *Economic Journal* (September).

Friedman, M. (1946), 'The Marshallian Demand Curve', *Journal of Political Economy* (December).

Hahn, F.H. (1973a), *On the Notion of Equilibrium in Economics* (Cambridge University Press: Cambridge).

Hahn, F.H. (1973b), 'The Winter of our Discontent', *Economica* (August).
Hahn, F.H. (1977a), 'Exercises in Conjectural Equilibrium', *Scandinavian Journal of Economics* (Vol. 79–2).
Hahn, F.H. (1977b), 'Keynesian Economics and General Equilibrium Theory: Reflections on Some Current Debates', in G.C. Harcourt (ed), *Microeconomic Foundations of Macroeconomics* (Macmillan: London and Basingstoke).
Hahn, F.H. (1978), 'On Non-Walrasian Equilibria', *Review of Economic Studies* (February).
Harrod, R. (1973), *Economic Dynamics* (Macmillan: London and Basingstoke).
Hayek, F. (1935), *Prices and Production* (Routledge and Kegan Paul: London).
Hicks, J.R. (1937), 'Mr. Keynes and the Classics: A Suggested Interpretation', *Econometrica* (April).
Hicks, J.R. (1946), *Value and Capital*, 2nd edition (Clarendon Press: Oxford).
Hicks, J.R. (1965), *Capital and Growth* (Clarendon Press, Oxford).
Hicks, J.R. (1973), 'Recollections and Documents', *Economica* (February).
Hicks, J.R. (1974), *The Crisis in Keynesian Economics* (B. Blackwell: Oxford).
Hicks, J.R. (1977), *Economic Perspectives: Further Essays on Money and Growth* (Clarendon Press: Oxford).
Kaldor, N. (1956), 'Alternative Theories of Distribution', *Review of Economic Studies* (Vol. 23, no. 2).
Kaldor, N. (1957), 'A Model of Economic Growth', *Economic Journal* (December).
Kaldor, N. (1961), 'Capital Accumulation and Economic Growth', in F. Lutz (ed), *The Theory of Capital* (Macmillan: London and Basingstoke).
Kaldor, N. (1962), 'A Comment', *Economic Journal* (September).
Kaldor, N. (1966), 'Marginal Productivity and the Macro-Economic Theories of Distribution', *Review of Economic Studies* (October).
Kaldor, N. (1972), 'The Irrelevance of Equilibrium Economics', *Economic Journal* (December).
Kaldor, N. (1980), *Essays on Value and Distribution*, 2nd edition (Duckworth: London).
Kaldor, N. and Mirrlees, J.A. (1962), 'A New Model of Economic Growth', *Review of Economic Studies* (Vol. 29, no. 3).

Kalecki, M. (1935), 'The Mechanism of the Business Upswing', in M. Kalecki (1971), *Selected Essays on the Dynamics of the Capitalist Economy* (Cambridge University Press: Cambridge).
Keynes, J.M. (1930), *A Treatise on Money* (Macmillan, Royal Economic Society edition, 1971: London and Basingstoke).
Keynes, J.M. (1936), *The General Theory of Employment, Interest and Money* (Macmillan, Royal Economic Society edition, 1973: London and Basingstoke).
Keynes, J.M. (1973), *Collected Writings Vol. XIV* (Macmillan: London and Basingstoke).
Leijonhufvud, A. (1968), *On Keynesian Economics and the Economics of Keynes* (Oxford University Press: Oxford).
Leijonhufvud, A. (1973), 'Effective Demand Failures', *Swedish Journal of Economics* (March).
Lucas, R.E. (1978), 'Unemployment Policy', *American Economic Review*, (May). Reprinted in R.E. Lucas (1981), Studies in Business-Cycle Theory (B. Blackwell: Oxford).
Malinvaud, E. (1977), *The Theory of Unemployment Reconsidered* (B. Blackwell: Oxford).
Marx, K. (1954). *Capital, 3 Vols*. (Lawrence & Wishart: London).
Matthews, R.C.O. (1968), 'Why Has Britain Had Full Employment since the War', *Economic Journal* (September).
Muus, L.T. (1981), *Aspects of Modern Disequilibrium Theory* (Institute of Economics, University of Aarhus: Denmark).
Negishi, T. (1960), 'Monopolistic Competition and General Equilibrium', *Review of Economic Studies* (Vol. 28).
Pasinetti, L.L. (1962), 'Rate of Profit and Income Distribution in Relation to the Rate of Economic Growth', *Review of Economic Studies* (October).
Pasinetti, L.L. (1966), 'New Results in an Old Framework', *Review of Economic Studies* (October).
Robinson, J. (1962), *Essays in the Theory of Economic Growth* (Macmillan: London and Basingstoke).
Robinson, J. (1969), 'Review of "On Keynesian Economics and the Economics of Keynes" '. *Economic Journal* (September).
Rowthorn, B. (1981), 'Demand, Real Wages and Economic Growth', *Thames Papers in Political Economy* (Autumn).
Samuelson, P.A. and Modigliani, F. (1966), 'The Pasinetti Paradox in Neo-classical and More General Models', *Review of Economic Studies* (October).
Skott, P. (1981), 'On the "Kaldorian" Saving Function', *Kyklos* (Vol. 34, no. 4).

Skott, P. (1986), 'On General Equilibrium Theory, Rationality and the Costs of Spurious Generality', *British Review of Economic Issues* (Vol. 18).

Skott, P. (1989a) *Kaldor's Growth and Distribution Theory* (Peter Lang Verlag: Frankfurt a. M.)

Skott, P. (1989b) *Conflict and Effective Demand in Economic Growth* (Cambridge University Press: Cambridge).

Solow, R.M. (1979), 'Alternative Approaches to Macroeconomic Theory: A Partial View' (mimeograph).

Weintraub, E.R. (1979), *Microfoundations – The Compatibility of Microeconomics and Macroeconomics* (Cambridge University Press: Cambridge).

3. The Political Economy of the Phillips Curve

Malcolm Sawyer

INTRODUCTION

Most discussion on inflation and its causes over the past quarter of a century has involved reference to the Phillips curve. Indeed it could be said that the discussion of inflation has been dominated by the notion of the Phillips curve, even if there were several notions of Phillips curve which were sometimes only loosely related to the original concept of Phillips (1958). This chapter seeks to answer the question of why the Phillips curve has exerted such a strong influence over the discussion of inflation. It could, of course, be answered that the reason for the dominance of the Phillips curve is simply that it has strong theoretical and empirical bases. We have addressed the issue of the theoretical basis of the Phillips curve elsewhere (Sawyer, 1985) and do not repeat those arguments here. However, we do discuss the different interpretations which have been given to the term Phillips curve. The use of several interpretations is suggestive of, at least, confusion over the theoretical basis of the Phillips curve. We have also discussed the empirical support for the Phillips curve (e.g. Sawyer, 1982a, pp. 156–161) and again do not repeat the full argument here.

The next section of this chapter is a brief discussion of the origins of the Phillips curve. The third section discusses four different concepts of the Phillips curve whilst the fourth section outlines the way in which the Phillips curve is presented in textbooks. The concept of a 'natural' rate of unemployment (or more generally a non-accelerating inflation rate of unemployment, hereafter NAIRU) is closely related with the Phillips curve. The fifth section is devoted to a discussion of the concept of a 'natural' rate or a NAIRU. The penultimate section makes some suggestions on the reasons for the popularity and influences of the Phillips curve. The thrust of these suggestions is that the popularity of the Phillips curve did not (and could not) arise from its theoretical and empirical validity, but from the role it played within the economics profession. A short final section summarizes and concludes.

ORIGINS OF THE PHILLIPS CURVE

It is well-known that Phillips (1958) used data on wage changes and unemployment over the period 1861–1913 to discover a relationship between those two variables. This relationship was derived by seeking a non-linear function, which by trial and error best fitted the six grouped observations on wage change and unemployment, and this was found to be:

$$\dot{w} = -0.900 + 9.638U^{-1.394}$$

where w is money wages, U unemployment rate and a dot over a variable signifies proportionate rate of change of that variable. An important feature of this curve is that even as unemployment rate tends to 100 per cent, money wage change does not fall below −0.9 per cent; indicating a floor to money wage changes.[1]

The significance of the relationship estimated by Phillips arose in part from the fact that it represented a relaxation of the dichotomy between full employment with price rises and unemployment with prices constant which had previously been associated with Keynesian economics. But it did provide an empirical foundation for an asymmetry with downward rigidity of money wages even in labour markets characterized by low unionization in conditions of substantial unemployment (for discussion on this point by a key participant in the evolution of the Phillips curve see Lipsey, 1978, 1981)[2]. Further, the apparent stability of the Phillips curve over nearly a century could be viewed as the discovery of a long-run economic 'law' (Lipsey, 1962).[3] A relationship discovered for a period of history (pre-1914) when competitive conditions were assumed to have operated appeared to hold for both the inter-war period of depression and the post-1945 period with high levels of unionization and employment.

The general idea that the rate of change of wages was related to unemployment was in wide circulation prior to Phillips's article. Any claim of Phillips to an original discovery must here be based on the finding of an empirical relationship (see Lipsey, 1962; Summer, 1984). However, as Thirwall (1972) argues, Brown (1955) has a strong claim to this discovery. His diagram (Brown, 1955, p. 199) maps out the wage change, unemployment observations for the period 1880–1914, which generally display a negative relationship though with a definite floor to wage changes at −1.0 per cent.

The approach of Brown can be contrasted with that of Phillips in three respects. First, Brown places the statistical relationship into a much fuller discussion of the process of inflation, including the role of monetary expansion, level of demand and wage-price spiral. Second, Brown did not attempt to draw any curve through his data. In terms of textbook and policy discussion, the advantage of an estimated curve is that it can be used, without the accompanying data and caveats, to illustrate general relationships. Further, a loose statistical relationship was in effect translated into what appeared to be a precise empirical relationship. Third, Brown did not argue that the wage change-unemployment relationship observed for pre-First World War period held thereafter. He also noted that 'the institutional machinery by which prices and wages have been determined and changed has been quite largely different during the period of inflation from what had been assumed in most theoretical formulations . . . ' (p. v) and in Chapter 1 he discussed the difference between 'prices in a free market' and 'contractual and administered prices'. He also argued that '[t]he inflationary period [1939–1950], after unemployment had been reduced to a low level, displayed very little correlation between wage movement and the amount of remaining unemployment' (p. 96). In contrast, an implication of the work of Phillips (1958) was that the relationship between wage changes and unemployment held for nearly a century across many social and political changes. This could be seen as asserting the importance of the operation of underlying economic forces through varying institutional arrangements. 'The logic of the exclusion of institutional factors is clear. The contention is that the relationship between changes in wage rates and unemployment has remained constant for nearly a hundred years; thus since the institutions have undergone formidable changes in this period, they cannot be admitted as co-determinants' (Routh, 1959, p. 299).

Fisher is another author often advanced as a discoverer of the Phillips curve with his article of 1926 which was republished under the title *I Discovered the Phillips' Curve* (Fisher, 1926, 1973). However, we can note that his discussion was concerned with the correlation between the volume of trade/unemployment and the rate of change of prices rather than the rate of change of wages. Further the implied causation runs from inflation to employment (and the volume of trade). Indeed, the explanation given by Fisher is along the lines of what later became known as the 'surprise supply function'.[4]

Space precludes a full discussion of the strength of the empirical support for the Phillips curve. However, we can suggest that from an early stage there were reasons to doubt the empirical validity of the Phillips curve. Let us first note that there were some fairly spectacular divergences from the Phillips curve for war and immediate post-war periods, as in Table 3.1.

In part, the sharp non-linearity of the estimated Phillips curve helps to generate these large prediction errors. It can also be noted that every observation from 1933 to 1941 lies above the estimated Phillips curve.

Table 3.1

Year	*Actual inflation*	*Predicted inflation (given actual unemployment)*
1919	28 per cent	11/2 per cent
1921	−22 per cent	−1 per cent
1922	18 per cent	−1 per cent
1940	12 per cent	0 per cent
1946	11 per cent	2 per cent
1947	9 per cent	1 per cent

Lipsey (1960) concluded that '[t]he fitted relation between [$\dot{w}$] and U has changed substantially compared with the earlier period. . . . This indicates that the post-1922 experience was of less flexibility of wages in response to excess demand, whether positive or negative, than occurred in the pre-1914 period' (p. 27). Further, 'except for 1949 and 1950, there is evidence of a more rapid increase in wages in response to demand and prices in the period since the second world war than in the period prior to the first world war' (p. 30). Hence '[w]e must conclude that there is evidence that [$\dot{w}$] increased faster in the 1930's than in the pre-1914 period for comparable levels of U, $\dot{U}$ and $\dot{p}$' (p. 29).

Hines (1964) was one of the first to cast doubt on the role of unemployment in money wage change equations and he concluded that the level of unemployment did not appear to be an important factor in the determination of the rate of change of wage rates over the period 1921–38, 1949–61. He also quotes an equation from Lipsey (1960) for a similar period in which 'contrary to what is generally thought to be the case' (p. 241), unemployment is not statistically significant. Thus from an early stage there was reason to doubt the empirical validity of the Phillips curve, even before its celebrated collapse in the late 'sixties.

ALTERNATIVE CONCEPTS OF THE PHILLIPS CURVE

The purpose of this section is to establish that there are several distinct (and sometimes contradictory) meanings which have been attached to the term Phillips curve. We will later draw two suggestions from the existence of this variety of meanings. First, the different meanings given to and different theoretical justifications given for the Phillips curve is suggestive that there is not strong theoretical backing for the Phillips curve. Second, different meanings of the term Phillips curve allows a wider adherence to the Phillips curve as different people can accept different propositions, albeit all described by the term Phillips curve. We identify four different definitions and associated theoretical positions of the Phillips curve.

(i) Labour market disequilibrium

The Phillips curve has often been seen as reflecting labour market disequilibrium adjustment based on a Walrasian adjustment mechanism, with unemployment acting as a proxy for the excess demand for labour. This was clearly the theoretical justification provided by Lipsey (1960) for Phillips's findings, and led later on to the expectations-augmented Phillips curve in the work of Friedman (1968) and others.

The relationship between excess demand for labour and unemployment has generally been accepted as unproblematic. However, there are in my view substantial reasons why the mapping from the excess demand for labour to unemployment is neither firmly established nor necessarily a negative one. This line of argument has been advanced in Sawyer (1982a, chapter 4) and more extensively in Sawyer (1985), and the argument will not be repeated here.

Friedman (1968) criticized the original work of Phillips (1958) and Lipsey (1960), in which money wage changes were related to the excess demand for labour as being an incorrect specification and that real wages should be used rather than money wages. The basis for this argument is that real wage is the relevant price in the labour market. We can note as an aside that it is not self-evident that it is real wages rather than money wages adjust in the labour market. The view that money wages (and changes therein) are determined in the labour market is consistent with Keynes's *General Theory*, and in that sense with a Keynesian approach to economics. Keynes argued that whilst money wages are determined in the labour market, real wages are not since they depend on product market conditions as well as money wages and the shape of cost curves.[5]

Friedman's view that real wages are determined in the labour market, whilst apparently widely accepted, has very little grounding even in neoclassical economic theory. In the context of general equilibrium, it would not be possible to identify any sub-set of markets as the ones in which real wages (or any other price) were determined. It would be rather that the demand and supply situation in labour and product markets in equilibrium which determine all relative prices including the real wage. In disequilibrium situations (to which the Phillips curve relates) with money wages and prices changing then whilst money wage movements relative to expected prices may be determined by conditions in the labour market, output price movements relative to expected costs including wages would be seen as related to conditions in the product market.

The general version of the Phillips curve treated as labour market disequilibrium phenomenon is $\dot{w} = f(U) + b\,\dot{p}^e$. The original Phillips curve would correspond to $b = 0$, and $b = 1$ corresponds to the expectations-augmented Phillips curve with no long- run trade-off. At one level the value of b can be viewed as an empirical matter. But it has considerable theoretical importance. For if b is less than unity then not only is the labour market seen as setting the money wage and not the real wage, but also the economy is not seen as constrained to operate in the long-run at some 'natural' rate of unemployment.

(ii) Trade-off between inflation and the level of economic activity

The Phillips' curve has often been seen as an aggregate level relationship between the rate of inflation and the level of economic activity (as indicated by employment, output, etc.), which represented a trade-off facing an economy. Phillips (1954) introduced such a relationship between price changes and the level of production (pp. 307–8).[6] Samuelson and Solow (1960) converted the wage change-unemployment relationship into a price change-unemployment relationship, with the addition of constant productivity growth and the growth of real wages in line with productivity growth. This type of argument has often been retained (e.g. Turnovsky, 1977) by seeing prices as set as a constant mark-up over unit labour costs.

Samuelson and Solow (1960) would appear to be the first to have turned the Phillips curve into a trade-off or in their words 'the menu of choice between different degrees of unemployment and price stability' (p. 192). They did, however, see this as a short-term menu which would gradually change. They did not indicate how they moved from a relationship which had been established on the basis of a disequilibrium adjustment mechanism and/or business cycle relationship to a stable menu of choice. For the menu of choice suggested that the economy could be held at any particular level of unemployment indefinitely. This should have been dismissed along the line of what later became known as the Lucas critique, namely that the operation of the economy is not policy invariant. The Phillips curve had been justified theoretically as a disequilibrium relationship in which wages are changing in response to the level of excess demand (positive or negative). Thus any observed combination of wage change and unemployment is only a temporary position for the economy on its route to somewhere else; the changes in wages will lead to changes in excess demand and thereby unemployment. Observing the swings of a pendulum tells us nothing about what happens when the pendulum is held steady.

(iii) Industrial 'reserve army' arguments

The notion that wage changes will be negatively influenced by the level of unemployment can also arise from the common sense notion that the bargaining position of workers will be weaker when unemployment is high. Marx provided a strong statement of this view when he wrote that 'taking them as a whole, the general movements of wages are exclusively regulated by the expansion and contraction of the industrial reserve army, and this in turn corresponds to the periodic alternations of the trade cycle' (Marx, 1976, p. 790).[7] Indeed it could be argued that this 'common sense' view with its apparent realism helped in the acceptance of the concept of the Phillips curve.

In the labour market disequilibrium approach, the adjustment mechanism is that the level of excess demand (negatively proxied by unemployment) determines rate of change of (real) wages, which sets the new level of real wages, which in turn determines the subsequent level of excess demand. The system is of course assumed to be stable. But in the industrial reserve army approach, a different type of mechanism is involved. One version would involve the process of accumulation. A low level of unemployment leads to a rise in real wages, which eventually dampens down the rate of investment and the level of aggregate demand. A fall in aggregate demand generates a rise in unemployment and the higher level of unemployment helps reverse the rise in real wages.

When unemployment is seen as influencing wage determination through weakening the power of workers, then other variables (such as level of trade unionization, strike intensity) may be relevant as well. Further, there is no reason why the level of unemployment as a measure of the excess supply of labour should be the relevant variable; other variables such as the rate of change of unemployment, specific types of unemployment (e.g. those unemployed for less than twelve months) which may be appropriate. In a sense this becomes an empirical question, i.e. which variable in practice affects wages?

(iv) The 'surprise supply function'

The term Phillips curve has also been used to describe one of the components of the 'surprise supply function'. The approach developed by Lucas and Rapping (1969) and the theorizing and empirics of Fisher (1926, 1973) are in this vein. The idea here is that unanticipated changes in prices generate employment decisions, but with the direction of causation running from price changes to (un)employment. It is not appropriate to examine the defects of the 'surprise supply functions' here, (but see Sawyer, 1984). The key point for our argument here is that the term Phillips curve was invoked even though the direction of causation was the reverse of the original Phillips curve and only unanticipated (rather than total) inflation is involved.

TEXTBOOK TREATMENT OF THE PHILLIPS CURVE

The confusion over the meaning of the Phillips curve is reflected in the treatment of the Phillips curve given in economics textbooks. An examination of textbooks should provide an indication as to what students are taught (without any claim that lecture and textbooks present an identical picture) and also to reflect the conventional wisdom of the economics profession. We have aimed to cover some of the main texts, without aiming for a comprehensive coverage. Limitations of space and availability of texts in local libraries have restricted the coverage. We have included a selection of textbooks designed for introductory undergraduate courses and some more advanced specialist macroeconomics texts.

This discussion is undertaken in three stages. First, to what extent was the Phillips' curve (however defined) presented as well-established truth and what implications were derived for policy purposes? Second, what was the nature of the Phillips curve taken to be (e.g. wage change/unemployment, price change/output relationship)? Third, what was the theoretical justification given for the Phillips curve? For example, some authors present the Phillips curve as based on the labour market, whilst others present it as a economy-level relationship based on the interaction of aggregate demand and supply.

It is notable that the translations between wage and price changes and between unemployment and output are frequently made. The justification for the first translation is usually appeal to some notion of full-cost pricing, with little or no demand effects on the rate of price change (relative to rate of wage change). The justification for the second translation is the 'common sense' view that the level of economic activity influences both which therefore vary together. This raises two points. First, over a long period of time there is no reason to think that the degree of excess capacity would move with the level of unemployment; for simply there may be inadequate capital stock to fully employ labour so that full capacity may coincide with substantial unemployment. Second, a positive association between excess capacity and unemployment accepts a Keynesian view of the world (with both excess capacity and unemployment determined by aggregate demand considerations). In a neoclassical world, excess capacity (representing excess supply of output) and unemployment (representing excess supply of labour) would be inversely related.[8]

We first illustrate that the Phillips curve has often been presented as well-established fact. For example, 'In 1958 Professor A.W. Phillips of the London School of Economics *demonstrated* that there was a strong statistical relationship between the annual rate of inflation and the annual unemployment rate in the U.K.' (Begg, Fischer and Dornbusch, 1984, p. 619, italics added). Gordon (1981, p. 212) gives similar support and authors such as Samuelson (1980, p. 797) and Branson (1979, p. 397) define the Phillips curve without any expression of doubt on its empirical validity. There are also strong suggestions that the long-run Phillips curve is vertical. For example, '[t]here remains a tradeoff between inflation and unemployment . . . In the short run, of say 2 years, there is a relation between inflation and unemployment. . . . That *short-run Phillips curve*, however, does not remain stable. It shifts as expectations shift. In the long run, there is no tradeoff worth speaking about between inflation and unemployment. In the long-run, the unemployment rate is basically independent of the long-run inflation rate' (Dornbusch and Fischer, 1981, p. 14).

This illustrates the degree of confidence in the existence of some kind of Phillips curve. It is rare to find any doubts expressed on the existence of, at least, a short-run Phillips curve, or that economies are constrained either by a long-run Phillips curve or to operate at the ' natural' rate of unemployment. One of the few authors of mainstream textbooks (the only one which was found) who cast doubt on the validity of the Phillips curve is Ackley (1978). On the statistical relationship, he states that '[t]he notion that there is *some rough relationship* between the unemployment rate and the existence and speed of inflation *of course* was not new with Phillips.' Many other scholars had looked but 'were, at first, mainly impressed not with the regularity of the phenomenon but with its unregularity and looseness' (pp. 439–40, italics added). Ackley further notes that 'Phillips' work touched off an extensive effort to establish whether "Phillips curves" could be found in empirical data for other economies. Apparently they could, at least if you selected the right years' (p. 440).

The policy implications of the Phillips curve drawn by textbooks vary from noting a possible trade-off between inflation and economic activity possibly involved to stressing the role of the 'natural' rate of unemployment. 'An "income policy" is needed to supplement fiscal and monetary policy – in order to *give the mixed economy a better long-run Phillips curve or natural rate*' (Samuelson, 1980, p. 781). 'The *Phillips curve* shows that a higher inflation rate is accompanied by a lower unemployment rate, and vice versa. It suggests we can *trade off* more inflation for less unemployment, or vice versa' (Begg, Fischer and Dornbusch, 1984, p. 620).

Other authors present a different view. For example, 'there is no such trade-off [between unemployment and inflation] in the long-run. The economy's self-correcting mechanism ensures that unemployment eventually will return to the "natural rate", no matter what happens to aggregate demand. In the long run, faster growth of demand leads only to higher inflation, not to lower unemployment; and slower growth of demand leads only to lower inflation, not to higher unemployment' (Baumol and Blinder, 1982, p. 303).

We now briefly look at the interpretation given to the term Phillips curve. Some authors (e.g. Branson, 1979) use the term to mean a relationship between wage changes and unemployment. But a much more widely used definition is in terms of a negative relationship between (output) price changes and unemployment (e.g. Baumol and Blinder, 1982, and Begg, Fischer and Dornbusch, 1984) or a positive relationship between price changes and output (e.g. Gordon, 1981 and Lipsey, 1983).

Finally, we turn to the question of the theoretical derivation given by the texts for the Phillips curve. It should be said here that the derivation of the Phillips curve often involved a good deal of what could be called 'hand-waving', i.e. jumps in the argument which are glossed over.

Some authors view the Phillips curve relationship as resulting from shifts in the aggregate demand curve whilst shifts in the aggregate supply curve would destroy any Phillips curve relationship (e.g. Baumol and Blinder, 1982; Begg, Dornbusch and Fischer, 1984). Branson (1979) begins with a link between wage changes and with excess supply of labour and price changes. Unemployment is used as a proxy for excess supply and a price equation introduced which preserves constant income shares (apart from supply shocks). These are combined to provide an equation in which wage changes are a function of unemployment, productivity growth and supply shocks. The derivation of Dornbusch and Fischer (1981) is rather similar but an equation linking price level with previous price level and capacity utilization, which is described as the short-run aggregate supply schedule.

Lipsey (1983) adopts a rather different tack. The Phillips curve (which relates price changes with the level of output) is derived from 'the theory of short-run oligopoly pricing . . . firms absorb cyclical demand fluctuations by varying output rather than their prices' and 'the theory that wage costs do not fall rapidly in the face of excess supply of labour, although they can rise rapidly in the face of excess demand for labour' (p. 736).

Parkin and Bade (1982) argue that '[T]he neo-classical theory of price adjustment, as a macroeconomic proposition, was introduced by A.W. Phillips'. Then, '[e]xcess demand is thought of as being related to the unemployment rate, so that the neo-classical theory of wage adjustment – usually called the Phillips' curve – says that the rate of change of money wages will vary inversely with the unemployment rate' (pp. 346–7).[9]

The purpose of this brief discussion of textbook treatment of the Phillips curve is to indicate the considerable confusion which has surrounded the Phillips curve as well-established.

THE 'NATURAL' RATE OF UNEMPLOYMENT

The 'natural' rate of unemployment, often closely linked with the Phillips curve, can be interpreted as corresponding to the Walrasian general equilibrium level of employment (at which according to Walrasian adjustment mechanism real wages would be constant) or as the level of unemployment at which inflation would be constant (i.e. the non-accelerating inflation rate of unemployment, NAIRU). The first concept of the 'natural' rate includes both the general equilibrium and essentially voluntary level of unemployment as well as the notion of non-accelerating inflation, whereas the second concept is limited to the non-accelerating inflation aspect. In either case, in practice, the 'natural' rate of unemployument is calculated from an equation such as $\dot{w} = f(U) + \dot{p}^e$. The 'natural' rate (hereafter labelled U_N) is then calculated from $f(U) = 0$ or g (the growth rate of productivity). Clearly the validity of the estimates of U_N depend on the validity of the estimated equation. For the purpose of this argument we will assume that the estimation of such an equation is econometrically acceptable.[10] A regression equation is only a 'best fit' line drawn through a scatter of points, and the question arises as to what significance should be attached to such a line.

The basis of our argument here is twofold. We first argue that it is highly likely that the estimate of the U_N will lie around the middle of the observed range of unemployment levels, whether or not the notion of the expectations-augmented Phillips curve is valid. Secondly, we will argue that it could be the case that the expectations-augmented Phillips curve is mis-specified, leading to estimates of NAIRU which are invalid both in the sense of being inaccurate and also do not correspond to any 'equilibrium' level of unemployment.

We start with the first argument indicated above. An estimate of the Phillips curve is made from a collection of statistics on wage and price changes and unemployment levels. It may be the case that it is not possible to achieve an econometrically acceptable estimate of the Phillips curve. This would correspond roughly to the position reached by the mid-seventies (cf. Henry, Sawyer and Smith, 1976). But when an expectations-augmented Phillips curve has been successfully estimated, what significance do we attach to the value of U_N calculated from such an estimate? The share of wages and salaries in national income has often been thought to vary relatively little. Insofar as that is true and the expectations-augmented Phillips curve is successfully fitted to the data, then it must be the case that the 'natural' rate of unemployment or NAIRU will be calculated to lie towards the centre of the range of unemployment observed. Given that the share of wages and salaries is roughly constant, i.e. if wL/pQ varies little, then to some extent w/p varies with Q/L, we can note that if there are relatively limited cycles such that Q/L varies pro-cyclically then w/p may vary pro-cyclically and thus move counter to unemployment.

It might be expected that the rate of change of real wages fluctuates around the trend growth of productivity. The expectations-augmented Phillips relationship is: $\dot{w} - \dot{p}^e = f(U)$. It is taken that price expectations are unlikely to be seriously out of line with actual inflation. The solution to the equation $f(U) = g$ (with real wages assumed to grow in line with productivity) must fall within the range of unemployment observed. It would then be expected that the estimated 'natural' rate of unemployment or NAIRU will move in sympathy with the general rate of unemployment observed. When, as after 1973, unemployment is generally higher than previously, then it would be anticipated that the calculated 'natural' rate will move higher. The circumstances under which that would not happen would be if with the higher levels of unemployment there was a distinct trend in the share of wages and salaries in national income. It is difficult to see the economic system being able to function for a substantial period of time with a distinct trend in wage and salary share. 'There is a disconcerting tendency for estimates of NAIRU to rise in line with the actual level of unemployment' (Worswick, 1985, p. 10). The thrust of the argument above is that upward shifts in the calculated 'natural' rate (or NAIRU) as observed unemployment rises tells us no more than unemployment has risen without there being a distinct long-term trend in labour share. It tells us nothing about what would happen if lower levels of unemployment were achieved.

This argument can be reinforced by a numerical example. The coefficient on unemployment in an expectations-augmented Phillips curve has often been found to be the range 0.5 to 2.0 (wage and price changes measured at an annual rate and unemployment rate measured as a percentage). Over a five year period (starting with a labour share in national income of 70 per cent) if the rate of unemployment was 1 percentage point above the NAIRU, then the share of labour would fall by between 1.7 and 6.6 percentage points. A rate of unemployment 5 percentage points above NAIRU would generate falls in labour share of between 8.1 and 26.5 percentage points. Labour's share has often been regarded as constant; but if not constant then a slowly changing ratio. It is likely that changes of the order of magnitude indicated above would generate political and social reactions and would have substantial impact on the composition and level of demand. These calculations suggest that it is rather unlikely that a linear Phillips curve is a relationship which would survive large changes in the level of unemployment. The original Phillips curve was non-linear with a floor of −0.9 per cent to money wage changes, and even at an unemployment rate of 10 per cent money wage change would be predicted as −0.5

per cent. Thus higher levels of unemployment would have a minor impact on wage changes.

The second line of argument proceeds as follows. There are several alternatives to the expectations-augmented Phillips curve interpreted as $\dot{w} = f = (U) + \dot{p}^e$. The alternatives would include (a) unemployment relative to recent levels, (b) changes in unemployment (but not the level of unemployment) and (c) inclusion of the difference between actual real wages and some target real wage. If the expectations-augmented Phillips curve is in fact a misspecified version of either (a) or (b), then the calculated NAIRU would be quite misleading. In the case of (a), clearly any calculated NAIRU would be relative to recent levels of unemployment. For case (b) it would yield a 'natural' rate of *change* of unemployment.

In case (c), an equation linking the level of real wages with the level of unemployment can easily be derived for which real wages grow in line with productivity. Then there is no unique NAIRU but rather for each level of real wages a level of unemployment which would hold real wage rises in line with productivity growth. However, a pricing equation can be introduced which has implications for real wages. The combination of the wage and price equations (cf. Sawyer, 1982b) can be used to yield equilibrium levels of economic activity and real wages. But it is then clear that it is the interaction of wage and price formation which serves to determine the level of economic activity (and unemployment) rather than solely the labour market.

Thus it is not only a question of whether unemployment has an influence on wage determination but what form that influence takes. A belief that unemployment may have some influence on wage determination (and employee and employer behaviour more generally) is not the same as a belief in the expectations-augmented Phillips curve (with $b = 1$ in the equation used above). But it is only the Phillips curve in that form which yields a NAIRU or 'natural' rate of unemployment whose absolute level is determined by the labour market.

WHY WAS THE PHILLIPS CURVE SO POPULAR?

It is difficult to establish why any single person adopts a particular view, and even more difficult to establish why a large number of people do. Thus inevitably our discussion of the popularity of the Phillips curve will be rather speculative. Underlying the discussion in this section is the view that the Phillips curve was never firmly based either theoretically or empirically. The discussion above has hinted at the theoretical weaknesses (which are more extensively discussed in Sawyer, 1985). Further, 'the extraordinary influence [of the Phillips curve] cannot be attributed to either a more fully articulated statement of the theory to be tested or a more sophisticated technique than in some earlier and many contemporary studies' (Sumner, 1984, p. 170). The differences in interpretation of the Phillips curve is further support for this view in that a strong theoretical basis would not have generated a range of conflicting interpretations. It is clear though that some general notion labelled the Phillips curve has had a wide popularity, being quickly incorporated into textbooks and the conventional wisdom. We do not have space to discuss the weakness of the empirical evidence on the Phillips curve, though we could point to the widely perceived collapse of the Phillips curve in the late 'sixties (for example Trevithick and Mulvey, 1975, pp. 74–5) and we have indicated the doubts cast on whether unemployment influenced wage changes in the inter-war and early post-war periods.

McCloskey (1986) has argued that '[e]conomists have two attitudes towards discourse, the official and the unofficial, the explicit and the implicit' (p. 5) and further that economists do not adhere in practice to the positivist methodology ('modernism'). Indeed one of his sections is headed 'modernism itself is impossible and not adhered to' (p. 16). In effect McCloskey argues that there are many ways (e.g. argument by analogy) by which economists seek to persuade their fellows of the validity of a particular theory or approach. The basis of the argument here is that the Phillips curve drew strength from factors such as its easy representation as a diagram, its use as a trade-off combined with a social welfare function and its links with a competitive view of the economy rather than drawing support from empirical and theoretical arguments.

The acceptance of the Phillips curve on grounds other than its empirical validity is not necessarily to be decried. McCloskey (p. 17) points out that the Keynesian view of macroeconomics was widely accepted many years before any empirical evidence was advanced to support it. As a further example McCloskey (pp. 58 *et seq.*) puts forward eleven reasons why economists find the Law of Demand persuasive, of which only the first three reasons relate to statistical tests (and those are recognized to not always support the Law of Demand). The development of the Phillips curve differs from that of both Keynesian economics and the Law of Demand in that it began as an empirical proposition for which a theoretical explanation was sought.

The first suggestion for the popularity of the Phillips curve is that it could be seen as completing the Keynesian model by incorporating price change. Initially it 'seemed to most economists . . . to provide the missing element in the Keynesian model. Now there was a theory of inflation which could be integrated into the IS–LM framework and the Keynesian edifice was complete' (Desai, 1981, p.4). Lipsey (1978) states as one of his conclusions on the nature of the original Phillips curve that 'the curve provided a theoretical link between the Keynesian I-S, L-M, macro-model and the labour markets. This link made it unnecessary to assume rigid money wages in order to make the Keynesian macromodel work. The labour market was effectively integrated into the Keynesian model . . .' (p. 55).

Keynesian economists had generally felt uncomfortable when confronted with the view that their models depended on the assumption of rigid wages and/or prices. The dichotomy of constant prices/wages with high levels of unemployment on the one hand and rapid inflation with full employment on the other was also unappealing. The Phillips curve offered an escape from that dichotomy as well as an empirically based observation on the degree of price flexibility.

Lipsey (1981) has indicated that 'Phillips, for example, calculated the asymptotic rate of decrease in UK money wages as unemployment went to 100 per cent as 1 per cent per annum' (p. 558), which served to provide an empirical basis to the proposition of downward wage rigidity. Since the curve had been originally estimated for the period 1861–1913, this downward rigidity could be said to be endemic to the economic system rather than attributable to the role of trade unions or minimum wage legislation (which were either weaker or non-existent in that period than in the post-First World War period).

The second suggestion is that the Phillips curve represented a long-term stable relationship. '[T]he Phillips curve, which predicts wage inflation at different unemployment rates on the assumption that the labour market still functions as it did in the nineteenth century, fitted the post-war observations more closely than it fitted the original nineteenth century data' (Sumner, 1984, p. 171). This view was apparent in the original paper of Phillips, though we have noted above that there was always doubt about the accuracy of that observation.

The third suggestion is related to the second one. If economists are able to identify the causes of inflation in terms of variables traditionally thought of as economic, then there is no need for non-economic explanations. 'The day may come when [a radical departure from accepted economic theory] is necessary, but a great deal of evidence which is currently only partially visible in mimeographed conference papers, etc., needs to be accumulated and sifted before cautious scientists will be forced to follow their more impulsive colleagues such as Professors Harrod (1972) and Wiles (1973) in a rush for the sociology laboratories' (Lipsey, 1978, p. 70).[11] One is tempted to comment adversely on the 'impulse' economists who rushed to ascribe to the Philips curve before a careful sifting of evidence.

Elements of the second and third suggestion can be found in Lipsey (1962). 'A casual glance at the time series for these two variables [wages changes and unemployment] suggests that there is some relation.' But further investigation is disappointing and reveals 'some sort of a vague relation but it does not seem to be a very strong one.'

> At this stage mental attitudes become critical. If we believe in the arguments against constant human behaviour patterns, we say, 'just as I thought', and we give up. But, if we believe there is a stability to be found, then we go back to the data and we try again.
>
> We might then reason somewhat as follows: the near chaos is only apparent, there *must* be some order here. . . . Let us try dating the points and observe the sequence in which they occur. When we do this we observe the most remarkable phenomenon. The points form from very clear loops . . . on the upswing of a trade cycle when U is falling, [$\dot{w}$] is high, while on the downswing when U is rising, [$\dot{w}$] is low.
>
> Now our original chaos has resolved into truly remarkable order! . . . One is left, at the end of all this, with a feeling of the possibility of a truly scientific study of human behaviour in the economic sphere and with an attitude of optimism about the long-term development of such a science Lipsey (1960) (pp. 272–3).

The fourth suggestion is that the Phillips curve represented the reassertion in macroeconomics of the operation of competitive market forces. This was not important at the beginning but gathered strength in the late 1960s and during the 1970s. One strain of Keynesian economics involved the rigidity of prices through an appeal to the growth of oligopoly and the practice of administered prices and of trade unions and collective bargaining over wages injected considerable elements of price and wage inflexibility, in the same sense of being insensitive to demand pressures.

The Phillips curve involved the reassertion of the importance of competitive forces in two respects. First, it was strongly suggested that the Phillips curve applied not only in the pre-First World War period when competitive forces were assumed to be in operation but also in the post-First World War and indeed the post-Second World War period as well. The reverse argument could also be applied, namely that the way in which wages and prices are determined involve many forces other than traditional market forces (such as social convention, fear of upsetting customers) which applied even in the pre-1914 period. However, the presence (and presumed statistical significance) of unemployment pushed the argument in the direction of competitive and/or economic forces.

Second, as was first seen in Lipsey (1960), there is an

emphasis on demand and supply and the role of excess demand. It is only within the context of perfect competition that supply and demand functions (and hence excess demand functions) can be given a meaning. A theory of inflation clearly must involve price change and someone to undertake the changing of prices. Hence such a theory (and specifically any analysis based on the Phillips curve) has to involve some departure from perfect competition in that perfect competition assumes all agents are price-takers. Thus there is an incompatibility between perfect competition and theories of inflation which can only be resolved by some 'fudge' by which some parties are able to change prices (unless there really is an auctioneer involved whose role is to change prices in response to excess demand). Further, in the approach of Friedman (1968) some of the institutional features of developed capitalist economies (specifically the American one) are introduced, particularly the notions that money wages rather than real wages are the basis of negotiations and that money wages are agreed for a significant period of time ahead.

The fifth suggestion relates to the Phillips curve viewed as a trade-off between wage/price inflation and unemployment which had the attraction that it fitted with some conventional notions widely used in micro-economics. Policy discussions could be discussed in terms of maximizing a social welfare function which depends negatively on unemployment and inflation subject to the constraint represented by the Phillips curve. There is a clear analogy between that and the general approach in neoclassical microeconomics of optimization subject to constraints.

The Phillips curve also represents some re-establishment of economics as 'the dismal science', with economists able to point to the constraints on the economy which had not been widely appreciated by the public and which prevents the economy operating with very low levels of unemployment because of the inflationary consequences. It also fits in with the general dismissal of the possibility of a 'free lunch'. Lower levels of unemployment can only be obtained at the cost of higher inflation (and in the expectations-augmented Phillips curve case by accelerating inflation). The collective guilt felt by economists at promoting the Keynesian ideas which appeared to offer the 'free lunch' (increased government expenditure permitted not only gains from that expenditure but also the benefits of the multiplier effects) could now be assuaged.

There is the related 'benefit' for economists that the positive and normative aspects of macroeconomics could apparently be sharply separated. With the normative aspects represented by the social welfare function which the economist can postulate as taken from the views of politicians, the public or whoever. The positive aspects relate to the Phillips curve which can be ascertained by the use of regression analysis.

The sixth suggestion is that the confusion over what was meant by the Phillips curve allowed different economists to hold different views and yet believe that they all subscribed to the notion of a Phillips curve. This has in part been illustrated by our discussion above on the alternative meanings given to the Phillips curve and the textbook treatment of the Phillips curve. The question of which type of inflation (e.g. demand pull or cost-push) was explained by the Phillips curve provides a further example. Lipsey (1981) argues that '[n]eo-Keynesians always saw the Phillips curve as representing the pressure of excess or deficient demand on wages . . . It is worth noting that the Phillips curve was persistently misunderstood on this [the American] side of the Atlantic as a cost-push phenomenon' (p. 556).

There are a number of ideas or notions which are widely used by economists or in the teaching of economics, despite many objections having been raised against them. No doubt, economists would differ as to which are the ideas which continue to have some kind of respectability despite the doubts raised against them. I would cite as one example the kinked demand curve theory of oligopoly (Sweezy, 1939). It has proved of limited empirical and theoretical validity (Stigler, 1982),[12] and would appear to be of limited interest in an era of rising prices since it attempted to provide an explanation of stable prices. Yet, it continues to feature widely in introductory texts where it is presented as a (if not the) major theory of oligopoly.

The Phillips curve comes into this category. It has survived numerous attacks on its empirical validity (beginning with Routh, 1959) and the announcement of its demise followed by that of its reappearance (Sumner and Ward, 1983). It is well-known that the response of many to a break-down of the original Phillips formulation (i.e. money wage changes as a function of unemployment) was a search for alternative measures of excess demand for labour (e.g. vacancies, modifications to measured unemployment), the introduction of additional variables (e.g. profits, trade union activity) and modifications (notably the introduction of inflationary expectations). One honest statement of this was Thirlwall (1975) who wrote that '[f]or two years after the traditional inverse relation between wage-rate changes and unemployment first went awry in 1967, Jim Taylor saved us from rewriting our lecture notes on the Phillips curve (at least, I didn't rewrite mine) by adding hoarded labour to the registered unemployment and rehabilitating the Phillips relation' (p. 139).

The general reaction of the economics profession is described by Trevithick and Mulvey (1975). 'This development [the breakdown of the Phillips curve in the late sixties] caused a good deal of consternation amongst economists at the time, since they appeared to have lost one of the *tidiest economic relationships* in an otherwise untidy world. There was therefore in the late 1960s a *need* to discover the nature of the breakdown of the Phillips relation and to find an alternative way of explaining the theoretically expected relationship between domestic excess demand and wage inflation' (pp. 74–5, italics added).

One popular methodology advocated by many economists runs along Popperian falsificationist lines so that an hypothesis is only provisionally accepted pending dis-proof by empirical evidence. It would be unrealistic to support that one piece of 'rogue' evidence apparently disproving a theory would be sufficient to overthrow the provisional acceptance of that theory. In the age of computers, it is easy to generate numerous regression results some of which (if only by chance) would run counter to the maintained hypothesis. However, the response to the apparent collapse of the Phillips curve was at the other end of the spectrum, namely substantial attempts to modify variables (alternative measures of unemployment, use of vacancies data, introduction of other variables relating to union strength, etc.) to maintain a relationship which could be described as a Phillips curve. But it should also be noted that the history of the Phillips curve suggests that the interaction between theory and evidence does not always follow the Popperian route.

Besides tenaciously holding onto the Phillips curve in the face of contrary evidence, there is also the element of evidence preceding theory. Lipsey (1962) wrote that 'the important breakthrough [by Phillips] was the discovery of order where before there seemed to be only chaos. The next stage is, of course, to advance a theory explaining this order; this Phillips also did. After that the new theory must be tested and, if it is refuted, this means that new knowledge (the observations which refuted the theory) has been brought to light. A new theory must then be put forward which explains the original phenomenon . . .' (p. 275).

The purpose of this section has been to suggest that there were reasons why there was such a strong adherence to the Phillips curve despite its theoretical and empirical weaknesses. These suggestions perhaps explain why there has been such an unwillingness amongst most economists to give up their faith in the Phillips curve.

SUMMARY AND CONCLUSIONS

The use of the term Phillips curve to cover a wide variety of relationships involving wage and price change and the level of economic activity can only lead to confusion. The policy conclusions which can be drawn depend heavily on, for example, whether causation runs from inflation to economic activity or vice versa, whether it is the level of or rate of change of economic activity which is relevant for the rate of inflation. This confusion is indicative of the general confusion over the nature of the Phillips curve which we have illustrated above. We have further indicated that the empirical and theoretical support for the Phillips curve is not strong. We have argued that the Phillips curve has survived and prospered because of the role which it has played for the economics profession, rather than through its intrinsic merits.

NOTES

I would like to thank Philip Arestis for helpful comments on a variety of earlier drafts of this paper.

1. For further discussion on the data used by Phillips, see Routh (1959), and on his method of estimation see Desai (1975).
2. For example, 'Phillips wrote down the relation that subsequently became famous as the "Phillips curve" and built it into his early models in order to remove this dichotomy [between output only change at less than full employment and price only changes at full employment]' (Lipsey, 1978, p. 49).
3. 'Phillips's claim to fame rests on the stability of the relationship he estimated between unemployment and the rate of change of wages . . . When that curve [estimated for 1861–1913] was superimposed on a scatter diagram showing the post-Second World War observations, for 1948–57, they were found to lie very close to the curve. Indeed, the Phillips curve, which predicts wage inflation at different unemployment rates on the assumption that the labour market still functions as it did in the nineteenth century, fitted the post-war observations more closely than it fitted the original nineteenth-century data. This is a remarkable result. Few economic relationships exhibit unchanged parameters over a period of almost a century. . . . The stability of the Phillips curve was all the more remarkable in that it relates to a market which has experienced major institutional and organisational changes in the interval between the fitting period and the prediction period . . .' (Sumner, 1984, p. 171).
4. 'The principle underlying this relationship is, *of course, familiar*. It is that when the dollar is losing value, or in other words when the price level is rising, a business man finds his receipts rising as fast, on the average, as this general rise of prices, but not his expenses, because his expenses consist to a large extent of things which are contractually fixed. . . . For this and other reasons, the rise in expenses is slower than the rise in receipts when inflation is in progress and the price level rising . . . Employment is then stimulated – for a time at least. . . . On the other hand, when prices are falling, expenses

likewise lag behind and reduce profits, for exactly the same reason turned about. Consequently, during periods of falling prices profits are reduced, bankruptcies are increased, concerns shut down entirely or in part, and men thrown out of work' (Fisher, 1973, p. 498; italics added).

5. For example, Keynes (1936) argued that '[n]ow ordinary experience tells us, beyond doubt, that a situation where labour stipulates (within limits) for a money-wage rather than a real wage, so far from being a mere possibility, is the normal case' (p. 9). 'There may exist no expedient by which labour as a whole can reduce its *real* wage to a given figure by making revised *money* bargains with the entrepreneurs. This will be our contention. We shall endeavour to show that primarily it is certain other forces which determine the general level of real wages' (pp. 12–13).
6. Whilst Phillips mentioned the possible impact of varying marginal costs on prices arising from differences in the level of output, he mainly focused on the impact of the level of demand on factor prices, and thereby on product prices. There is some confusion in the argument over changes in the level of production and differences in the level of production.
7. The quote from Marx is clearly unspecific as to whether it is money or real wages which are regulated and whether it is the level of or changes in the level of unemployment which are important.
8. According to Walras' Law, the sum of excess demands is zero. Hence in a simple world of labour and output, excess demand for one would be found alongside excess supply for the other, i.e. the negative relationship suggested in the text.
9. Parkin and Bade (1982) continue with the following: 'You should be clear that these neoclassical propositions about price and wage adjustments are different from Keynes's theory. Keynes assumed that wages and prices would not move downwards at all and that they would move upwards instantaneously to clear any excess demand' (p. 347). No justification is given for this extraordinary statement.
10. Many of the estimates of the Phillips curve made in the early 'sixties displayed serial correlation for which adjustments were not made leading to biased estimates of standard errors of parameters.
11. Harrod and Wiles were basically arguing for the importance of social and political factors in explaining the upsurge of inflation in the late 'sixties and early 'seventies.
12. 'What I would have thought was the most interesting and puzzling attribute of the literature on the kinked demand curve is . . . [that] the kinked demand curve flourishes in textbooks and languishes in the professional study of oligopoly and industrial organisation' (Stigler, 1982, p. 204).

REFERENCES

Ackley, G. (1978), *Macroeconomies: Theory and Policy* (Collier Macmillan: New York).
Baumol, W.J. and Blinder, A.S. (1982), *Economics: Principles and Policy*, Second Edition (Harcourt Brace Jovanovich: New York).
Begg, D., Fischer, S. and Dornbusch, R. (1984), *Economics* (McGraw-Hill: London).
Bergstrom, A.R., Catt, A.J.L., Peston, M.H. and Silverstone, B.D.J. (eds), (1978), *Stability and Inflation* (Wiley: Chichester).
Branson, W. (1979), *Macroeconomic Theory and Policy*, Second Edition (Harper: New York).
Brown, A.J. (1955), *The Great Inflation, 1939–1951* (Oxford University Press: Oxford).
Desai, M. (1975), 'The Phillips Curve: A Revisionist Approach', *Economica* (February).
Desai, M. (1981), *Testing Monetarism* (Pinter: London).
Dornbusch, R. and Fischer, S. (1981), *Macroeconomics,* Second Edition (McGraw-Hill: New York).
Fisher, I. (1926, 1973), 'A Statistical Relation between Unemployment and Price Changes', *International Labor Review*, (June). Reprinted in *Journal of Political Economy* (March/April). (Page references in the text refer to the reprint.)
Friedman, M. (1968), 'The Role of Monetary Policy', *American Economic Review* (March).
Gordon, R.J. (1981), *Macroeconomics,* Second Edition (Little Brown: Boston).
Harrod, R. (1972), 'The Issues: Five Views' in R. Hinshaw (ed), *Inflation as a Global Problem* (Johns Hopkins Press: London).
Henry, S.G.B. Sawyer, M. and Smith, P. (1976), 'Models of Inflation in the United Kingdom: An Evaluation', *National Institute Economic Review* (August).
Hines, A.G. (1964), 'Trade Unions and Wage Inflation in the United Kingdom, 1983–1961', *Review of Economic Studies* (July).
Keynes, J.M. (1936), *The General Theory of Employment, Interest and Money* (Macmillan: London).
Lipsey, R.G. (1960), 'The Relations between Unemployment and the Rate of Change of Money Wage Rates in the United Kingdom, 1862–1957: A Further Analysis', *Economica* (February).
Lipsey, R.G. (1962), 'Can There be a Valid Theory of Wages?' in

B.J. McCormick and E.O. Smith (eds), *The Labour Market* (Penguin: Harmondsworth).

Lipsey, R.G. (1978), 'The Place of the Phillips Curve in Macro-economic Models' in Berstrom *et alia* (1978).

Lipsey, R.G. (1981), 'The Understanding and Control of Inflation: Is there a Crisis in Macro-economics?', *Canadian Journal of Economics* (November).

Lipsey, R.G. (1983), *Introduction to Positive Economics,* Sixth Edition (Weidenfeld and Nicolson: London).

Lucas, R.E. and Rapping, L.A. (1969), 'Real Wages, Employment and Inflation', *Journal of Political Economy* (September/October).

McCloskey, D.N. (1986), *The Rhetoric of Economics* (Harvester Press: Brighton).

Marx, K. (1976), *Capital, vol. 1* (Penguin: Harmondsworth).

Parkin, J.M. and Bade, R. (1982), *Modern Macroeconomics* (Phillip Allan: Deddington).

Parkin, J.M. and Nobay, A.R. (eds), (1975), *Contemporary Issues in Economics* (Manchester University Press: Manchester).

Phillips, A.W. (1954), 'Stabilisation Policy in a Closed Economy', *Economic Journal* (June).

Phillips, A.W. (1958), 'The Relations between Unemployment and the Rate of Change of Money Wage Rates in the United Kingdom, 1861–1957', *Economica* (November).

Routh, G. (1959), 'The Relations between Unemployment and the Rate of Change of Money Wage Rates in the United Kingdom, 1861–1957: Comment', *Economica* (November).

Samuelson, P. (1980), *Economics*, Eleventh Edition (McGraw-Hill: New York).

Samuelson, P. and Solow, R. (1960), 'Analytical Aspects of Anti-Inflation Policy', *American Economic Review* (May).

Sawyer, M. (1982a), *Macro-Economics in Question* (Wheatsheaf: Brighton).

Sawyer, M. (1982b), 'Collective Bargaining, Oligopoly and Macro economics'. *Oxford Economic Papers* (November).

Sawyer, M. (1984) 'The Surprise Supply Function: A Critique', *British Review of Economic Issues* (Autumn).

Sawyer, M. (1985), 'On the Nature of the Phillips' Curve', *British Review of Economic Issues* (Spring).

Stigler, G. (1982), 'Review of G. Reid *The Kinked Demand Curve Analysis of Oligopoly,* (Edinburgh University Press: Edinburgh)', *Economic Journal* (March).

Sumner, M.T. (1984), 'The History and Significance of the Phillips Curve' in D. Demery, N.W. Duck, M.T. Sumner, R.L. Thomas and W.N. Thompson, *Macroeconomics* (Longmans: London).

Sumner, M.T. and Ward, R. (1983), 'The Re-appearing Phillips' Curve', *Oxford Economic Papers* (November, Supplement).

Sweezy, P. (1939), 'Demand Under Conditions of Oligopoly', *Journal of Political Economy* (August).

Taylor, J. (1975), 'Wage Inflation, Unemployment and the Organised Pressure for Higher Wages in the United Kingdom, 1961–71', in Parkin and Nobay (1975).

Thirlwall, A. (1972), 'The Phillips Curve: A Historical Note', *Economica* (August).

Thirlwall, A. (1975), 'Discussion of Taylor (1975)', in Parkin and Nobay (1975).

Trevithick, J.A. and Mulvey, C. (1975), *The Economics of Inflation* (Martin Robertson: London).

Turnovsky, S. (1977), *Macroeconomic Analysis and Stabilization Policy* (Cambridge University Press: Cambridge).

Wiles, P. (1973), 'Cost Inflation and the State of Economic Theory' *Economic Journal,* (June).

Worswick, D. (1985), 'Jobs for All?', *Economic Journal* (March).

4. Market Structure and Firm Behaviour: An Empty Box?

Paul Auerbach

INTRODUCTION

The main concern of this chapter is to examine the extent to which the concepts of 'market' and 'industry' as used in economic theory serve as suitable bases for a research programme into the question of the state of competition in the modern economy. The author strongly believes that the only meaningful way of dealing with the question of business competition in the modern world is from a dynamic perspective. This would seem to be an uncontroversial position. After all, who would not prefer to be 'dynamic' rather than 'static'? We have all come across Hayek's powerful strictures against perfect competition. He notes (Hayek, 1948) that the latter paradoxically rules out all manifestations of agents actively *competing*: 'Advertising, undercutting, and improving ("differentiating") the goods and services produced are all excluded by definition – "perfect competition" means indeed the absence of all competitive activities'. Economists usually nod their heads in agreement when confronted with such criticisms of the mainstream theory.

What accounts, then, for the overwhelming dominance of the static neoclassical approach of Cournot, Edgeworth and Walras in economic theory, and of that bastard hybrid of classicism and neoclassicism – the 'Marshallian' model found in intermediate microeconomics textbooks – as the major influence on empirical work in industrial economics? The answer given by Stigler (1957) is that the static market structure approach offers superior 'precision' (and is therefore more 'scientific' than any dynamic analysis of the competitive process.

But in what sense is the mainstream theory thought precise? The following propositions seem relevant:

(a) Competition is conceived in a manner that makes it amenable to objective measurement: the degree of competition can be measured by the inverse of some index of the concentration of firms within a market.
(b) Decisive predictions can be derived of an inverse relation between profitability within the market and this measure of competition.
(c) It is possible to construct statistical tests with this measure of competition as the key independent variable which (successfully) explain the level of profitability within an industry.

Proposition (c), until recently a powerful weapon in the legitimation of mainstream textbook theory, has had its underlying methodology seriously questioned.[1] Proposition (b) has proved more robust. The standard theory, emblazoned in textbooks, poses a strict uni-causal relationship:

Market structure → *Behaviour of firms*

Many attempts have been made to derive this proposition analytically (see Waterson, 1984), and serious weaknesses may be pointed out (Auerbach and Skott, 1988). But our main concern in this paper is proposition (a). The impossibility of delineating the market in an objective and consistent manner makes measures of market concentration worthless, and renders proposition (b) unworkable, whatever its presumptive logic. While a great deal of effort in the economics literature has been devoted to alternative measures of concentration (concentration ratio, Herfindahl index, entropy index, etc.), the literature on the delineation of the object being measured – the market itself – is remarkably thin. It is not our opinion that these problems have been ignored because they are of trivial consequence.

There has grown up an empirical literature of enormous magnitude and influence which makes use of 'market concentration' as a key independent explanatory variable. Such investigations have been of two kinds: first, cross-sectional studies of the kind envisaged in proposition (c), where the variable being 'explained' is average industry profitability, but similar work has been carried out to account for levels of industry research, advertising, wages, etc. (see, for instance, Philips, 1971). Such research, however, is worthless if it does not give serious consideration to the problems of the measurement of 'market' or 'industry' extent. The problem with time series research (the second kind of investigation) is no less serious! Studies measuring trends in economy-wide averages of concentration in different markets over time show a long term upward trend in manufacturing industry, especially in the UK (e.g. Hart and Clarke, 1980). Such research serves as the basis for the 'stylised fact' that there is a secular tendency towards lower levels of competitiveness – towards 'monopoly capitalism'.[2] This research is based on the implicit presumption that the extent of the market – the arena of competitiveness – *can be taken to have remained constant over decades*. If there are reasons to believe in a long term tendency for 'market extent' to expand over time, one may argue that such 'stylised facts' point in *precisely the wrong direction*. But such argument is beyond the scope of this paper. Our conclusion is that the foundations of the static theory of competitiveness are ill informed and ill thought-out. In the last section we provide some hints at a reconstruction of the concept of competitiveness.

MARKET DELINEATION AND MAINSTREAM THEORY

The problem of market delineation

In a formal sense, it is possible to construct models of an economy which incorporate the 'invisible hand' process of competition without any reference to the concepts of 'market' or 'industry' (see Auerbach, 1988 chapter 4). But the burden of market delineation was taken on by the Marshallian approach, since in this conceptualization of the competitive process it is industrial or market 'structure' which critically shapes the performance of firms. The centrality of the role of market structure can be seen most clearly in the construction of the most crucial variable of structure, the index of market concentration, which is often used by itself as a surrogate for the degree of competition within a market. There are two ways in which the Marshallian approach is at a disadvantage with respect to general equilibrium or pure transactions-based models such as those derived from Edgeworth: first, with its greater pretence to realism, it has more difficulty than do the latter models in sweeping away real world problems simply because they are found to be troublesome, and secondly, the explicit introduction of a time dimension in the Marshallian model raises difficulties not present in neoclassical transactions approaches.

What in fact would be the prerequisites for a successful market measure in the Marshallian context? The following characteristics would seem to be crucial in answering the question – what is a market?

(a) *Qualitative delineation.* It must be possible to separate these markets *qualitatively* one from the other, with unambiguous lines of demarcation
(b) *Consistent delineation.* The criterion/criteria used for delineation must be *consistent* between markets and over 'time', the latter concept referring both to:

1. Marshallian 'time' in which we distinguish between the short and long run, and
2. Historical time. Here, if the measure is not to be constant over different periods, we have to be able to demonstrate that a systematically and uniformly applicable methodology for showing changes in the boundaries of the market is available.

(c) *Independent specification.* The market must be specified in a manner which makes its delineation independent of the behaviour of the participants in that market, if the statement 'market structure affects conduct' is to be meaningful in the powerful form in which it is put forth in standard theory.

We believe it is impossible to fulfil these criteria in the context of the Marshallian paradigm, and that the research programme which flows from it is incapable of completion. This is all in the context of the grand purposes of economic theory. For practical pursuits, it has always been *implicitly* recognized that the above criteria are incapable of realization, so that, for instance, the drawing of industry boundaries for anti-monopolies or anti-trust purposes, have always *implicitly* made use of an interaction of 'structural' and 'behavioural' variables, but often rather apologetically, as if a pure structural approach would be possible *if only enough information were available.*

Alternative approaches to market delineation in economic theory

How, then, is the problem of delineation of the market dealt with in economic theory? Discussions are in fact very rare, as may be seen by a perusal of the more prestigious current publications. The question as a rule is:

(a) defined away,
(b) or considered to have 'practical' difficulties which require 'practical' solutions.

Strategy (a) is certainly the best route to a Nobel Prize. Thus, in a pure general equilibrium model, goods are simply labelled qualitatively, as well as in time and space. In this context, all problems of market delineation are eliminated:

1. There are no firms in the pure model, so we exclude the practical and conceptual difficulties caused by diversification: the linkages between products in the context of the firm's internal locus of decision-making, on the one hand, and in the context of its external market environment, on the other.
2. The good is defined in space, so that the delineation of the market is identical with the delineation of the product (as a result these problems are often conflated in the literature); geographical questions can be avoided. Having defined the 'commodity' we have defined the *market* for that commodity.
3. The market *is* where exchanges actually take place – there is no problem of *ex ante* and *ex post* delineation of the market, because it is defined only for the instantaneous moment of transaction. Since the instantaneous model has none of the problems related to time, it can avoid as host of Marshallian conundrums:

   (a) Over what time dimension do we measure the relevant parameters? For instance, if we need to calculate elasticities of demand as a method of market delineation, are they long or short run elasticities?
   (b) Is our delineation on the basis of markets (the 'short run') or in terms of industries (the 'long run')? There may be a 'market' for biscuits which is relevant for the construction of a concentration measure, but such a domain may be too narrowly defined for the appropriate entry barriers. On the other hand, the tobacco 'industry' might be overly broad for delineating functional 'market' concentration, even if it contains the relevant domain for the measurement of entry barriers.[3] This implies not only alternative, and possibly conflicting systems of

classification of products based, on the one hand, on substitution in consumption (elasticity of demand) and in production (elasticity of supply), but as well as a geographical conflict between where goods are consumed and where they are produced.

(c) How do we deal with changes over time, such as movements in technology, which challenge the validity of our initial categories?

(d) Most significantly, how can we maintain our market delineations in a consistent, independent way over time *when these markets are inevitably shaped by the behaviour of participants?*

The perspective adopted from the transactions model is that conceptual difficulties in market delineation do not really exist, and such 'practical' problems as are present may be dealt with by way of *ad hoc* solutions to the problem. These latter solutions have received a great deal of attention in economics, first, as a result of the pressing need for some sort of solution to the problem of market delineation in various practical contexts such as the analysis of monopoly situations, but, secondly, because of *the clear implication from general equilibrium theory that the problem of market delineation is one of relatively trivial consequence*. This lighthearted approach has influenced the Marshallian tradition, and through the latter's pretence at practical relevance has made its effect upon the mainstream of industrial economics.

The situations in the two models are, however, very different. In the transactions model we may speak without ambiguity of 'the market' simply by specifying where buying and selling actually take place, since without the dimension of time there can be no distinction between *ex ante* and *ex post* measures of this concept. In the Marshallian model, however, the introduction of continuous time makes it impossible to delineate the market simply by specifying where trade takes place, since to be meaningful as a behavioural variable in continuous time *the market must be considered (like the cost curve) as an ex ante concept*. When we use market analysis to explain and predict economic outcomes, we are interested in how this parameter constrains and affects the behaviour of participants within this domain. So, for instance, if there were only two shops selling food in a particular section of London, we would hesitate to apply a duopoly analysis to this 'market', even if almost every household in this neighbourhood purchased its food in these shops, unless we had clarified for ourselves what kind of access customers had to shops in other neighbourhoods, and were certain that *objective conditions* (distance, cost of transport, etc.) had dictated that they were functionally limited to neighbourhood shops. If with small price differentials purchasers were in a position to break their habit of neighbourhood shopping and use an alternative, it would seem pointless to delineate the neighbourhood as the relevant unit of analysis for explaining and predicting the behaviour, prices and profits of the two shops. In other words, it would be impossible to delineate the market until we had separated necessity from convenience (see Steiner, 1968) for the shoppers in this case, and, more generally, had specified the market's domain *independently of the actual behaviour of its participants*. In order to have coherent explanatory power, market analysis must be capable of such independent *ex ante* delineation. The impossibility of this task in the Marshallian framework[4] is, as we shall see, one of its central failures and has been reflected in problems in the development of industrial analysis.

Of the several attempts to deal with this problem perhaps the most venerable is that attributed to Cournot and to Marshall, whereby the domain of the market is set where the price (inclusive of transport costs) of the commodity is uniform. There is an important sense in which this is a useful way of looking at the world, since, for instance, one of the most pointed indications of the internationalization of world grain production and the elimination of insulated submarkets (especially in the Third World) since the end of the Second World War has been the development of universally applicable international grain prices. For all its attractiveness, this notion cannot be the foundation of a market measure, as it precludes, by definition, the possibility of testing the usefulness and applicability of the perfectly competitive model's prediction that deconcentrated markets will tend to price uniformity.[5] It makes nonsense of any attempt to explore, for instance, why two brands of aspirin, side-by-side on the counter shelf sell for different prices, since we would have to declare them to be in different markets in order to be consistent. In this case the definition would exclude many central issues in market analysis concerning the possibility of price discrimination, countervailing power, consumer ignorance or other forms of 'market failure'. Unfortunately, therefore, the long list of assumptions about the *behaviour* of both producers and consumers which would be needed to generate this elegant solution to the problem of market extent make it inappropriate as a *structural* measure.

The other attempt at a 'straightforward' operational solution to the problem is to specify the domain of the market so that it includes all those firms which are conscious of each others' behaviour.[6] Once again this may be a useful way of dealing with problems in the context of a case study of 'short-run' pricing behaviour within an apparently oligopolistic market. It cannot in any way, however, serve as a more general solution to the problem, since the delineation of the market as a structural parameter cannot be successfully separated from the behaviour of its participants. Neither of these 'practical' approaches to the problem of market delineation can be considered as serious candidates for a solution: it is to the most formidable contender that we now turn.

MARKET ANALYSIS: ATTACK AND DEFENCE

The elasticity of demand and its critics

The (cross) elasticity of demand is the central device suggested for the delineation of the market in almost every textbook where the issue is raised. Despite the fact that it has rarely been used in practice it has retained its status as a principled solution to the problem on the grounds that obstacles could be overcome if sufficient information were available. This is indeed a curious state of affairs, since the arguments presented below suggesting the unviability of the elasticity of demand *in principle* are extremely well known. It is perhaps worthy of note as an aspect of the history of ideas that an intellectual discipline will preserve even an impractical and logically incoherent tool of analysis in the absence of a viable alternative.

The underlying and essential problem with the use of cross-elasticities to delineate market boundaries is that the level of 'cut-off' is totally and completely arbitrary from the point of view of economic theory, and that they cannot be applied in a consistent and meaningful way. One of the authorities to whom the cross-elasticity solution has been attributed is Kaldor (1935), but it is clear that Kaldor's concern, in the context of the monopolistic competition debate was to distinguish different 'types' of markets ('pseudo-monopolistic'), and that his proposed solution was a 'practical' and not a principled, theoretical one. In fact Kaldor's earlier comment on this question highlights some of the crucial issues:

> [Mrs. Robinson's concept of an 'industry'] implies the assumption that the products of different firms consist of a 'chain of substitutes' surrounded on each side by a 'marked gap' within which the demand for each firm's product is *similarly sensitive* with respect to the price of any of the others. The 'boundary' is thus defined as the limit beyond which this sensitiveness ceases or at any rate becomes a different order of magnitude. No doubt for each *particular* producer there exists such a boundary. But there is no reason to assume (except in some very special cases, involving a peculiar grouping of consumers) that this boundary is the *same* for any group of producers: or that the sensitiveness of demand for the products of any particular producer is of the same order of magnitude with respect to the prices of *any* group of his rivals. Some producers will be 'nearer' to him, others 'further off'. *If the demand for cigarettes in a particular village shop is more affected by the price of beer in the opposite public-house than by the price of cigarettes in the shop at the nearest town, which of the two would Mrs. Robinson lump together into 'one industry': the seller of cigarettes plus the seller of beer in the village, or the seller of cigarettes in the village plus the seller of cigarettes in the town?*
>
> (Kaldor, 1934, emphasis added.)

The first point to note here is why Kaldor's question is a paradox at all. While the discussion of this question proceeds purely in terms of elasticity of demand, it is implicit that there would be something a bit absurd about aggregating cigarettes and beer, to the exclusion of cigarettes more geographically separated, since these 'market' categories based on elasticity of demand will have to serve as 'industry' delineations (Mrs. Robinson's seller-oriented concept) as well.

Kaldor's very discussion of the question of the aggregation of goods using a cross-elasticity measure points to the most fundamental issue: *cross-elasticity cannot be used in any systematic way to delineate goods*. Let us say we were looking for a delineation between two classes of products, $M^1 \ldots M^6$ we call 'meat' and $B^1 \ldots B^{10}$ we call bread':

$$M^1, M^2, M^3, M^4, M^5, M^6, B^1, B^2, B^3, B^4, B^5, B^6, B^7, B^8, B^9, B^{10}$$

The simple fact is that since all demand elasticities are contingent on the level of aggregation, *they cannot be used to determine the initial level of aggregation in a consistent way*. If M^3, for instance is 'poultry', why have we decided to use such a category instead of separate ones including chicken, turkey, etc., or even more narrow ones contingent on the packaging, quality, etc. of these products? Now in the real world, these problems will be decided for us by the levels of initial aggregation set by the Standard Industrial Classification system (see below) which, being largely decided on 'supply' considerations are irrelevant to the needs of a consistently demand based criterion. We would base our cut-off on the 'intrinsic' difference between, say, M^6 and B^1, but this is not really playing the game, and not very helpful in the context of using this tool to decide the geographical delineation of the market, where of course the same problem is posed.

The criticisms contained here are those which exist *in principle*, and since at an applied level there are a host of further problems that have prevented this tool from ever having been made operational, we feel no particular need to be merciful on grounds of practicality. Furthermore, the issue is invariably discussed as *if a resolution to the problem could be made in this purely static context*. In the real world, one has to decide whether one is referring to a relatively short run or long run concept of (cross) elasticity of demand. In any attempt at empirical estimation, one will probably have to make use of observations over whatever time span is available and hope that they are sufficiently comparable between different products. Once we enter into the dimension of time, it is impossible to ignore the Marshallian distinction between short and long run, since market delineations based on substitution in demand may be very different from industry (long run) delineations based on substitution in supply. This sometimes results in the rather casual comment that delineation should be based upon elasticities of demand *and* (!) supply,[7] though the integration is never clearly specified. The market-industry distinction may cause a problem in the conflict between a demand oriented butter–margarine delineation and the supply-oriented delineation between butter and cheese. Moreover, the geographical domain of production may differ from the geographical domain of consumption; below we shall be discussing the complications brought about by the existence of international trade.

The defence of the industry and practical applications

The use of market (industry) analysis in economic theory is indeed so ubiquitous that spirited defences of the concept are hard to come by:

> Flippant examples purportedly destructive of the industry concept in a product differentiated economy (such as the alleged close substituted of nightclub admissions, pleasure cruises and cold showers) are not persuasive; for each of these there can be twenty queries such as those concerning the evident degree of substitutability between cigarettes and kitchen sinks, automobiles and roller skates, or concrete and gunpowder. A serious endeavour to couple our powers of observation with our knowledge of the concept of cross-elasticity of demand might have shut off a great deal of pseudomethodological quibbling over the acceptability and validity of the industry concept in a price theory that deals with a product-differentiated economy.
>
> (Bain, 1972, p. 192)

It is easy to be sympathetic with practical economists such as Bain who, after all, have to 'get on with the job', whatever the objections of high-falutin theorists: in the absence of a usable alternative, the industry, whatever objections are posed, will retain its central role because of the need felt to order firms (or the activities of firms) in some other way than as an arbitrary conglomeration.

We now explore the actual statistical data that are used to designate the industry. Our overall hesitation with their ubiquitous use in an unquestioning manner is as follows: there are quite enough difficulties involved with the implementation and interpretation of firm data *even without* the further set of arbitrary assumptions, conjectures and surmises necessary for the construction of industry statistics. The system of industrial classification is international, with the problems and philosophy of implementation especially close between the US and the UK, though differences make straightforward national comparisons difficult.

If we look at the UK classification system, we note that it

> . . . has been prepared to conform with the organisation and structure of industry and trade as it exists within the United Kingdom. All relevant factors such as the commodity produced or service given, the raw materials used and the nature of the process or the work done has been taken into consideration.[8]
>
> (Central Statistical Office, 1968)

Clearly, what we have here is some sort of 'industry' or supply-side delineation. The economist confronting these rather loose criteria for the first time may demand to know why they can not be made more 'rigorous'. The main reason is that the Industrial Census is made to serve multiple purposes and a certain vagueness is therefore inevitable. A common grouping on the basis of supply characteristics would take a different form if its purpose were to register industrial competitiveness than if it were used to measure raw materials use or trends in the evolution of the labour market between manual and non-manual work. In reality, it must be made to serve all these needs.

If we look at the 1968 Standard Industrial categories, we see that they break down into 27 broadly based Orders such as

Order IV – Coal and petroleum products
Order VI – Metal manufacture

Within these Orders may be found 181 Minimum List Headings. So within Order III – Food, Drink and Tobacco, we may find (partial listing):

217 Cocoa, chocolate and sugar confectionary
218 Fruit and vegetable products
219 Animal and poultry foods
221 Vegetable and animal oils and fats

These Minimum List Headings are sometimes further broken up into 'product' listings. It has been implied upon occasion that the Minimum List Headings can be used to represent 'industry' or supply characteristics while product designations closely approximate 'market' or demand delineations. A brief glance at the SIC catalogue makes it clear that this is not so, and that the main purpose of the product listings is to disaggregate further the supply-based Minimum List Headings. As we can see under MLH 217, for instance, there are two further divisions, the first of which, especially, is unlikely to be thought to describe a 'market' in a meaningful way:

(i) *Cocoa and chocolate*
Manufacturing cocoa powder, drinking chocolate and chocolate confectionary of all kinds. Cocoa butter is included.

(ii) *Sugar confectionery*
Manufacturing boiled sweets, toffee, caramels, marzipan, liquorice, chewing gum and all other types of sweets.

In a world made simple for the Census (and for Marshallian theory) each firm would have its activities allocated to a specific classification. As firm activity becomes progressively more diversified, the need for allocation of these activities becomes more pressing, though the problem may be somewhat eased by long term improvements in the quality of firm accounting data. The Census takes its unit of classification to be the 'establishment', and 'the whole of the establishment is classified according to the main activity' (Central Statistical Office, 1968).

The allocation for all of an establishment's activity to one product category could lead to an overestimate of the importance of principal activities, or a misrepresentation of the distribution of the production of certain products where a large percentage of output is produced by firms as ancillary activities. In the case of the 1963 UK Census, however, the average 'industry homogeneity' for all manufacturing establishments was 90 per cent (Sawyer, 1976), which would seem to indicate that the problem was of a trivial order of magnitude. It is worth noting, however, that the 1947 US Census, which reported the same level of average industry homogeneity found it necessary to incorporate a 'resistance factor' so that 'abrupt and unrealistic' small changes in the balance of an establishment's activities would not result in industry code changes (Conklin and Goldstein, 1955), which would indicate that this problem is somewhat worrisome to those close to the source of data collection. The rubric from the Census to enterprises does not indicate what measure they should use to designate 'principal activity', such as sales, value added, total assets, net assets, or labour employed (each of which would imply a different theory of business behaviour). Wherever it is possible to do so, ancillary activities such as transport, wholesale and retail distribution are listed as separate establishments (the necessary detail likely to be forthcoming only from the larger firms). Failing that, they are allocated to existing establishments. In the 1963 and 1968 Census products with sales of less than £10 million have been excluded: the outputs of certain establishments have been aggregated in a more or less arbitrary way when the products seemed to be reasonably 'homogeneous' (Hart and Clarke, 1980, pp. 131–2).

Lastly, it is important to observe that changes in industry definitions and product designations, the introduction of new categories and the elimination of obsolescent ones dictate that only a proportion of them are available for any comparison over an extended time span (Hart and Clarke, 1980, chapter 2). It is likely that some of these changes are responses to the evolution of the competitive process and, most especially, technological innovation, so that they take place in a non-random fashion, leaving the remaining categories unsuitable as a sample to illustrate or measure changes in competition over time (Hart, Utton and Walshe, 1973, p. 24). On the whole, the Census categories, which are fairly consistently based on supply characteristics are more useful than the muddle which would result if the advice of some economists were followed and greater aspects of demand were incorporated (as in Suits's comment on Conklin and Goldstein, 1955). Our intuitive feeling about the Census classifications is that they may be usable for indicating certain trends in industrial development (e.g. diversification), but they are totally unsuitable as fundamental measures of the 'competitiveness' of the economy.

THE MARKET: INTERACTION OF STRUCTURE AND BEHAVIOUR

The Phillips critique and the problem of entry

In Bain's pioneering study (Bain, 1956), the 'largest' barrier to entry in consumers' goods industries was that of product differentiation due to advertising. This raised for Phillips the disturbing possibility that, in the oligopolistic sector of the economy at least, it might well be possible to reverse the presumptive lines of causation in the structuralist model where, for instance, technological factors generate high minimum efficient scale in an industry, which acts as a barrier to entry and results in high concentration. Phillips suggests that an oligopolistic industry *may* adopt a *strategy* designed to exclude entry through collective agreements, the creation of product differentiation barriers to entry, and a host of other practices (Phillips, 1972b). In Phillips's words – 'Structure, Conduct, and Performance – and Performance, Conduct, and Structure?' (Phillips, 1972a).

In recent years, it has become even more clear that such apparently 'structural' variables as the level of excess capacity in an industry may well in part be an aspect of oligopolistic manipulation of the environment which might be faced by potential rivals (see Williamson, 1963 and Spence, 1977). Bain was able to maintain a purely structuralist conception of his barriers to entry partially because the levels were based on his own subjective determination. When explicit statistical estimates were attempted of the barriers to entry in various industries, these problems became more difficult to ignore. It might be barely possible to accept in structuralist terms of reference that high barriers to entry into, say, the sulphur industry might be due to control of the raw material by dominant firms, or into the ethical drugs industry due to patent protection, but must one consider the product differentiation barrier in the chewing gum industry (Mann, 1966) as being of the same kind? Similarly, one *may* choose to consider an estimate of the capital requirements and the 'risks' of an industry as first approximations to structural barrier to entry parameters, but what is one to do in a purely structural context with such variables as the intensity of research and development and of advertising?[9]

The Phillips critique and extensions thereon have emphasized that when firms have substantial market power, it is impossible to describe economic outcomes in 'structural' terms with those minimal assumptions about behaviour hitherto thought sufficient, since indeed it is that very behaviour which will shape the environment in which firms exist. It is our contention, however, that this is a more general proposition – one that cannot be confined to oligopolistic and monopolistic markets: when we view economic behaviour from a perspective that explicitly embodies the passage of time, *it is not meaningful to conceive that the behaviour of participants is determined by a set of market parameters which are exogenous to this behaviour.*

'Uncertainty, evolution and economic theory'

Our critique of the structuralist approach under all conditions, whether oligopolistic or not, is best explained with reference to the well-known article by Alchian (1950). Therein is established, in its most extreme form, the basis of the structure-performance paradigm: Alchian argues that concerns about the internal workings of a firm, about whether they actively or consciously pursue the goal of profit maximization are irrelevant. In a *competitive environment* the survivors will be those who successfully adapt. In this context – essentially a Social Darwinist one – reservations about the standard theory which stem from the impossibility of profit maximization in a world of uncertainty, or about the 'unrealistic' nature of the assumptions in an empirical sense are irrelevant. The pressure to survive will in the long run dictate the 'behaviour' of firms, since only those following a 'correct' course will continue to exist. We can thus describe and predict the 'behaviour' without reference to the desires and propensities of the individual entrepreneur.

We may describe Alchian's conception in terms of a purely static model, which somewhat distorts its probabilistic character but embodies the essential message: in the long term equilibrium, the firm in the perfectly competitive market can only survive by producing at what is in fact the profit maximizing output and selling it at the market price. Any factor which prevented the firm from selling at this price, be it due to inefficiency or benevolence,[10] would cause it to disappear.

The key difficulty with this formulation[11] may be seen by imagining a county in England in the late Middle Ages, populated by villages each of which possesses its own (solitary) shoemaker. Let us assume that transport costs are inconsequential, so that the market as 'objectively' measured covers more or less the whole county. What if, as a result of habit, tradition and ignorance on the part of all concerned, shoes are only purchased and sold *within* each village, with the resultant price, set by custom and tradition substantially above 'minimum long run average cost' (whatever that may mean in this context)? It is clear here that the 'objective' specification of a [deconcentrated] market environment is not a sufficient condition to predict either the *functional* delineation of the market, or the price resulting in such a 'market'.

The market environment implicitly specified by Alchian includes not only the physical possibilities for exchange (as dictated by transport costs, etc.) but a repertoire of abilities, attitudes and propensities on the part of the participants in the market ('entrepreneurs' and consumers) which would make the environment in which business takes place competitive. As is well known, even in a purely static context, market outcomes must be *initiated* by one or another participant. This is even more obvious in a context that exists over time. As Scherer succinctly put it '. . . if no firms in the industry happen to conform to the optimal pattern, the selection process can bog down altogether for there will be no "fit" to expand, multiply and drive out the less fit' (Scherer, 1980, p. 38). Thus until we have a precise idea of the pattern of behaviour to which firms *do* adhere, it will be impossible to delineate in a meaningful way the boundaries of the very 'industry' to which these firms belong.

It may be suggested that we have misrepresented or misunderstood the Alchian argument, and that its very purpose is to illustrate that only 'minimalist' assumptions about business behaviour are necessary to generate a competitive environment – they involve only the lowest level of self-seeking and desire to survive:

> . . . suppose that, in attempting to predict the effects of higher real wage rates, it is discovered that every businessman says he does not adjust his labour force. Nevertheless, firms with a lower labour-capital ratio will have lower cost positions and to that extent, a higher probability of survival. The force of competitive survival, by eliminating higher-cost firms, reveals a population of remaining firms with a new average labour-capital ratio
> (Alchian, 1950).

In other words, a 'natural selection' process combined with only minimal (implicit) assumptions about firms' self-seeking behaviour (those necessary to create the 'force of competitive survival') are enough to generate a competitive *outcome*. Alchian's article converged nicely with Friedman's contemporary attack on the role of 'assumptions' as opposed to predictions in economic theory (Friedman, 1953). Our objection here to the Alchian model is that because of its (implicit) static framework, it focuses exclusively upon *outcomes* as opposed to processes, and it therefore has a rather rigid, all or nothing quality. Let us, for the sake of argument assume that a minimal amount of self-seeking on the part of our shoemakers would *eventually* result in a 'competitive' outcome by virtue of the Darwinian iterative process outlined by Alchian. But *what is the time dimension necessary to bring about this outcome?* Is it one year or a hundred? How quickly will this process have to reach its conclusion for us to declare that the environment in which it takes place is 'competitive'? Alchian's analysis of competition in static terms, with its focus on final outcomes, ignores the critical dimension of time, which can only be understood in the context of competition as a dynamic process of equalization.

The static approach in this extreme form posits that, given the most minimal assumptions about the behaviour of individual firms, we can use exogeneously specified market structure to predict (final) outcomes. On the contrary, we argue that whatever the 'long run' static outcome, the behaviour and attitude of firms will crucially affect the process of competition and functional specification of 'the market' as surely as a change in the 'objective' variables affecting market structure – a change towards 'rational' self-seeking profit maximizing behaviour on the part of our shoemakers, an increase in the efficacy of their business practices, a widening of their horizons in a geographical sense away from the traditional village will affect the actual 'extent of the market' and the *rate* at which profits tend to equalise between firms as surely as a reduction in transport costs.

Markets and international trade

A recognition of the problematic nature of the distinction between *ex ante* and *ex post* delineations of the market is implicitly recognized in some statistical work, and may be seen in a study by Weiss (1972) where geographical submarkets are defined not *ex post* where sales are seen to take place, but in terms of an *ex ante* delineation based upon an index of transport costs. In international trade, as we have pointed out, even the crude *ex post* corrections for market delineation (subtracting production which is exported and adding imports) are often not performed even for open economies like the UK. The arguments made (besides those that relate to data limitations) are that:

(a) Some imports are not competitive, since they are merely inputs into domestic production. (This may not be clear from the SIC categories.)
(b) Some imports are controlled by domestic producers and multinationals (cars and matches being prominent examples).
(c) The *threat* of imports may be as important as the imports themselves.

These arguments are often used to suggest that the whole question can be ignored.[12] However, when import corrections are made, the conventional conclusions suggesting a rising level of market concentration for the 1960s and 1970s in Britain seem to be reversed. This result holds even when it is assumed that as much as one quarter of these imports are controlled by domestic companies (Utton and Morgan, 1983, chapter 2). Unfortunately, as hinted at in argument (c), such a procedure is not even approximately valid, since a market as an *ex ante* concept must dictate a sphere of *potential* competition. It is no more legitimate to decide on the level of international incursion into a domestic market by examining the level of imports than it would be to plot a demand curve for a product by looking at sales figures. If domestic firms react to the threat of foreign competition by lowering their prices, then no actual imports may be recorded. If, however, domestic firms maintain uncompetitive prices, then import penetration may well be rising as foreign competitors move in. In other words, a lack of competitiveness may show up in a decline in profitability or an increased import penetration. Even if we should observe such multinational control, so that the functional level of market concentration remains unchanged, does this mean that nothing has changed in the competitive environment? In the US, television manufacturers in the late 1960s responded to the threat of Japanese competition by shifting their production 'off-shore' to foreign subsidiaries and affiliates of US-owned firms (Millstein, 1983). This shift in behaviour was a competitive response to an increasingly competitive environment, with important implications for many aspects of firm behaviour. In static, market structure terms, nothing has changed in the competitive environment almost by definition if market concentration is unchanged, but the presumption of an objective statistical measure is illusory.

Thus practical economists have been left to themselves to try to improvise a usable definition of the market for empirical purposes. At a level of 'intermediate' theory, attempts to come up with practical but reasonably principled approaches to market definition (which might be usable in an anti-monopolies or anti-trust, if not in a global, context) make invariable concession to the fact that any such measure must embody both structural and behavioural parameters. *An ultimate solution to the problem of market delineation is not to be found, however, because a market is not a 'thing' to be measured but a behavioural relation.*[13] Practical solutions may be useful and necessary in particular contexts, but the 'market' or 'industry' cannot serve as a primary unit of analysis in economic theory.

CONCLUDING REMARKS

The corpus of microeconomic theory in its various manifestations is complex and sophisticated, but in the context of industrial economics the issues directed by the theory reduce to one straightforward question: what determines the behaviour of firms and, in particular, what are the constraints on their pursuit of profit (or other objectives)? As we have noted above, mainstream theory attempts to give clear answers to these questions through the use of the theoretical construct of the 'market'. Industrial economics has adapted market analysis to create practical tools such as the concentration ratio for the analysis of concrete situations. Are these constructs useful, or do they cause us to focus on minor irrelevant or even deceptive aspects of the problem?

Our responses to these questions should now be unambiguous: the 'market' or 'industry' cannot be used as the basis of a research programme into the competitive process as suggested by mainstream analysis. *Nothing* here should be taken to suggest any criticism of research efforts which delineate areas of study into the tobacco industry, metal box industry, etc. (as in Prais, 1981). It is not the delineation *per se* to which we object, but the presumption of mainstream analysis that it can form the basis of a 'structural' determinant of behaviour.

What alternatives exist to the static, market-based approach to competition? An important beginning is to note that the key agency for economic decision making in modern economies is *the firm*, which is the most primitive source from which the bulk of high quality business data is likely to emerge. Instead of analysing dubiously constructed 'industry profit rates', we should deal with the lesser, but sufficiently troublesome questions surrounding the rate of profit and valuation of individual firms. Once the firm is the focus of our study, it is clear that it is not merely subject to an exogeneously specified (market) environment, but is a key instrument through which that environment is formed and by which it evolves. Only by a much more thorough analysis than has hitherto been thought necessary of the external and internal forces impinging on firm behaviour – managerial, technological and financial – can real progress be made into the nature of the competitive process.

NOTES

1. A crucial change in the relatively uncritical acceptance of this approach was signalled by the publication Phillips (1976); see as well the series of articles on this topic in the *Journal of Industrial Economics* for June, 1984.
2. Recent examples of this literature include Cowling (1982) and Aaronovitch and Sawyer (1975). An examination of the central

propositions of the monopoly capitalist doctrine may be found in Auerbach and Skott (1988).
3. These examples are taken from industries used in statistical tests by Hart and Morgan (1977).
4. Note that even in our example we have made an implicit assumption about 'price rationality' on the part of buyers – we have presumed that if objective conditions permit them to pursue cheaper alternatives they will do so, and not persist in their present behaviour out of custom, laziness, or consumer loyalty. This aspect of the problem is brilliantly discussed in Kaldor (1935).
5. Once again, see Steiner (1968) for critiques of this and many of the other attempts to construct objective 'market' measures.
6. Steiner (1968) reconciles himself to this 'practical' solution. Earlier supporters of this approach are Robinson (1931, p. 12) and Mason (1939): '(a seller's market) includes all buyers and sellers of whatever produce whose action he considers to influence the volume of sales'.
7. '. . . In economic theory, an industry is a collection of firms making products which are highly substitutable; formally they have high cross-elasticities of demand *or* supply', and '. . . the Census of Production industry used here . . . is not in practice always closely related to the economists's definition of an industry as a group of products with high cross price-elasticities of demand *and* supply'. Both quotations are from Hart and Clarke (1980), pp. 2 and 11 (emphasis added).
8. This publication offered the most detailed, albeit brief, description of the rationale of the classification system. For 1980, '. . . an attempt was made to align the United Kingdom classification as closely as practicable to the NACE, the classification in use by the Statistical Office of the 'European Community' (Business Statistics Office, 1980). Our emphasis on the international standard industrial classification of the United Nations (which formed the basis of the pre-1980 UK and the present US system) is in order to link it to existing empirical work in these countries.
9. Orr (1974) treats these latter variables as purely exogeneous 'structural' constraints. He also includes market concentration as a barrier to entry.
10. In a probabilistic model it may be due to (randomly distributed) bad luck.
11. Other difficulties exist which are peripheral to our main consideration, such as Winter's (1964) clarification that 'survivability' is not necessarily to be identified with profit maximization in a world of uncertainty. Alchian's article has had its most direct influence upon industrial economics in the literature concerning the 'survivor technique', the case for which is most strongly asserted in Stigler (1958).
12. See Hart and Clarke (1980) pp. 105–6 and Cowling (1982) chapter 6.
13. An analogy can be made with those foolish attempts to make scalar measurements of human intelligence, which can only be meaningfully observed as an on-going *process* interacting with the environment (see Rose, *et al* 1984).

REFERENCES

Aaronovitch, S. and Sawyer, M. (1975), *Big Business* (Macmillan).

Alchian, A. (1950), 'Uncertainty, Evolution and Economic Theory', *Journal of Political Economy*, LVIII.

Arrow, K. (1959), 'Towards a Theory of Price Adjustments', in Abramovitz, M. (ed), *The Allocation of Economic Resources* (Stanford).

Auerbach, P. (1988), *Competition* (Basil Blackwell).

Auerbach, P. and Skott, P. (1988), 'Concentration, Competition and Distribution – A Critique of Theories of Monopoly Capital', *International Review of Applied Economics* 2.

Bain, J. (1956), *Barriers to New Competition* (Harvard).

Bain, J. (1972), *Essays on Price Theory and Industrial Organization* (Little, Brown and Co., US).

Business Statistics Office (1980), *Report on the Census of Production Business Monitor*, PA-1002 (HMSO).

Central Statistical Office (1968), *Standard Industrial Classification* (HMSO).

Conklin, M. and Goldstein, H. (1955), 'Census Principles of Industry and Product Classification in Manufacturing Industries' in National Bureau of Economic Research, *Business Concentration and Price Policy* (Princeton).

Cowling, K. (1982), *Monopoly Capitalism* (Macmillan).

Friedman, M. (1953), 'The Methodology of Positive Economics', *Essays in Positive Economics* (University of Chicago).

Hart, P. and Clarke, R. (1980), *Concentration in British Industry, 1935–1975* (Cambridge).

Hart, P. and Morgan, E. (1977), 'Market Structure and Economic Performance in the United Kingdom', *Journal of Industrial Economics* 25.

Hart, P., Utton, M. and Walshe, G. (1973), *Mergers and Concentration in British Industry* (Cambridge).

Hayek, F. (1948), 'The Meaning of Competition', as reprinted in *Individualism and Economic Order* (University of Chicago).

Hefleblower, R. and Stocking, G. (eds), (1958), *Reading in Industrial Organization and Public Policy* (Richard D. Irwin).

Kaldor, N. (1934), 'Mrs. Robinson's "Economics of Imperfect Competition" ', *Economica*, August, as reprinted in Kaldor (1980).

Kaldor, N. (1935), 'Market Imperfection and Excess Capacity', *Economica*, February, as reprinted in Kaldor (1980).

Kaldor, N. (1980), *Essays on Value and Distribution*, second edition (Duckworth).
Mann, H.M. (1966), 'Seller Concentration, Barriers to Entry and Rates of Return in Thirty Industries', 1950-1960, *Review of Economics and Statistics* 48.
Mason, E. (1939), 'Price and Production Policies of Large-Scale Enterprises', *American Economic Review* XXIX Suppl., as reprinted in Hefleblower and Stocking (1958).
Millstein, J. (1983), 'Decline in an Expanding Industry: Japanese Competition in Colour Television' in Zysman, J. and Tyson, L. (eds), *American Industry in International Competition* (Cornell).
Orr, D. (1974), 'An Index of Entry Barriers and its Application to the Market Structure Performance Relationship', *Journal of Industrial Economics* XXXIII.
Philips, L. (1971), *Effects of Industrial Concentration* (North-Holland).
Phillips, A. (1972a), 'Structure, Conduct and Performance – and Performance, Conduct and Structure?' – in Markham, J. and Papenek K. (eds), *Industrial Organization and Economic Development: Essays in Honour of E.S. Mason* (Houghton-Mifflin).
Phillips, A. (1972b), 'An Econometric Study of Price-Fixing, Market Structure and Performance in British Industry in the Early 1950s' in Cowling, K. (ed), *Market Structure and Corporate Behaviour* (Gray-Mills).
Phillips, A. (1976), 'A Critique of Empirical Studies of Relations Between Market Structure and Profitability', *Journal of Industrial Economics* XXIV(4) (June).
Prais, S. (1981), *Productivity and Industrial Structure* (Cambridge).
Rose, S., Kamin, L. and Lewontin, R. (1984), *Not in Our Genes:* Biology, Ideology and Human Nature (Pelican).
Robinson, E. (1931), *The Structure of Competitive Industry* edition of 1950 (Cambridge).
Sawyer, M. (1976), 'Concentration in British Manufacturing Industry', *Oxford Economic Papers* 23.
Scherer, F. (1980), *Industrial Market Structure and Economic Performance*, second edition (Rand-McNally).
Spence, A. (1977), 'Entry, Capacity, Investment and Oligopolistic Pricing', *Bell Journal of Economics* 8(2).
Steiner, P. (1968), 'Markets and Industries' entry in the *International Encyclopedia of the Social Sciences* Volume III (Macmillan, US).
Stigler, G. (1957), 'Perfect Competition, Historically Contemplated', *Journal of Political Economy* LXV(1) (February).

Stigler, G. (1958), 'The Economies of Scale', *Journal of Law and Economics* I.

Utton, M. and Morgan, E. (1983), *Concentration and Foreign Trade* (Cambridge).

Waterson, M. (1984), *Economic Theory of The Industry* (Cambridge).

Weiss, L. (1972), 'The Geographical Size of Markets in Manufacturing', *Review of Economics and Statistics* LIV(3).

Williamson, O. (1963), 'Selling Expense as a Barrier to Entry', *Quarterly Journal of Economics* 77.

Winter, S. (1964), 'Economic "Natural Selection" and the Theory of the Firm', *Yale Economic Essays* (Spring).

5. Competition, Monopoly Power and the Prices of Production

Amitava Krishna Dutt

INTRODUCTION

The classical economists – Smith, Ricardo and Marx – analysed the laws of motion of capitalist economies in terms of their concept of competition. Following the changes in industrial structure due to the concentration and centralization of capital, a tradition of Marxist economists originating in Lenin and Hilferding, and culminating in the work of Kalecki, Steindl, Baran and Sweezy, argues that the laws of competition have to be replaced by those of monopoly capitalism, according to which the capitalist system was ultimately regulated by the balance of power relations between workers, capitalist firms and the state. While accepting the empirical facts regarding changes in industrial organization, another group of Marxist writers using, somewhat paradoxically, ideas developed by Lenin, argues that such tendencies merely intensified the forces of competition in a capitalist economy, so that the framework of the classical economists, with their concept of competition, remains the appropriate one for the analysis of modern economies with large firms. The framework has been given a formal representation using the Sraffa–Leontief–Dmitriev–Schwartz analysis of the prices of production in an input-output system.

The purpose of this chapter is to show that the monopoly power view is not necessarily inconsistent with the concept of competition incorporated in the prices of production model, and that changes in industrial organization resulting from the concentration and centralization of capital may nevertheless imply that the theory of prices in a capitalist system has to be radically altered. To do so, the chapter reviews the central features of the classical (and neoclassical) notion of competition, the implications of monopoly power, and the debate between the two divergent Marxist views described above. It also develops a simple model incorporating the work of Kalecki and Steindl in the prices of production framework, and examines its consequences for the Marxian debate.

COMPETITION

This section examines the evolution of the concept of competition and its role in price theory, from the precursors of Adam Smith to Marx, and then to the neoclassical economists.[1]

While many accounts of the study of competition begin with Adam Smith,[2] McNulty (1967) has argued convincingly that '(n)either the concept itself nor its analytical function was original to him'. Becher, the seventeenth-century German mercantilist, had written that monopoly would result in high prices and competition in the form of many sellers would result in lower prices. Subsequently Petty, Boisguillebert, Cantillon and Harris had discussed the relationship between competition and 'intrinsic value'. They had discussed competition as a bargaining type of economic rivalry, competition increasing with the number of bargainers such that none had a direct influence on price.[3] Quesnay (1758) had described the formation of competitive prices as being 'independent of men's will . . . far from being an arbitrary value or a value which is established by agreement between the contracting parties'. Turgot (1766) had discussed how keen competition among rich entrepreneurs for renting land would make them pay all of their surplus profits to landlords as rent. Finally, Steuart (1767) had examined competition amongst buyers and competition amongst sellers, the former raising prices and the latter reducing them; competition on both sides or 'double competition' prevents an excessive rise or fall in prices.

Smith's (1776) contribution was to make the notion of competition the centerpiece of a general theory of prices. According to him, prices always tended to their natural levels, defined as those just 'sufficient to pay the rent of land, the wages of labour, and the profits of the stock employed . . . according to their natural rates', which were their ordinary or average levels. While actual market prices would deviate from the natural prices due to temporary shortfalls, the forces of competition would make them tend to the natural levels. Competition took the form of the mobility of labour and stock between different uses; if the market price of a commodity was above (below) the natural price, some components of its price (rent, wages or profits) would be greater (less) than their natural levels, resulting in the movement of land, labour, or stock into (away from) that use. The implication of this mobility was the equalization of rent, wages and the rates of profit, in different sectors. In these adjustments, individual buyers and sellers changed prices in response to market conditions. For example, when quantity supplied exceeded that demanded, 'some part must be sold to those who are willing to pay less . . . (and) the market price will sink more or less below the natural price, according as the greatness of the excess increases more of less the competition of the sellers, or according as it happens to be more or less important to them to get immediately rid of the commodity'. Smith did, however, acknowledge that due to several reasons, including concealed demand, secret technical advantages, monopoly granted to individuals or trading companies, and 'exclusive privileges of corporations, statutes of apprenticeship, and all those laws which restrain, in particular employments, the competition to a smaller number than might otherwise go into them', market prices could deviate for a substantial length of time from natural prices, creating differentials in the rate of profit.

In Smith's analysis of competition, landlords, capitalists and workers had symmetrical roles as active agents of mobility. The rate of profit, just like the wage rate, could be different between sectors due to 'the agreeableness or disagreeableness of business', although 'the average and ordinary rates of profits in the different employments of stock should be more nearly upon a level than the pecuniary wage of the different sorts of labour'. With Ricardo (1817) the emphasis shifted to the distinctive role of capital in competition:

> It is, then, the desire, which every capitalist has, of diverting his funds from a less to a more profitable employment, that prevents the market price of commodities from continuing for any length of time either much above, or much below their natural price.

Ricardo also departed from Smith's analysis of natural prices; for him, the centre of gravity of prices was given by the direct and indirect labour requirements, although only in an approximate sense, since there were several reasons due to which relative prices could differ from relative labour values. Ricardo's analysis of prices using the notion of competition in which capital mobility had a tendency to equalize rates of profit across uses, was confined to the vast majority of commodities the quantity of which could be increased by 'the exertion of human labour, and on the production of which competition operates without restraint'. He did recognize that all commodities did not satisfy these conditions (paintings, rare books and rare wines being examples) and the prices of these was determined by their scarcity alone; he used the term 'monopoly price' for them and argued that these prices had no necessary connection with their natural value.

Marx formulated a more general and dynamic concept of competition than Smith and Ricardo, although it was based on their approach. Marx, like Smith and Ricardo before him, saw the role of competition as being played through the intersectoral mobility of capital, which resulted in the tendency to equalize the rates of profit in all sectors. However, there are several important differences and developments that are worth noting.

First, in his work, competition is related to his particular vision of the working of the capitalist economy and played a much broader role than it did in Smith and Ricardo. It is related not just to the circulation of commodities, but to production (competition between capitals producing surplus value by raising the productivity of labour), distribution (between owners of capital), and the realization (by aiming to enlarge the market share and improving market conditions) of surplus value.

Second, unlike Smith's and Ricardo's notions, the regulating centres of market prices were the prices of production, given by the average costs of production and the average rate of profit (equalized between sectors by competition).

Third, competition, through the mobility of capital, does not bring about a smooth process of adjustment and convergence to the centres of gravitation, but results in disequilibria and deviations from them due to disequilibrium of supply and demand and a long time of turnover of capital in particular spheres of production (which would prevent production responding to demand), barriers to the entry and exit of financial capital (although this could be overcome somewhat by the credit system), and differences in the efficiency of individual units of capital within industries. Thus Marx did not assume that competition will equalize rates of profit between sectors, but used the concept of equalized profit rates (and competition) as a benchmark against which to examine actual price formation in a capitalist economy. But insofar as it was used as a benchmark, and considered useful as such, there seems to be the suggestion that there was a long-run tendency for the deviations to be evened out over time.

Fourth, Marx took a historical view of competition, and related it to the rise to dominance of the capitalist mode of production. He wrote:

> While free competition has dissolved the barriers of earlier relations and modes of production, it is necessary to observe first of all that the things which were a barrier to it were the inherent limits of earlier modes of production, within which they spontaneously developed and moved. These limits became barriers only after the forces of production and the relations of intercourse had developed sufficiently to enable capital as such to emerge as the dominant principle of production. The limits which it tore

down were barriers to its motion, its development and realization. It is by no means the case that it suspended all limits, nor all barriers, but rather only the limits not corresponding to it.

(Marx, 1976)

Competition was encouraged by and grew with the development of capitalism, removing legal and extra-economic impediments to the freedom of movement of capital.

Fifth, there are some implications that can be drawn from the distinction that Marx made between the categories of value and exchange value and between exchange value and price, distinctions that were never made consciously or consistently by Smith and Ricardo.[4] It may be argued that the implication of these distinctions is that Marx presumes that individual producers set prices on the commodity *at the point of production* and *prior to exchange*, and it is the subsequent process of exchange in the market that will inform independent producers of the social validity or invalidity of the prices that they set. Marx states in volume 1 of *Capital* (Marx, 1867) that the expenditures of 'socially necessary labour' determine to what extent individual prices are socially sanctioned, and in volume 3 (Marx, 1895) he states that the expenditure of 'capital' in a competitive framework, that is, the prices of production, that provide the social criteria for price formation. This implies that Marx's value theory provides a clear view of the role of individual price setting, although ultimately modified by social laws.

Finally, and although the relevance of this to the notion of competition was not clearly examined by Marx, his analysis focused on an economy in which money played a fundamental role. In the earlier classical writers money was simply a veil. Ricardo (1817) espoused what was later to be called Say's law, which argued that individuals produced only in order to buy other goods, so that there could never be a generalized excess supply of goods; money merely facilitated these transactions. Marx (1905) criticized this Ricardian notion, arguing that commodities were produced with an initial amount of money, attempting to make more money out of it. The anarchical nature of production, and the separation of the acts of sale and purchase brought about by the existence of money resulted in the *possibility* of crisis due to overproduction.[5] He showed, especially in Marx (1885, chapter 20), using his reproduction schemes that the aggregate demand resulting from output may not be enough to purchase the output produced in the economy.[6] While Marx did not complete the theory of crises and show how they actually occurred (a task left for Kalecki and Keynes to explore, as discussed below), he did show a clear understanding of the problem of effective demand and the possibility of crises. While the relevance of these developments to this debate will become clear later, two points should be noted here. One, the possibility of crises in Marx's analysis implies that the adjustment to a competitive equilibrium may not be smooth and continuous, and be subject to discontinuity and possible breakdown due to crises. Two, in Marx's system crises are the basis of the processes of concentration and centralization which, as we shall discuss below, are principally associated with the development of monopoly.

To return to competition itself, Marx's notion of the prices of production, incorporating the classical notion of competition with equalized rates of profit, can be formalized using the approach developed by Dmitriev (1974), Sraffa (1960) and Schwartz (1961). Let A be the matrix of input-output coefficients with elements a_{ij} referring to the amount of the ith good used in the production of a unit of the jth good, a_o the column vector of labour requirements per unit of output, p the column vector of the prices, w the equalized money wage rate in all sectors, and r the equalized rate of profit. Then, if following Sraffa we assume that wages are paid after production takes place, there are no joint products (and no fixed capital), and homogeneous labour is the only primary input in production, we can write:

$$p' = p'A(1 + r) + a_o' w \tag{1}$$

Given A, a_o, one of the distributional variables w or r, and a rule for normalizing prices (perhaps setting the price of one good equal to unity) we can use the system of equations to solve for the other distributional variable and the prices. With the rates of profit equalized between sectors, these prices are obviously Marx's prices of production. Sraffa's approach was to follow the classical tradition in price theory, which involved taking (1) technology, (2) the level and composition of output, and (3) distribution as data, and using the theory of competition (equalized rates of profit) to understand the nature of the prices of production as centres of gravity. The first two elements of the set of data fixed A and a_o (no assumption was thus necessary about returns to scale), while the third element fixed either w or r.[7]

Five observations summarize the classical theory of competition. First, for Smith, Ricardo and Marx, the central feature of competition refers to the mobility of capital (stock) between different branches of competition, and the resulting tendency towards an equalization of the rates of profit between sectors. Second, competition does entail active competition among sellers and individual capitals. Third, the behaviour of individual producers as sellers and bargainers is usually hidden under their role as agents of capital mobility,[8] (although this is not the case for many pre-Smithian writers on competition). Fourth, and as a corollary of this, the classical economists do not have a treatment of the effect of industrial structure of a particular industry on the behaviour of individual sellers. To be sure, Smith and the others did point out that restrictions on entry would result in high prices, due to the fact that production would be low; but they did not examine carefully the behaviour of individual firms as decision makers regarding prices and quantities, and how these decisions would be affected by the number of competing sellers. By not discussing such issues their analysis seems to imply that industrial structure was of no consequence for prices. Finally, the classical approach seems to suggest that one can analyse prices (at the social level) without analysing production levels and their rates of growth in the capitalist economy; there is thus a dichtomy between the theory of price and the theory of quantities and macroeconomic balance.[9]

The marginalist theories of the neoclassical economists – beginning with Cournot, and continuing with Jevons, Edgeworth, Walras, J.B. Clark and Knight – also used the notion of competition, which has been inherited by the modern neoclassical economists as the concept of perfect competition. Instead of describing a process towards equalized profits rates, this concept makes several precise assumptions about the structure of perfectly competitive markets in an economy as follows: agents were 'atomistic' in the sense that there were many buyers and sellers in it so that each one perceived that it could trade any quantity it wanted to at the going price; the product in a market was homogeneous; agents had perfect knowledge about their environment (and in some versions of future states of the economy); and factors and agents were perfectly mobile in the sense that there were no barriers to their mobility from one use (or market) to another. The assumption of perfect competition in all markets, together with the assumption of optimizing behaviour on the part of all agents (some definitions of perfect competition include this as one of its assumptions – see Knight, 1921, for example), and some other assumptions, have been used for proving the existence of equilibrium and its Pareto optimality.

It should be remarked that one implication of the assumptions of perfect competition is that each agent is a price taker. A seller, for example, will sell only at the going price it knows that at a higher price it would be able to sell nothing since perfectly informed, perfectly mobile, and optimizing buyers would rather buy the homogeneous product from a seller which sells at the going price; it need not sell at a lower price since it can sell all it wants to at the going price. This implies that under perfect competition the economy cannot be in a state of excess supply or demand for even the shortest instant of time, since then agents would then cease to believe in their atomistic status. Further, since all agents are price takers, there can be no price changes effected by individual agents; hence the necessity of the auctioneer. It follows that the assumptions of perfect competition are consistent with only a state of equilibrium (or the result of a particular process), but do not describe a process which takes the economy to that state, and in fact are inconsistent with a process which allows for excess supply or demand and price changes without the fictitious auctioneer.[10]

The classical and neoclassical notions of competition are different in several ways. First, it follows from what we have just said that the latter truly refers to a state, while the former refers to a process.[11] Second, the classical notion did not involve the assumption of atomistic or many agents since, as seen above, but it did allow firms to change prices, and to compete with each other actively; the neoclassical notion ruled out any kind of active competition involving business rivalry. Third, the neoclassical notion is much more precise, and so it necessitates the making of the two assumptions of perfect knowledge and homogeneous product. The classics did not make any analogous assumptions explicitly, but their notion of long period equilibria implicitly assumes an assumption of perfect information, and the existence of one price for a commodity requires the assumptions of homogeneous product. Fourth, in the neoclassical notion of competition, the behaviour of a firm (and other agents) is carefully spelt out: it maximizes profits as a price-taker, and can enter and exit in response to profits. Finally, the perfect mobility assumption of neoclassical perfect competition comes closest to the classical idea, but there are differences. For instance, in the classics, the mobility emphasized is the mobility of finance capital, and does not necessarily imply the movement of firms or factors of production (especially 'capital') in a neoclassical sense.[12]

MONOPOLY POWER

Important changes took place in the nature of advanced capitalist economies towards the last decade of the nineteenth century and the first decade and a half of the twentieth century. Industry, which had earlier been composed of numerous small family enterprises, increasingly came to be in the hands of giant corporations. In the US and Canada, in Europe and Japan, capital stock in manufacturing underwent consolidation in mergers, and very large industrial firms tended to outcompete smaller firms. This rise in big business resulted in a plethora of popular descriptive protest literature, and economic theorists from different perspectives began to analyse the changes.[13]

Marx had shown an early understanding of these developments when he perceived that accumulation went hand in hand with the twin processes of concentration (the absolute growth of individual capitals accompanying the expansion of social wealth as a whole) and centralization (the relative growth of particular firms due to the absorption and liquidation of smaller firms) of capital. These processes were brought about through economies of scale which allowed larger capitals to have cost advantages over smaller ones, and were speeded up by the credit structure of capitalist society. Marx saw the growth of joint stock companies as a natural consequence of this process of centralization. At the turn of the century Engels, after Marx's death, was also describing the genesis of trusts and corporations in European countries, as well as the importance of the industrial securities market for these developments.[14]

Veblen, as early as 1904, began developing many of the central concepts and features of what was later to emerge as the theory of monopoly capitalism.[15] In his works on North American capitalism he examined the decline of price competition, the tendency for monopolistic margins to widen at the expense of weaker firms and workers, the emergence of excess capacity and unemployment, problems of underconsumption and demand shortfall, and stagnation. Although influenced by Marx's work, Veblen was not himself a Marxist.

Within the Marxist fold the first to systematically analyse the rise of monopoly capital was Hilferding (1910). In his analysis, increasing concentration in production and circulation and the collusion and cooperation among capitalists because of mergers, cartels and trusts were the main causes of the development of monopoly capitalism. He also analysed the barriers to capital mobility across industries, the main reasons for these being increasing organic composition and the accumulation of fixed capital. To him, competition among capitals was transitory, giving way to the organization of production and income distribution by cartel arrangements. Decreasing competition thus went hand in hand with an increasing regulation of capitalism by cartels and the state. The forces of competition had to be replaced by those of power relations in the understanding of capitalism. Bukharin (1915) and Lenin (1916) also examined the replacement of free competition by monopoly capital, and they extended the analysis to encompass the problem of accumulation and conflict on a world scale. Despite these developments, however, these early Marxist analysts of monopoly capital did not analyse, in a theoretically systematic manner, the changes brought about in the dynamics of capitalism in advanced capitalist economies by the replacement of the forces of competition by the forces of power relations.

Economic theorists in the neoclassical tradition also responded to the changes in the nature of capitalism, developing theories of monopoly and monopolistic competition. To neoclassical economists, the assumption of perfect competition, which implied, among other things, that atomistic firms were price takers, had to be replaced by large firms which realized that the price of their product would depend on the quantity they sold. Using partial-equilibrium analysis, Robinson (1933) and Chamberlain (1933) analysed the cases of monopoly and monopolistic competition, respectively and showed that with downward-sloping demand curves price would exceed marginal cost, so that the equilibrium would be very different from the perfectly competitive one: *ceteris paribus*, the price would be higher and the quantity lower. Chamberlain merely relaxed the assumption of homogeneous products (but still assumed many sellers and perfect mobility): this highlights the fact that even with perfect mobility the equilibrium could be different from that under perfect competition.

Theoretical developments from the Marxist perspective followed with Kalecki (1939, 1943, 1954, 1971), who examined how changes in the structure of capitalism implied by the rise of monopoly capital could change the functioning of capitalist economies. The central features of Kalecki's system can be examined by discussing his theory of monopoly pricing, his theory of saving, and his theory of investment demand, in a one sector model of the capitalist economy.

While some of his earlier work proceeded along neoclassical lines, in the final phase of his work he jettisoned the optimizing apparatus, arguing that in view of the uncertainties inherent in the process of pricing (due to reactions from other firms) firms could not be assumed to maximize profits in any precise manner.[16] Instead, he assumed that they fixed prices taking into consideration prices charged by other firms and their own prime costs, so that the price of the product was marked up on the prime costs of production. Assuming, for simplicity, that labour is the only factor of production other than capital (which will be assumed to be physically the same as the produced good), and that technology is fixed coefficients and constant returns to scale, we may write:

$$p = (1 + z)wa \tag{2}$$

where p is the price of the good, z the rate of mark-up, w the wage rate and a the technologically-given labour-output ratio. With w given in the short run, and with z given by the 'degree of monopoly power', the price level was determined. The degree of monopoly power depended on factors such as the concentration ratio in the market, government policies, and the state of class struggle between workers and capitalists, and could be assumed to be fairly stable over time. The theory implied that the price was thus affected by the balance of power between capitalists, and between them and workers and the state. The assumption that the price level was fixed by equation (2) implies that firms responded to changes in demand by changing the levels of output.

This is shown in Figure 5.1, where for a representative firm, wa is the prime cost, $(1 + z)wa$ is the price level, and given our simplifying assumption of fixed coefficients, X^* is the level of output corresponding to full capacity. Assuming that demand is less than X^*, the firm will always produce to the level of demand without changing its price. Notice that if it does not do so, the price level will show a tendency to change. An immediate corollary is that if demand exceeds X^*, the price will be higher than $(1 + z)wa$. To make his theory consistent,

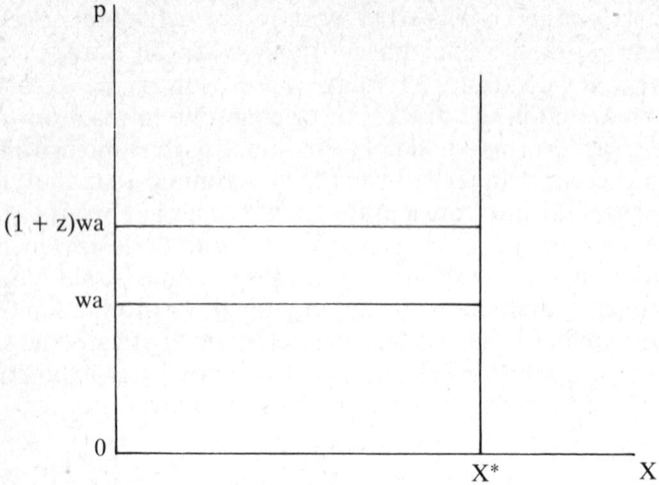

Figure 5.1

we have to assume that demand is less than X^*, or that excess capacity exists.

To complete his theory, Kalecki needed a theory of the determination of output, which he sought in the demand side, that is, in saving and investment. His theory of saving was that workers who earned wage income had a lower propensity to save than capitalists who earned mark-up income. A simple case is to assume that workers do not save, and capitalists save a constant fraction, s, of their income. Regarding investment, Kalecki assumed its dependence on the gross savings of firms and an index of changes in the level of activity; the crucial assumption was that investment was not equated to saving by variations in interest rates. The simplest assumption to emphasize this exogeneity is to assume a given level of real investment. Macroeconomic balance required saving to be equal to investment, and given our assumption, this implied:

$$X = [(1 + z)/z]\,(I/s) \tag{3}$$

where X is the level of output and I the given level of investment. It follows that a rise in the degree of monopoly power, increasing z, depresses the level of output. This occurs through the redistribution of income from workers to capitalist with a lower propensity to consume, reducing aggregate demand and hence output.

Kalecki's analysis of aggregate demand can be seen as a development of Marx's analysis of crisis due to the lack of demand, as discussed in the previous section. It should be remarked that Kalecki's model is demand driven in the same sense as are models of Keynesian economics; but Keynes's unemployments problem had nothing to do with the rise of monopoly. This implies that the analysis of aggregate demand – including that by Marx – is quite independent of the analysis of monopoly power. However, we see that the theory of aggregate demand is an essential component of the theory which examines the macroeconomic consequences of the emergence of monopoly in Kalecki's analysis, explaining why we found it necessary to draw attention to the difference between Marx's analysis and the Say's law approach to aggregate demand in the previous section.

Steindl (1952), continuing in the direction taken by Kalecki, believed that the utilization of productive capacity was fundamental to the investment planning of monopolistic firms. Confronted with a decline in demand, firms would cut back output (as in Kalecki) rather than prices, but the resulting fall in output would reduce capacity utilization, and therefore reduce investment and growth rates. The resulting secular stagnation was directly seen to be related to monopoly capital. Steindl's essential ideas can be expressed by extending the model developed above, to allow investment spending to depend positively on the rate of profit (as in Kalecki) and capacity utilization (as in Steindl). We assume that

$$g = g(r,u) \tag{4}$$

where $g = I/K$, $u = X/K$, r the rate of profit, and K the capital stock, and both partial derivatives are assumed to be positive. Using (2) the rate of profit can be shown to be given by

$$r = [z/(1 + z)]\, u \tag{5}$$

The saving-investment equality implies that

$$g = sr \tag{6}$$

which, using (4) and (5) can be written as

$$g[z/(1 + z)\, u, u] = s[z/(1 + z)]\, u \tag{7}$$

Given z, (7) solves for the equilibrium level of u. Total differentiation with respect to z shows that $dg/dz < 0$ if the stability condition that saving response is greater than investment response, is satisfied.[17] Thus a rise in the degree of monopoly power, given w, will raise the price level, and reduce the rate of growth of capital of the economy, g.

The same theme of monopoly power resulting in the breakdown of competition, regulation of the dynamics of the economy by power relations, and the tendency to stagnation is found in the writings of other Marxist writers such as Baran, Sweezy, Dobb, and Sherman. Baran (1957), and Baran and Sweezy (1966), for example, have analysed the rise of monopoly power and the resulting tendency toward stagnation in advanced countries due to the falling investment rates due to reductions in the rate of technological change and curtailment of output. Work similar to Marxist stagnationists was done independently by Sylos-Labini (1956), following the Keynesian ideas of Hansen, with demand deficiency and secular stagnation due to oversaving and underinvestment in the oligopolistic sectors of the economy.

We conclude this review of the monopoly power view with four comments. First, a large number of economists felt that capitalist economies had changed in structure: the laws of competition had to be replaced by the laws of regulation and monopoly power, due to the emergence of giant firms which behaved differently from the earlier smaller firms, the increase in barriers to mobility, and collusion between firms. Second, considerable attention was paid to how increasing monopoly power affected the behaviour of large firms. This departs from the classical practice of paying little attention to the firm, and is closer to the neoclassical notion of explicitly examining firm behaviour. Third, the analysis of pricing behaviour, at least in the world of Marxist economists, was closely tied up to the determination of output and rates of growth: monopoly power was related to lack of demand and stagnation. Finally, the analysis was usually macroeconomic in nature, so that no theoretical alternative to the prices of production framework, which showed how relative prices were formed in an economy in which competition reigned, was offered. To the extent that one of the aspects of monopoly power was barriers to the mobility of capital, some tended to argue that a uniform rate of profit was no longer to be expected.[18]

CLASSICAL COMPETITION VERSUS MONOPOLY POWER

The view of the Marxist theorists of monopoly power that capitalism passed from a competitive stage to a monopoly stage, which required fundamental changes in the nature of the analysis of capitalism, has been challenged by several Marxist economists who argue that despite the emergence of monopoly, capitalism is regulated by the self-expansion and competition of capital.

This group finds support in the work of Lenin. We saw in the last section that Lenin had described the process of concentration and genesis of monopoly power. However, Semmler (1984) writes that

> Lenin considered the capitalist mode of production as one of the self-expansion and accumulation of capital. He posited that competition is *not* abolished by concentration and collusion, but *resumed at a higher level* . . . Lenin regarded oligopolization as well as increasing competition and rivalry in the production, circulation and banking sectors as a necessary tendency in capitalists development.

Lenin's ideas are echoed in Varga's (1948) conclusion from his study of the monopolistic stage of capitalism in the 1930s, which was that concentration, barriers to capital mobility and collusion did not abolish competition but led to the creation of oligopolistic groups and to competition and rivalry among them; monopoly prices and monopoly profit rates were not overall phenomenon, but special cases.

Following Lenin and Varga, Shaikh (1978, 1979, 1982), Weeks (1981), Clifton (1977, 1983), and Semmler (1982, 1984), among others, have systematically explored this position. Their central ideas can be explored under four heads, as follows.

1. The position of the monopoly power view derives from a misunderstanding of the classical notion of competition and from confusing it with the neoclassical one. As discussed earlier, classical competition merely focussed on the tendency of the rate of profit to be equalized through the mobility of capital, and did not assume the existence of many sellers. Thus, concentration and centralization, and consequent changes in industrial structure, implied no changes as far as classical competition is concerned. Neoclassical perfect competition, which assumed the existence of many sellers, was the theoretical concept which had become obsolete.[19]
2. The institutional changes occurring with the concentration and centralization of capital have in fact heightened competition in the classical sense. This argument obviously finds direct support in Marx's views on the historical development of competition, referred to above. Mobility of capital, in the classical sense, does not require the movement of *firms*, but the movement of finance capital from sector to sector. Thus arguments relating the size of firms to restrictions on the mobility of capital are irrelevant as far as classical competition is concerned. The rise of giant corporations, as Clifton (1977) argues, facilitates the flow of capital, since the large corporation is more able to move its capital in search of profits, and has better access to information regarding opportunities for profit-making. Further, the development of communications networks, which has occurred *pari passu* with the development of capitalism,

makes the transfer of finance capital and spread of information easier. Clifton (1983) also argues that the rise of the institution of the multi-divisional corporation, controlled financially by the general corporate office, intensifies the forces equalizing the rate of profit. Often divisions exist in different sectors, and the corporate office investment decisions are made by examining the rates of profit in different divisions; this process hastens the equalization of profit rates between sectors. Additionally, Auerbach and Skott (1987) have argued that large firms are more able to overcome barriers due to geographical distance – both in locating their production operation and finding markets – and this also has tended to equalize profit rates.

3. The empirical arguments in favour of the monopoly view (for example, the preponderance of price setting practices and mark-up pricing) are unjustified. It has been argued by the monopoly view that the emergence of price fixing policies reflected by mark-up pricing rules; they have also shown that prices tend to be higher in more concentrated industries. Clifton (1983) has argued that the spread of price fixing strategies among large firms does not imply monopolistic price setting, but the greater ability of firms to set prices by examining their costs of production, so that prices are more quickly adjusted to the prices of production. Semmler (1984) has shown that the prices of production equations can be manipulated to produce mark-up pricing equations of the type estimated by the monopoly power view, concluding thereby that differences in mark-up rates are not contradictory with the equalization of rates of profit, since they may reflect differences in capital-output ratios between industries.
4. The empirical arguments against classical competition (for example, the overwhelming evidence regarding rates of profit differentials between sectors presented by Sherman, 1968, and Pulling, 1978) are incorrect and also miss the point. Semmler (1982, 1984) argues that such differentials are not incompatible with the classical notion of competition, which treated the prices of produc-

> tion as centres of gravity. As we have seen, Marx provided a detailed analysis of why rates of profit could diverge intersectorally, and also within industries. The empirical results showing differentials also do not show a stable and persistent hierarchy of profit rates related to industrial concentration; entry barriers seem to be a necessary condition for them to occur. Semmler demonstrates that these and other findings are quite consistent with Marx's analysis. Glick (1985) has argued that the data that monopoly theorists cite imply only short run differentials in profit rates. He proposes an alternative test of the existence of long run differentials and concludes that while the passage of time does not completely eliminate profit differentials, the size and persistence of differentials has been overstated by the short run studies.

The implication of all this is that this group would be quite content to use the prices of production framework, together with its implied concept of competition, in analysing the theory of price determination in capitalist economies. The genesis of monopoly capital did not cause the breakdown of competition in the sense used in this theory; rather it intensified it.

The rest of this paper argues that these arguments are not entirely convincing. To do so the next section develops a model incorporating some elements of the monopoly power view in a simple multi-sector model. The argument is not made that the classical competition view is wrong, but only that it is possible to have economies with large firms in which the prices of production framework is inadequate for understanding, and that an alternative framework focussing on the balance of power relations – as suggested by the monopoly power view – is required.

A MODEL

This section provides a simple two sector generalization of the one sector Kalecki–Steindl model examined earlier.[20] Discussion of relative prices requires a model with more than one sector, and a two sector model is chosen as the simplest such model in terms of which our essential ideas can be presented.

It assumes that there are two sectors producing one good each, one a pure consumption good and the other an investment good (and there are no intermediate goods). Each sector has a Leontief fixed coefficient technology, producing output with the capital good and homogeneous labour, which is assumed to be available in unlimited supply, and there is no depreciation of the capital good. Labour is assumed to be perfectly mobile between the two sectors, so that the wage rate is the same in both.

The behaviour of the model will be examined only in long-period equilibrium in which rates of profit are equalized between sectors (classical competition prevails) and the two sectors grow at the same rate. Three comments are necessary to clarify the role of this assumption. First, the concept of equilibrium with equalized rates of profit is invoked to allow classical competition – with the mobility of finance capital – to work even in an economy characterized by monopoly power. While recognizing that monopoly power may create some barriers to capital mobility, our strategy is to accept the idea of the classical competition school that profit rates tend to get equalized in an economy with large firms, and yet show the validity of the monopoly power view. Thus we do not invoke the argument of Sweezy regarding the non-equalization of rates of profit intersectorally, claiming that it is not an essential aspect of the vindication of the central result of the monopoly power view, that the theory of price determination should examine power relations. Second, exclusive attention to steady states implies a neglect of the behaviour of the economy out of the long period equilibrium state, an issue which has to be considered to deal with issues of stability and convergence.[21] The reason we eschew the formal analysis of explicit disequilibrium dynamics is that it is not our direct concern here.[22] Third, we do not necessarily mean to imply that a model of balanced growth is an appropriate construction to use for analysing classical and Marxian economic theory.[23] The device is used here only to provide a simple formalization of the quantity part of the system, and conclusions similar to the ones we shall draw could have been obtained without the assumption of balanced growth.

Our assumptions allow us to write two quantity equations and two price equations for the economy as

$$X_1 = c\,(a_{o1}X_1 + a_{o2}X_2) \quad (8)$$
$$X_2 = g\,(K_1 + K_2) \quad (9)$$
$$P_1 = P_2\,(K_1/X_1)\,r + Wa_{o1} \quad (10)$$
$$P_2 = P_2\,(K_2/X_2)\,r + Wa_{o2} \quad (11)$$

where X_i denotes the level of output of good i, P_i the price level for good i, K_i the level of stock of the capital good employed in sector i, a_{oi} the technologically fixed labour-output ratio in sector i, for i = 1 and 2; W the wage rate, r the rate of profit, g the growth of capital stock (these are equalized for the two sectors), and c the level of aggregate consumption per worker. Notice that equations (10) and (11) can be thought of as a simplified Sraffian prices of production model, since the K_i/X_i are input-output ratios.[24]

If we also assume, following classical tradition, that workers do not save and capitalists – who earn profit income – save a constant fraction s of their income, we get

$$c(a_{o1}X_1 + a_{o2}X_2) = (W/P_1)\,(a_{o1}X_1 + a_{o2}X_2) + (1\text{-}s)r(P_2/P_1)\,(K_1 + K_2) \quad (12)$$
$$sr = g \quad (13)$$
$$X_2/K_2 = g\,(K_1/K_2 + 1) \quad (14)$$
$$1 = (P_2/P_1)\,(K_1/X_1)\,r + (W/P_1)a_{o1} \quad (15)$$
$$P_2/P_1 = (P_2/P_1)\,(K_2/X_2)\,r + (W/P_1)a_{o2} \quad (16)$$

Equation (13) has been derived from (8), (9) and (12), so that if we use (13) and (14), which is derived directly from (9), equation (8) becomes redundant and does not have to be used separately. Equations (15) and (16) are derived from (10) and (11), with values expressed in terms of the consumption good; W/P_1 is the real wage, since good 1 is the only consumption good.

Three comments need to be made about this system of

equations. First, it embodies very little economic content, comprising mainly of accounting relations; the only *economic* assumptions made relate to consumption behaviour, the nature of technology, and the fact that we are studying equilibrium with equalized rates of profit and growth. Second, we do not require full utilization of capital, since X_i/K_i, the actual output-capital ratios, are allowed to vary, and not fixed at their technologically given maximum levels. Third, the model is not 'closed', since against four equations, we have seven unknowns, namely, W/P_1, P_2/P_1, X_1/K_1, X_2/K_2, r, g, and K_2/K_1. To 'close' the model we need three more equations, and we do so by introducing three additional equations along Kalecki–Steindl lines.

We assume the existence of market power of firms in each industry, so that prices in each industry are marked up on prime costs, with labour as the only input entering prime costs.

$$P_1 = (1 + z_1)\, Wa_{o1} \tag{17}$$
$$P_2 = (1 + z_2)\, Wa_{o2} \tag{18}$$

where z_i is the mark-up rate in sector i. The assumption is that the degree of monopoly power, which is a fairly stable element, fixes the mark-up rate in each sector. As discussed above, the mark-up rates can be assumed to depend on factors such as the degree of concentration in an industry, and the state of the class struggle. In a more general model with intermediate goods, both z_is would be affected by the wage bargaining process; in this model, since only z_1 affects the real wage, z_2 may not be affected by the state of class struggle. Both will be affected by concentration rates; since these could conceivably differ between sectors, the mark-ups in the two sectors may be different.[25] These equations embody a specific *theory* of price formation, in which large firms set prices as a mark-up on prime costs, and change the levels of output to meet demand; this is possible because of the existence of excess capacity. The mark-up rates are assumed to be constant at a level sufficient to yield an equilibrium for the model with excess capacity.[26]

A final equation examines investment behaviour. We assume

$$g = g(r, X_1/K_1, X_2/K_2) \qquad (19)$$

where g changes positively with respect to each argument. This equation should properly be thought not as a behavioural equation, but as a reduced form equation which shows how investment plans are made in equilibrium. The behavioural equations and the mechanisms on which it is based are not discussed formally in this paper, since it would be necessary to discuss the dynamic process which leads to the long period equilibrium, to examine them. We would then have to allow for differential rates of growth, g^1 and g^2, and also possibly differential rates of profit, r_1 and r_2, and examine the convergence to long period equilibrium which, as already noted above, is beyond the scope of the present paper.

However, a plausible mechanism needs to be discussed, if only in an informal manner, and that may be outlined as follows. Firms in each sector invest according to a function which makes the growth of capital stock depend on the sectoral rate of profit, the interest rate, and the degree of sectoral capacity utilization. Kaleckian and post-Keynesian reasons explain the profit rate, standard reasons explain the interest rate, and the degree of capacity utilization enters because of reasons examined given by Steindl (1952).

The classical assumption of competition due to the mobility of financial capital would equalize the rate of interest intersectorally, even in the short run, although rates of profit could diverge from it, and hence from each other. In long period equilibrium, in which the sectors have the same rate of growth of capital stock, the rates of profit would be equalized with the interest rate, and hence with each other.[27] The growth rate of capital stock would then depend on the common rate of profit and the degrees of capacity utilization. Specific forms of behavioural investment functions may have to be postulated to obtain this reduced form.

The model now has the same number of equations as variables, and can consequently be solved (assuming that the appropriate existence conditions, including those allowing equilibrium with excess capacity in both sectors, are satisfied). The real wage is solved from (17) as

$$W/P_1 = 1/[a_{o1}(1 + z_1)] \tag{20}$$

and (17) and (18) give us the price ratio

$$P_2/P_1 = [a_{o2}(1 + z_2)]/[a_{o1}(1 + z_1)\ ] \tag{21}$$

Substituting equations (17) and (18) into (10) and (11) implies

$$r = [z_1/(1 + z_2)]\ (a_{o1}/a_{o2})\ (X_1/K_1) \tag{22}$$

and

$$r = [z_2/(1 + z_2)]\ (X_2/K_2) \tag{23}$$

from which it follows that

$$X_1/K_1 = (z_2a_{o2}/z_1a_{o1})\ (X_2/K_2) \tag{24}$$

Substituting equation (19) in (16), and the value of r from (23) and the value of X_1/K_1 from (24) we obtain

$$s[z_2/1 + z_2)]\ X_2/K_2 = g\ (z_2/(1 + z_2)\ X_2/K_2,\ z_2a_{o2}/z_1a_{o1}\ X_2/K_2,\ X_2/K_2) \tag{25}$$

which has only one variable, X_2/K_2, which it solves for. The equilibrium solution is shown in Figure 5.2, where the S line shows the right hand side of (25) and the g line shows the left hand side, it being assumed that the latter line is flatter than the former. Notice that the g curve is rising because a higher K_2/K_2 makes all three arguments of the g function increase, all of them increasing the value of g. Substituting the equilibrium values of X_2/K_2 and g into (23) and (24) solves for r and X_1/K_1, and equation (13) then solves for K_1/K_1.

Two comments need to be made about this model. First, a fall in z_1, which can be caused by a fall in the degree of monopoly

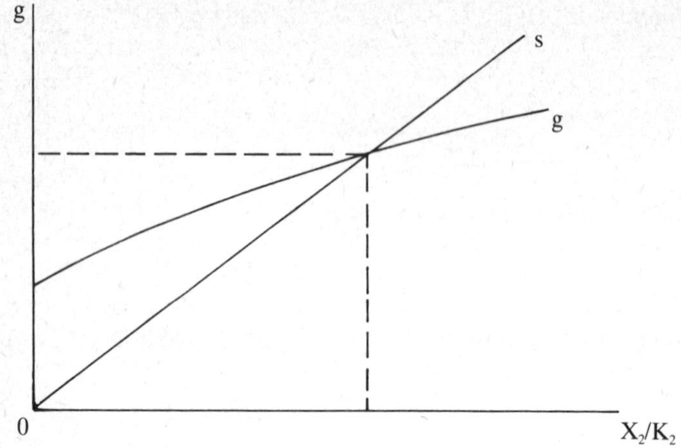

Figure 5.2

power in the consumer goods sector, will, by equation (20), increase the real wage. From equation (25) we see that the g curve in Figure 5.1 will be pushed up, so that the equilibrium values of X_2/K_2 and g will rise. From (23) and (24), the equilibrium values of r and X_1/K_1 will increase. We thus find that a higher real wage is associated with a higher growth rate. Also, the real wage-profit rate frontier is upward sloping, unlike the familiar downward-sloping curve found in Sraffa's work.[28] That downward sloping relationship could be derived from equations (10) and (11) of our model if we held as constant the levels of K_i/X_i. However, in our analysis of the parametric variation of z_1, we let the K_i/X_i vary. Since with the fall in z_1, K_i/X_is fell (capacity utilization increased in both sectors), the downward sloping wage-profit frontiers (with constant X_i/K_is) in effect shifted out, so that both the real wage and the rate of profit increased. The reason for these results is that a fall in the degree of monopoly power in sector 1 causes a rise in the real wage, which changes the distribution of income from high-saving capitalists to workers, increasing consumption expenditure, raising aggregate demand, reducing excess capacities, and raising both the profit rate and the rate of growth.[29]

Second, the equilibrium shows that a self-fulfilling long period state may exist with excess capacity. Excess capacity exists because of monopoly power which prevents prices from falling to restore full capacity; the degree of monopoly power also restricts aggregate demand below full capacity utilization by depressing consumption demand and hence investment demand. Note that if there are exogenous changes in the economy which lead it away from full capacity, there will be no automatic mechanism, with price stickiness, to return it to full capacity: in fact, if excess capacity reduces investment demand, it will lead the economy to greater excess capacity.[30] Classical competition equalizes rates of profit through the mobility of financial capital, but this equalization is quite consistent with excess capacity. Notice also, that with no reasons for firms going from one industry to another, there are no inherent causes for the industrial structure in any industry, and hence mark-up rates which depend on it, to change. The mark-ups may change over time in response to changes in the balance of power relations between workers and capitalists, and between capitalists and the government, and there are no reasons to believe that with excess capacity, they would fall to restore full capacity.[31] But for the purposes of our model, these changes are exogenous, and the mark-ups can be treated as stable elements.

Finally, we examine how the model developed has to be modified if we assume that long period equilibrium is characterized by the full utilization of capacity. A sufficient condition for the assumption of full capacity utilization in the model is that of price taking behaviour on the part of firms, an assumption made in neoclassical theory.[32] Excess capacity would be incompatible with such behaviour since producers would expect to sell all their output, and thus produce at full capacity, and excess supply would make the price level fall to whatever level is required for market clearing at full capacity. It was precisely the assumption of price fixing and quantity adjusting behaviour of the firms that was necessary for the emergence of excess capacity in our model. However, the assumption of perfect competition is not necessary for full capacity utilization. Even if monopoly power prevailed, if demand was very high (due to a 'high' investment function, low s, or low z), so that at the price compatible with monopoly power demand was higher than full capacity, the price would have to increase to clear the market since quantity response by firms would no longer be possible.

The full utilization of capacity in our fixed coefficients model would imply that the K_i/X_is in our model would be given at the technologically given capital output ratios, denoted by say a_{2j}. It follows that equations (15) and (16) could now be written as

$$1 = (P_2/P_1)a_{21}r + (W/P_1)a_{o1} \qquad (26)$$

$$P_2/P_1 = (P_2/P_1)a_{22}r + (W/P_1)a_{o2} \qquad (27)$$

In this case, these two equations provide a sub-model with three unknowns, the real wage, the rate of profit and the relative price. With the X_i/K_i technologically fixed, equation (25) would solve for the equilibrium value of r. Substituting for that value in equations (26) and (27) would determine W/P_1 and P_2/P_1. Equations (20) and (21) would simply solve for the implied 'mark-ups', from the solve values of W/P_1 and P_2/P_1.[33]

IMPLICATIONS OF THE MODEL FOR THE DEBATE

We are now in a position to evaluate the claims of the two views regarding the implications for the process of concentration and centralization for the laws of motion of capitalist economies. This evaluation, based mostly on the formal model developed in the last section, is made in terms of the following remarks.

1. Our model, with classical competition, but with firms setting prices as a mark-up over costs in a Kaleckian manner, adjusting quantities in response to changes in demand, and investing in a Steindlian manner, has shown that there is no necessary inconsistency between

competition as understood by the classical economists and the notion of monopoly power. Classical competition refers to the process of equalization of the rate of profit through the mobility of finance capital, while monopoly power as interpreted here is the ability of firms to set prices. It seems clear that it is possible to have a model where we may have prices of production equations in which given input-output ratios, and distribution, one can solve for prices of production with intersectorally equalized rates of profit (equations (14) and (15)), and also have prices as being given as marked up over prime costs.

2. For our model with monopoly power, classical competition and excess capacity, the question arises as to which of the equations – the prices of production or mark-up pricing ones – 'determine' prices, and thus which forces are relevant for studying the formation of prices. If we mean by 'determination', the solving of values of the variables to be determined in terms of some equations where the only other elements are the parameters of the model, then the prices of production equations (14) and (15) do not determine prices, since the equations contain elements other than relative prices which are variable in the model; equation (21) does, since the relative price is expressed as depending only on technology and the degrees of monopoly power, which are the parameters of the model. Thus, the balance of power relations between the workers and capitalists and between the capitalists and the state are important for the determination of prices (since they affect the mark-up rates), exactly as argued by the school of Marxists originating in Hilferding. It seems, therefore, that monopoly view may have been right in suggesting that the theory of prices had to be changed as a result of the rise of monopoly power.
3. If firms are price-takers, as would happen in economies with many sellers, our model shows that firms would always operate at full capacity. In this case, prices would be determined by equations (26) and (27), the prices of production equations. Thus, if the early stage of capital-

ism was characterized by markets with many sellers, the prices of production equations could be used as an adequate framework for understanding price determination.

4. If there are few sellers in each market, but if they work at full capacity, the prices of production will still be an adequate framework for studying the determination of prices. This implies that the changes in industrial structure need not out of logical necessity imply the theoretical obsolescence of the prices of production equation. The crucial issue is whether or not firms operate with excess capacity and fixed prices.[34]
5. That the rise in monopoly power and the emergence of large corporations could have increased competition in the classical sense, as argued in Clifton (1977) and others, may be true, but does not change the nature of our conclusions. In fact our model assumes the classical competitive mechanism and yet shows how monopoly power regulates capitalism through power relations. Even the argument about large firms overcoming geographical barriers and destroying the market power of some firms need not logically follow. Large firms could invade markets with several smaller, vigorously competing firms, and destroy whatever competition that existed; it could collude (even implicitly) with other large firms to stay out of that area, leaving to it some other market.
6. Attempts by Semmler (1984) and others to show that there is no stable hierarchy of profit rates, and classical competition does not require equalized profit rates all the time, may be quite valid; however, they seem to have no bearing on the debate as to whether the rise of monopoly power necessitated the abandonment of the prices of production framework for the determination of prices. This has been hinted at by Sherman (1983), but many, including Semmler (1983) and Glick (1985), continue to believe that it is central to the debate. Perhaps it is all for the best that this is not the case: the debates regarding the issue perhaps convince all except those completely committed that neither side has won in the

debate regarding the empirical issue – everything depends on how one actually measures one's theoretical categories, what time periods are chosen, and how stringent one is willing to be interpreting the term 'equalization'.

7. Attempts by Clifton (1983) and Semmler (1982, 1984) to make price fixing practices and Kaleckian mark-up pricing equations consistent with the prices of production equations are flawed. If firms fix prices as a mark-up on prime costs, where the mark-up depends on the degree of monopoly power, it is not the same as price fixing according to the prices of production equation. To go from one to the other, one needs to know the degree of capacity utilization, which is macroeconomically determined by demand in a general equilibrium framework. Semmler (1984) is right in showing that mark-ups can be calculated from prices of production equations, but do not necessarily show the existence of monopoly power or unequal rates of profit. His error in interpretation lies in arguing from this that he has ruled out the possibility of the mark-up playing a role in price determination. He simply assumes that the economy operates at full capacity, and mark-ups are determined once prices and costs are known from the prices of production equations, as in the version of our model with full capacity utilization. He does not allow for the possibility that with excess capacity, the mark-up equations (with exogenously determined mark-ups depending on the balance of power relations), determine prices, and the prices of production equations are consistent with them. Semmler (1982) writes that '(t)he mark-up over prime cost – in Kalecki's theory a measure of the degree of monopoly power – might be only another expression for the *uniform* profit rate . . . this mark-up must be different in industries where the capital-output ratio . . . is different, whereas the profit rate . . . may be the same in all industries.' Semmler is quite right; but what he fails to realize is that if capital–output ratios are determined, Kalecki's analysis implies that mark-ups, not prices of production

equations, determine prices *despite the equalization of rates of profit*.[35]

8. The failure of the group which believes that the forces of competition determine prices after the advent of monopoly capital to see the possibility of the role of monopoly pricing practices in price determination can be argued to arise from an uncritical return to the classical method of analysis. As noted before, this had two important characteristics: first, the theory of price determination – at least in the most influential interpretations – took as data the level and composition of output, technology, and distribution, and second, the theory did not consider the individual firm and its decision making in an adequate manner, except as an agent of capital mobility. The first one implies that it is acceptable to use the prices of production equation to determine prices. We have argued that this is not permissible if excess capacity exists (see also Dutt, 1986), since with levels of output responding to changes in demand, it is not useful to have a theory which takes output levels as data. Neoclassical theory broke this dichotomy, and the monopoly power theorists did the same in fact with a vengeance, generally being concerned with rates of growth, investment, output, and income distribution – that is macroeconomic categories – rather than relative prices. The second characteristic raises the possibility that the functioning of the economy in the classical system may be inconsistent with certain types of firm behaviour. The central feature of monopoly power, as interpreted in this paper, is the ability of firms to set prices, rather than being passive price takers. Price-fixing behaviour implies that firms must be able to vary output in response to changes in demand. Without explicit attention to output and price decisions of firms, classical theory was incapable of analysing the implications of such changes. Neoclassical theory considered decision making units much more carefully, and the theoretical implications of monopoly power (imperfections in competition) were explored in terms of that theory. Monopoly power theorists, especially Kalecki,

also carefully analysed the behaviour of firms, but did not incorporate that analysis in a model which examines the determination of relative prices. By attempting to do that in our model we have found that classical theory, by ignoring the decision of individual producers, was making implicit assumptions: that they were atomistic price takers, or for some other reason they worked with full capacity. Thus their price theory was inconsistent with price fixing and quantity adjusting behaviour of firms with monopoly power.

CONCLUSION

This paper has argued that the changes in structure of capitalism involving the concentration and centralization of capital may well have implied that the classical theory of price determination by the forces of competition, by which it is meant the examination of prices of production equation with equalized rates of profit, have to be replaced by a theory which examines the determination of prices by the balance of power relations between capitalists, workers and the state.

To develop our arguments we examined a simple model in the Sraffian tradition, and showed how its long period equilibrium position could be determined by using the theory of monopoly power and demand determined output developed by Kalecki and Steindl. The analysis used the classical notion of competition, but allowed for the existence of excess capacities in this long period equilibrium. It showed that relative prices were determined by the balance of power relations between different groups in the economy, rather than by the prices of production equations.[36] It thus showed that the rise of monopoly power may call for a theory of prices different from the classical one, even if one believes that the rise of large corporations increases competition in the classical sense.

NOTES

I am grateful to Edward Amadeo, Panagis Liossatos, Stephen Marglin, Murray Milgate, Lance Taylor, the participants of the Harvard-MIT seminar on Non-neoclassical Economics, and especially to an anonymous referee for this series for discussions and comments.

1. 'Competition' has other roles than those discussed in this exposition. Its role in enforcing minimum-cost production, and in generating technological change, are not dealt with here.
2. See Stigler (1957) and Clark (1961).
3. See Meek (1956) and McNulty (1967). See also Eatwell (1982), on which we draw heavily in this examination of the classical notion of competition.
4. I am grateful to the anonymous referee for the following interpretation.
5. See Kenway (1980).
6. See Foley (1986) for a modern treatment. See also Kalecki (1968).
7. See Eatwell (1977) for an account of classical price theory and its relation to Sraffa's work. Sraffa also extended his analysis to allow for different techniques, for joint products and land as a primary factor.
8. Several writers have remarked on the neglect of the role of the firm in classical theory. Levine (1980), for example, writes: 'Competition simply forces each firm, so far as it is to survive, to accept the fate of the system as a whole, conforming as best it can to that predetermined destiny . . . This same tendency to obliterate the active role of the firm within the conception of the price system and its development is revealed within the structure of the market and within the dynamic process of market price formation. This process, as it is established in its relation to the conditions of production, is fundamentally inconsistent with any conception of the firm as an institution whose sustenance is implied in the development and reproduction of the market.'
9. On this, see Eatwell (1977), Garegnani (1984) and Dutt (1986). This is not to say that the classical writers (in particular Marx) did not take into account the logical connection between price and output decisions at the level of the individual producer.
10. See Arrow (1959) and Fisher (1983) on this. This is not to imply that it is not possible to rigorously formulate assumptions which would generate a process resulting in an equilibrium approximated by perfectly competitive equilibrium. A model of monopolistic competition, for example, could supply these assumptions.
11. See McNulty (1967). A distinction, however, needs to be made between the two notions as they have been used in classical and neoclassical economics, and the visions underlying them. With neoclassical economics more concerned with precision, and with preci-

sion being more difficult in the analysis of processes than of states, neoclassical economists have formulated the notion of competition to analyse the latter. This does not mean that their notion of competition does not have an implicit process. See the previous footnote.

12. Roemer (1981) has shown that in a generalized Marxian economy with two classes (workers and capitalists), an equal rates of profit equilibrium with neoclassical assumptions competition (including price taking behaviour and profit maximization) can be shown to exist if capitalist firms have access to a perfect credit market. This shows that the equalization of rates of profit can be given a completely neoclassical interpretation. However, it does not show that price taking behaviour is necessary for classical competitive equilibrium. Alternative presentations, involving the mobility of capital responding to rate of profit differentials, are available in Nikaido (1983, 1985), Steedman (1983) and others.
13. See Foster and Szlajfer (1984) for a collection of readings by economic theorists in this tradition, including Sweezy, Kalecki, Dobb, Sherman, Sylos-Labini and Steindl.
14. Aside from these empirical issues, by rooting his analysis of prices in the price setting behaviour of individual firms [as pointed out in the previous section], Marx had developed a theory of prices under competition which was capable of being extended logically to the non-competitive environment.
15. See Veblen (1904, 1920, 1923).
16. See Kriesler (1987) for a critical analysis.
17. See Dutt (1984) (which draws on a 1981 paper included in a 1982 MIT PhD thesis) for a fuller exposition of this model, and Dutt (1987) for a comparison of this model with other macroeconomic growth models, following Marglin's (1984) work. Rowthorn (1981) has also independently developed a similar model.
18. Thus Sweezy (1968) wrote that 'the transition from competition to monopoly brings with it an increase in profits and hierarchy of profit rates' instead 'of the tendency to an equality of profit rates which is a characteristic feature of competitive capitalism'.
19. Shaikh (1978, 1979, 1982) has criticized also the neo-Ricardian school for confusing the classical and the neoclassical notions of competition. While such a criticism is valid for some of those in the neo-Ricardian tradition who have been discussing the choice of technology issue and its relation to the tendency for the rate of profit to fall, the concept of competition implicit in Sraffa is essentially the same as that employed in Marx, although all the details are not spelt out explicitly.
20. As will be clearer as we proceed, this model is an attempt to incorporate the work of Kalecki and Steindl in a Sraffian framework. There have been earlier attempts to synthesize Kalecki and Sraffa. Mainwaring (1977) examined a formal model, but the model was a short run one and – perhaps for that reason – did not allow for intersectoral capital mobility and the possibility of rate of profit

equalization. Bhaduri and Robinson (1980) also described a model synthesizing Sraffa, Kalecki and Marx. Although it did recognize the importance of excess capacity, it did not provide a formal depiction. Harcourt (1965) and Taylor (1983) have presented models similar to ours, but the former is a short run one model, and the latter makes different assumptions and draws different implications.

21. This does not necessarily involve the actual convergence of the economy to the long run equilibrium, but examination of the logical tendency of the economy to tend to its centre of gravity.
22. These issues are discussed in Dutt (1988a). It is shown there that except under rather stringent conditions, an economy of the type considered here will not converge to a position of equalized profit rates. Although there may be a tendency towards equalization, there may be one toward the opposite direction as well. Note that this is not inconsistent with the empirical finding that over the long run there may be a greater tendency toward equalization than in the short run.
23. See, for example, Sardoni (1981), who argues *against* such a position. However, there is a large tradition of writing in mathematical classical-Marxian economics which has used the assumption (see Sardoni, 1981 for references). We should also point out that a balanced growth model does not imply that we are examining an economy with all sector growing at the same rate: there could be systematic shifts in the parameters of the model which could make different sectors grow at divergent rates.
24. In Sraffa's analysis capital goods are dealt with as joint products and written on the left hand side of the price equations; we write them on the right hand side.
25. See Dutt (1987) for how class struggle and industrial structure can jointly determine the mark-up in a one sector model.
26. It will be seen from what follows that with sufficiently low mark-up rates, excess capacity may disappear. Then prices would have to be determined by the interaction of demand and supply forces, and equations (9) and (10) with the z_is constant would cease to apply. See, for example, Taylor (1983) and Rowthorn (1981). More of this later.
27. It is, of course, not inevitable that capital mobility, which equalizes financial rates of return between sectors, must necessarily equalize rates of profit between them; in a monopoly situation, particular industries may make profits above the rate of interest. We are assuming that accumulation occurs in such sectors and eliminates these differentials, so as to make the model exhibit classical competition with equalized rates of profit.
28. Note that the existence of the upward rising wage–profit frontier does not imply the non-existence of class conflict. Class conflict is the perception by workers and capitalists of conflict between them, and this would exist in the model since worker attempts at pushing up real wages would reduce mark-ups, and vice-versa. The rate of profit is

determined as a result of macroeconomic interactions which may not be perceived by the parties involved.

29. This analysis, which is quite opposed to Ricardo's is not inconsistent with Marx's, who, as we have noted above, emphasized the problem of aggregate demand. Marx (1885) wrote that '(t)he epochs in which capitalist production exerts all its forces are always periods of over-production, because the forces of production can never be utilized beyond the point at which surplus value can not only be produced but also realized.' In Marx (1894) he wrote that '(t)he falling tendency of the rate of profit is accompanied by a rising tendency of the rate of surplus value, that is, the rate of exploitation'.
30. See Amadeo (1985).
31. Excess capacity and unemployment could reduce the bargaining strength of workers and thus increase the mark-up in the consumption good sector. Further, greater excess capacity implies a higher burden of fixed costs, and as Kalecki (1971) argued, this could raise mark-ups. Finally, modern oligopoly theory suggests that periods of high demand could be associated with low mark-ups and conversely for periods of low demand; see Rotemberg and Saloner (1986), for example.
32. Perfect competition (that is, atomistic competition) can also be assumed and the neoclassical full employment assumption can be replaced by a desired accumulation function similar to equation (19), with full capacity equalization assumed. It is easy to see that for this model, the prices of production would still determine relative prices, after the desired accumulation function and the saving propensity of capitalists determines the rate of profit. (See Dutt, 1988b, for a fuller analysis.) This shows that the introduction of the aggregate demand problem into the analysis in the guise of the desired accumulation function does not in itself imply the abandonment of the prices of production apparatus.
33. This particular 'closure' is Marglin's (1984) neo-Keynesian closure. An alternative neo-Marxian closure would involve assuming the real wage to be determined by 'subsistence', and for g to be determined by sr, without an independent accumulation function. Intersectoral capital mobility would still need to be assumed. The relative price and rate of profit would be solved from equations (26) and (27), given the real wage.
34. Notice that we do not need excess capacity in both industries in our model for the prices of production model not to determine prices. Its presence in one industry could introduce an additional capacity utilization variable in the equations, preventing prices to be determined by them.
35. Kalecki (1942), in replying to Whitman's criticisms, makes it quite clear that capacity utilization would change to make differential mark ups compatible with equalized profit rates.

36. Since most of our arguments are based directly on the results obtained from the model, its assumptions ought to be scrutinized carefully. While the model is admittedly very simple, extensions to allow for many goods and intermediate goods, and technical substitution are not very difficult. The incorporation of asset markets and interest rates, and the study of non-balanced growth dynamics consistent with the model are tasks which seem important and non-trivial, but are not essential for our argument.

REFERENCES

Amadeo, E. (1985), *Keynes's Principle of Effective Demand and its Relationship to Alternative Theories of Distribution and Accumulation* (Unpublished dissertation, Harvard University).

Arrow, K. (1959), 'Toward a Theory of Price Adjustment', in M. Abramovitz *et al*, *The Allocation of Economic Resources* (Stanford University Press: Stanford).

Auerbach, P. and Skott, P. (1987), 'Concentration, Competition and Distribution – a Critique of Theories of Monopoly Capital', *International Review of Applied Economics* (Forthcoming).

Baran, P. (1957), *The Political Economy of Growth* (Monthly Review Press: New York).

Baran, P. and Sweezy, P. (1966), *Monopoly Capitalism* (Monthly Review Press: New York).

Bhaduri, A. and Robinson, J. (1980), 'Accumulation and exploitation: an analysis in the tradition of Marx, Sraffa and Kalecki', *Cambridge Journal of Economics* 4, 103–115.

Bukharin, N. (1915), *Imperialism and the World Economy* (Merlin Press: London, 1972).

Chamberlain, E. (1933), *The Theory of Monopolistic Competition* (Harvard University Press: Cambridge, Massachusetts).

Clark, J.M. (1961), *Competition as a Dynamic Process* (Brookings Institution: Washington).

Clifton, J. (1977), 'Competition and the Evolution of the Capitalist Mode of Production', *Cambridge Journal of Economics*, Vol. 1, No. 2, 137–151.

Clifton, J. (1983), 'Administered Prices in the Context of Capitalist Development', *Contributions to Political Economy* 2, 23–38.

Dmitriev, V. (1974), '*Economic Essays on Value, Competition and Utility*', in D. Nuti (ed), (Cambridge University Press: Cambridge).

Dutt, A.K. (1984), 'Stagnation, income distribution and monopoly power', *Cambridge Journal of Economics* (March).

Dutt, A.K. (1986), 'The classical dichotomy: the theory of prices with given output and distribution' (Mimeo).

Dutt, A.K. (1987), 'Alternative closures again: comment on "Growth, distribution and inflation" ', *Cambridge Journal of Economics* (March).

Dutt, A.K. (1988a), 'Convergence and equilibrium in two sector models of growth, distribution and prices', *Zeitschrift fur Nationalokonomie* 48(2), 135–58.

Dutt, A.K. (1988b), *Growth, distribution and uneven development* (University Press: Cambridge, forthcoming).

Eatwell, J. (1977), 'The Irrelevance of Returns to Scale in Sraffa's Analysis', *Journal of Economic Literature* (March).

Eatwell, J. (1982), 'Competition', in I. Bradley and M. Howard (eds), *Classical and Marxian Political Economy* (St. Martin's Press: New York).

Fisher, F. (1983), *Disequilibrium foundations of equilibrium economics* (Cambridge University Press: Cambridge).

Foley, D. (1986), *Understanding Capital* (Harvard University Press: Cambridge, Mass.).

Foster, J. and H. Szlajfer, (eds), (1984), *The Faltering Economy* (Monthly Review Press: New York).

Garegnani, P. (1984), 'Value and Distribution in the Classical Economists and Marx', *Oxford Economic Papers* 36, 291–325.

Harcourt, G.C. (1965), 'A two-sector model of the distribution of income and the level of employment in the short run', *Economic Record* (March).

Hilferding, R. (1910), *Finance Capital*, English translation (Routledge and Kegan Paul: London and Boston, 1981).

Kalecki, M. (1939), *Essays in the theory of Economic Fluctuations* (Allen and Unwin: London).

Kalecki, M. (1942), 'Mr. Whitman on the Concept of "Degree of Monopoly" – A Comment', *Economic Journal* (April).

Kalecki, M. (1943), *Studies in Economic Dynamics* (Allen and Unwin: London).

Kalecki, M. (1954), *Theory of Economic Dynamics* (Allen and Unwin: London).

Kalecki, M. (1968), 'The Marxian equations of reproduction and modern economics', *Social Science Information*, 7, (also in Foster and Szlajfer, 1984).

Kalecki, M. (1971), *Selected Essays on the Dynamics of a Capitalist Economy* (Cambridge University Press: Cambridge).

Kenway, P. (1980), 'Marx, Keynes and the possibility of crisis', *Cambridge Journal of Economics*, 4, 23–36.

Knight, F. (1921), *Risk, Uncertainty and Profit* (University of Chicago Press: Chicago, 1971).
Kriesler, P. (1987), *Kalecki's microanalysis* (Cambridge University Press: Cambridge).
Lenin, V. (1916), *Imperialism: the Highest Stage of Capitalism* (Foreign Languages Publishing House: Moscow, 1950).
Levine, D. (1980), 'Aspects of the classical theory of markets', *Australian Economic Papers* (June).
McNulty, P. (1967), 'A note on the history of perfect competition', *Journal of Political Economy* (August).
Mainwaring, L. (1977), 'Monopoly Power, Income Distribution and Price Determination', *Kyklos*, Vol. 30, Fasc. 4, 674–690.
Marglin, S. (1984), *Growth, Distribution and Prices* (Harvard University Press: Cambridge, Mass.).
Marx, K. (1867), *Capital*, Volume 1 (International Publishers: New York, 1967).
Marx, K. (1885), *Capital*, Volume 2 (International Publishers: New York, 1967).
Marx, K. (1894), *Capital*, Volume 3 (International Publishers: New York, 1967).
Marx, K. (1905), *Theories of Surplus Value*, Volume 2 (Lawrence and Wishart: London, 1972).
Marx, K. (1976), *Grundrisse* (Penguin: Harmondsworth).
Meek, R. (1956), *Studies in the Labour Theory of Value* (Lawrence Wishart: London).
Nikaido, H. (1983), 'Marx on Competition', *Zeitschrift fur Nationalokonomie*, Vol. 43, 4, 337–362.
Nikaido, H. (1985), 'Dynamics of Growth and Capital Mobility in Marx's Scheme of Reproduction', *Zeitschrift fur Nationalokonomie*, Vol. 45, 3, 197–218.
Pulling, K. (1978), 'Cyclical Behaviour of Profit Margins', *Journal of Economic Issues* (June).
Quesnay, F. (1758), *Tableau Economique*, English Translation, M. Kuczynski and R.L. Meek (eds), (Macmillan: London, 1972).
Ricardo, D. (1817), *Principles of Political Economy and Taxation* (ed), P. Sraffa (Cambridge University Press: Cambridge, 1951).
Robinson, J. (1933), *The Economics of Imperfect Competition* (Macmillan: London).
Roemer, J. (1981), *Analytical foundations of Marxian economic theory* (Cambridge University Press: Cambridge).
Rotemberg, J. and Saloner, G. (1986), 'A Supergame–Theoretic Model of Price Wars during Booms', *American Economic Review* (June).

Rowthorn, B. (1981), 'Demand, Real Wages and Economic Growth', *Thames Papers in Political Economy* (Autumn).
Sardoni, C. (1981), 'Multi-Sectoral Models of Balanced Growth and the Marxian Schemes of Expanded Reproduction', *Australian Economic Papers* (December).
Semmler, W. (1982), 'Competition, monopoly, and differentials of profit rates: Theoretical considerations and empirical evidence', *Review of Radical Political Economics* (Winter).
Semmler, W. (1984), *Competition, Monopoly and Differential Profit Rates* (Columbia University Press: New York).
Schwartz, J. (1961), *Lectures on the Mathematical Method in Analytical Economics* (Gordon and Breach: New York).
Shaikh, A. (1978), 'Political economy and capitalism: Notes on Dobb's theory of crisis', *Cambridge Journal of Economics*, 2.
Shaikh, A. (1979), 'Marxian competition versus perfect competition: further comments on the so-called choice of techniques', *Cambridge Journal of Economics*, 4.
Shaikh, A. (1982), 'Neo-Ricardian Economics: a Wealth of Algebra; A Poverty of Theory', *Review of Radical Political Economics*, 14:2, 67–83.
Sherman, H. (1968), *Profits in the United States* (Cornell University Press: Ithaca).
Sherman, H. (1983), 'Monopoly Power and Profit Rates', *Review of Radical Political Economics* (Summer).
Smith, A. (1776), *An Inquiry into the Nature and Causes of the Wealth of Nations*, 2 Vols (Oxford University Press: Oxford, 1976).
Sraffa, P. (1960), *Production of Commodities by Means of Commodities* (Cambridge University Press: Cambridge).
Steedman, I. (1984), 'Natural prices, differential profit rates and the classical competitive process', *Manchester School*.
Steindl, J. (1952), *Maturity and Stagnation in American Capitalism* (Monthly Review Press: New York).
Steuart, J. (1767), *An Inquiry into the Principles of Political Oeconomy* (A. Millar and T. Cadell: London).
Stigler, G. (1957), 'Perfect Competition, Historically Contemplated', *Journal of Political Economy*.
Sweezy, P. (1942), *The Theory of Capitalist Development* (Monthly Review Press: New York, 1970).
Sylos-Labini, P. (1956), *Oligopoly and Technical Progress* (Harvard University Press: Cambridge, Mass.).
Taylor, L. (1983), *Structuralist Macroeconomics* (Basic Books: New York).

Turgot, A. (1766), *Turgot on Progress, Sociology and Economics*, (ed), R.L. Meek (Cambridge University Press: Cambridge, 1973).

Varga, E. (1948), *Changes in the Economy of Capitalism Resulting from the Second World War* (Mimeo.).

Veblen, T. (1904), *The Theory of Business Enterprise* (Scribners: New York).

Veblen, T. (1920), *Vested Interests and the Common Man* (Huebsch: New York).

Veblen, T. (1923), *Absentee Ownership and Business Enterprise in Recent Times: the Case of America* (Huebsch: New York).

Weeks, J. (1981), *Capital and Exploitation* (Princeton University Press: New Jersey).

6. G. C. Means's Doctrine of Administered Prices

Frederic S. Lee

INTRODUCTION

A decade ago, Alfred Eichner noted that the foundation of post-Keynesian price theory was not to be found at Cambridge, but at Oxford, the home of M. Kalecki, J. Steindl, P.W.S. Andrews, and the Oxford Economists' Research Group during the formative years (1935–1950) of the theory's development (Eichner, 1978). In his efforts to draw attention to Oxford, he did not mention the non-orthodox American economist whose work influenced him greatly. Being a student at Columbia in the late 1950s, Eichner had never heard of Gardiner Means when he decided in the Spring of 1959 to attend the administered prices hearings taking place before the Senate Subcommittee on Antitrust and Monopoly. At the hearings, Means was presenting his views of administered price inflation. Taken with his arguments, Eichner perused many of Means's books and articles, including *The Corporate Revolution* (1962) and *Pricing Power and the Public Interest* (1962), from which he drew the distinction between industrial pricing and commodity pricing, his basic conception of the megacorp, and his model of industrial pricing. However, coming early in his research which eventually resulted in *The Megacorp and Oligopoly*, he overlaid the arguments he drew from Means with ideas, arguments, empirical evidence, and models gleaned from over 500 books, articles, documents, and manuscripts. Consequently, Means's imprint on *The Megacorp and Oligopoly* and on Eichner's work in general is not easily discernible.[1]

Means's imprint on the work of other post-Keynesian price theorists is even less discernible – in fact it does not really exist. For example, excluding references to *The Modern Corporation and Private Property*, there have been less than ten citations of Means's work in all the volumes of the *Journal of Post Keynesian Economics*, *Cambridge Journal of Economics*, and *Contributions to Political Economy* (see the *Social Science Citation Index* for the years 1966 to 1987). Moreover, of the many books which have appeared in recent years concerned with issues in post-Keynesian price theory (e.g. Hodgson, 1988; Acs, 1984; Moss, 1981; Semmler, 1984; Sylos-Labini, 1984; Levine, 1981; Sawyer, 1985; and Kriesler, 1987), most do not mention Means at all and none devote any significant amount of space to discussing his work. Thus, in spite of the importance Eichner attributed to it, Means's work has not in any meaningful way found its way into the discussions of post-Keynesian price theory. Why this happens to be the case is due to many reasons, not the least being the parochial view held by many post-Keynesian regarding ideas not originating from Cambridge, England. However, given the near exclusion of Means's ideas from American graduate economic programs, coupled with the absence of any systematic presentation of them, either by Means or anyone else, their absence from the ongoing discourse surrounding post-Keynesian price theory is primarily due to ignorance on the part of the economists involved. Lifting the veil of ignorance is the purpose of this chapter. In particular, the chapter will deal with a specific part of Means's work – his doctrine of administered prices – because of its importance influence on Eichner and its relevance to the current discourse on post-Keynesian price theory.

As a graduate student, Means was taught that the economy was a self-regulating machine which ensured that in the short term all national resources were fully utilized and the general price level varied directly with the money supply; and in the long term economic waste was eliminated, income distributed according to the marginal productivity principle, and the effective use of resources realized. He was also taught that these macro results were predicted on the economy being inhabited by small competitive owner–worker enterprises which employed little fixed capital, made a single good, and produced a negligible share of market output; and on the profit motive, which by compensating the owners for risking their capital and managing their enterprise, was the guiding force in directing the enterprises' economic activity. Most importantly, it was impressed upon Means that for the economy to be self-regulating, the co-ordination of all economic activities and, thus, a policy of non-intervention had to occur in the market and was predicated on all prices and wage rates being perfectly flexible. While he thought neoclassical economic theory was clearly relevant to the British economy of Smith and Ricardo's time, to the American economy prior to 1840, and to the economic activities of the oriental bazaars, Means found it completely irrelevant to the American economy of the twentieth century, in which large corporate enterprises and administered prices were pervasive. As a result, he concluded, the co-ordination of economic activity as pictured in neoclassical economics ceased to occur and with it the ending of the economy as a self-regulating machine which ensured the full, efficient, and effective use of resources and a stable price level.

For Means, the clearest evidence of the collapse of the 'traditional' co-ordination of economic activity was the Great Depression. Thus, he set out to determine the manner in which economic activity was actually co-ordinated in a corporate-enterprise, administered-price dominated economy and the manner through which economic policy was actually made so as to achieve non-market determined levels of economic activity. In recasting economic theory in a more realistic vein, Means centred his attention on the role administered prices played in the co-ordinating of economic activity. Consequently, his doctrine of administered prices was primarily concerned with the fundamental problem of setting forth the forces, such as administered prices, which affected the co-ordination of economic activity and determined the actual operating characteristics of the modern corporate economy. To delineate the doctrine, it is necessary to first outline the structural characteristics of the type of corporate economy that underlies administered prices. Thus the first section of the chapter will deal with the structure, organization and co-ordination of economic activity. The next section will delineate the price-setting behaviour of the atomistic and corporate enterprises. The third section will discuss the short-term impact administered prices has on the level of economic activity and employment and the general price level. The final section will discuss the relationship between the doctrine and the making of industrial policy.

THE STRUCTURE, ORGANIZATION AND CO-ORDINATION OF ECONOMIC ACTIVITY

Means developed his doctrine of administered prices within the context of a specific conception of the American economy. Concerned with identifying the relatively permanent features of the archetype corporate economy which gave it its salient characteristics, he observed that in the US economy most economic activity was repetitive or continuous over short periods of time and changed relatively slowly over longer periods of time. Hence he concluded that one salient characteristic of a functioning economy was that of economic continuity, meaning that consumers and business enterprises generally repeated their economic activities over time. With this concept in hand, Means then identified those characteristics of the US economy which structured its economic activity.

The first characteristic that Means identified was the structure of consumer wants. Adopting a lexicographic approach, he argued that the consumer ranked his/her wants according to biological and social needs. Then assuming that the general biological and social needs, hence the ordering of wants, were broadly the same for all consumers, Means aggregated the individual orderings and denoted the new synthetic ordering as the structure of wants for the economy.

The second characteristic that Means identified was the structure of resources and production. With respect to resources, Means identified six categories: three – natural resources, productive plant, and labour power – which were consumed in the process of satisfying wants, and three – physical environment, technology, and social institutions – which conditioned production without being consumed in the process. For production, Means delineated its geographical structure, its structure of the physical flow of produced goods, and its structure of money flows; and as for the second structure, Means argued that the physical flow of produced goods consisted of one way and *circular flows*, with the one-way flows being specific to consumption goods, while the circular flows were found in the agricultural and manufacturing industries. Consequently, as long as the consumed but not reproducible resources remained in abundance, the structure of production automatically ensured that the material inputs and capital goods needed for the production of consumer goods were continuously reproduced (Means, 1938a and 1939a).

Overlying the structure of the physical flow of produced goods of a corporate economy, Means argued, was a continuous flow of money and series of money transactions, including a circular flow between producers and consumers in the form of producers dispersing money for labour services and its return to them through the purchase of their goods by the consumers. It also included a circular money flow between producers reflecting interindustry transactions, and a quasi-circular flow between producers and consumers with respect to savings and the return on savings. The importance of the various money flows was that, by mirroring the production flows, they ensured that both production and consumption were continuous and repetitive and that monetary market transactions were always taking place. In particular, the series of money transactions allowed a wide variety of monetary prices to act as mechanisms for the co-ordination of market activity between producers and consumers.

Since both production and consumption were continuous and repetitive in a functioning monetary economy, Means noted that market transactions were always taking place and taking place in historical time. Consequently, business enterprises were continually producing goods for demand which they knew, in general, would exist, and buyers were always entering the market to buy goods which they knew were being produced for them to buy. Thus each specific market in the economy was clogged with sequential transactions in historical time and each business enterprise which entered it was also engaged in sequential production and transactions in historical time.

To facilitate the continual rush of economic activity within the business enterprise, Means argued, canalizing rules and goals become established. Similarly for Means, rules and goals also facilitated the co-ordination of market transactions between business enterprises and buyers in the market. However, of all the mechanisms for the co-ordination of market activity which he identified, Means placed most of his emphasis on the market mechanism and administrative co-ordination. He referred to the former as the organization and co-ordination of the economic activities of many separate producers and consumers through price, and buying and selling. As for the latter, administrative co-ordination referred to situations where a common authority, such as an owner or manager of a business enterprise or government bureau, organized economic resources under its control and co-ordinated the resulting economic activity. For Means, the clearest example of administrative co-ordination was found in the internal operations of the large modern corporation (Means, 1939a).

Although he separately discussed the four organizing and co-ordinating mechanisms – canalizing rules, goals, market mechanism, and administrative co-ordination – Means realized that they operated in combination in a functioning economy. In particular, he realized that even large administrative units used the market in co-ordinating their activities, especially with respect to the prices and wage rates they set for goods they sell and labour they hired. That is, Means noted that in a functioning monetary economy, market co-ordination of economic activity took place through a continuous series of money transactions:

> . . . [the] circuit [of money] flows are made up of a series of money transactions which facilitate the organized use of resources. Through these money transactions, manpower and capital funds are made available to producers; raw materials, semifinished products, and capital goods are transferred from one producer to another, and finished products or services are made available to consumers. These money transactions also provide a system of prices which are stated in terms of a common money medium and which act as a guide to the use of resources, stimulating some uses and repressing others.
>
> (Means, 1939a, p. 108.)

Consequently, by providing the context in which the system of prices operated, the flow of money transactions permitted the organization and co-ordination of economic activity via prices regardless of whether the prices were flexible and determined within the market or inflexible and administered to it. Thus the flow of money transactions permitted administrative units to use prices to co-ordinate and organize economic activities between themselves and with small business enterprises that did not have the market power to determine their own prices. However, Means noted, the 'adequacy' to which the flow of money transactions were co-ordinated in the market depended on the extent to which flexible market prices dominate market transactions.

In considering this question, Means noted that the specific organization and co-ordination of economic activity in a market economy depended upon the relative dominance of each of the four mechanisms and of the specific canalizing rules and common goals in existence. Using the degree of aggregate and market concentration of economic activity as a basis, Means identified two basic types of market economies – atomistic economy and corporate economy. He defined an atomistic economy as one with virtually no aggregate or market concentration. In such an economy, the form of production was owner–worker enterprises producing a single good to sell on the market to equally small buyers, and the mode of transaction was higgling and bargaining through which an agreed upon price and quantity was determined. He equated the atomistic economy with the competitive economy described by Marshall and subsequent neoclassical economists. Means defined corporate economy, which he felt began emerging in the United States in the 1890s, as one in which both the degree of aggregate and market concentration had greatly increased and the corporate form of enterprise controlled a significant portion of the economy's economic activity. Here, the corporation administered its internal economic activities, the prices at which it sold its goods and the wages it paid its workers (unless it had to bargain with unions over them). Moreover, the mode of transaction of one-price no bargaining was instituted. In addition, unlike in the atomistic economy, the owners of the corporate enterprise did not necessarily control or manage it, thus undermining the role of the profit motive in the organizing and co-ordinating of economic activity. Finally, in the corporate economy, the interest rate and the price of new security issues were also administratively determined (Means, 1939a and 1962; and Ware and Means, 1936).

In delineating these two types of economies, Means fully realized that the American economy of the twentieth century did not match any one precisely. Rather, it was a hybrid in which some markets were unconcentrated and thus behaved as if in an atomistic economy, while others were relatively concentrated and behaved as if in a corporate economy. However, he felt, that as an analytical device, the US economy could be divided into two sectors – the administered sector in which internal and market co-ordination was the dominant mechanism behind economic activity, and the market sector in which the market mechanism was the dominant co-ordinating mechanism.[2] Before examining the role prices play in the co-ordination of economic activity within and between the two sectors, it is first necessary to delineate the price setting behaviour of the archetypical business enterprise in each sector.

PRICING AND THE BUSINESS ENTERPRISE

For Means, the structure of production and costs of the business enterprise, and the pricing procedures it adopted, were determined by its time horizon and business strategy, which, in turn, were determined by its scale of production and the degree to which an enterprise could assert its presence in the market. These latter two factors were ultimately determined by the interaction of technology and the managerial and organizational structure of the enterprise. Thus, for example, if the interaction of technology and organization created a small enterprise with virtually no market power, then, as Means argued, the enterprise would adopt a very restricted time horizon and devise an appropriate business strategy in light of it, which would manifest itself in the structure of production and costs and pricing procedures adopted by the enterprise. Inherent in this argument was that varying degrees of enterprise size were correlated with relative degrees of market concentration, implying that pricing, prices, and the enterprise itself differed between the market and administered sectors. Therefore to delineate the role of prices in the co-ordination of economic activity adequately, it is necessary to do so in the context of (i) the atomistic enterprise found in the market sector and (ii) the corporate enterprise found in the administered sector.

Atomistic enterprise

The atomistic enterprise, which Means considered to be the archetypal neoclassical competitive firm, is an owner–worker enterprise whose scale of production is very small. Consequently the owner faces a very large market in which his contributions to market output are extremely small. As a result, he does not possess any market power to determine his fate, such as determining the price for his goods based on his specific market situation.[3] Therefore in devising business strategy, the owner of the enterprise is forced to limit his time horizon in regard to making profits to the immediate transaction under consideration. In particular, the owner has to approach each market transaction as an isolated event in which his objectives is to get the best price for their goods and leave the market empty-handed. Then using the market price of the previous transaction as a proxy for the next transaction, he would produce the amount of goods that would maximize his profits for the upcoming transaction, which means producing the amount that equates the enterprise's upward sloping marginal cost curve to the expected market price. As a result, production takes place in discrete batches which are taken to the market to be sold. Finally, in selling his goods on the market, the owner is essentially engaged in an act of trading or higgling and bargaining over the price with prospective buyers in an effort to reach the best price possible that would also clear the market of his goods.

The importance for Means of the trading or higgling and bargaining pricing process for reaching a transaction price was that the price was determined in the pricing process itself. Hence it reflected the particular and largely episodic economic forces operating in the market at that time rather than the needs of the atomistic enterprise. Moreover, because of this, the transaction price for a series of transactions was extremely sensitive to variations in these economic forces, especially those from the side of demand, since the amount of goods supplied to the market was largely fixed for any particular transaction. Consequently, transaction prices would vary with nearly every transaction, increasing or decreasing in response to increases and decreases in demand. However, as long as the transaction prices remained above the enterprise's average pay-out costs, the owner could and would continue to engage in subsequent acts of production and exchange, at least for a limited period of time; but if the transaction prices persistently failed to cover the enterprise's capital costs, he would leave the market. Thus while the pricing procedures of the atomistic enterprise produced profit-maximizing and market-clearing prices, they also produced extremely flexible prices which did not reflect the owner's desire to maintain his enterprise over time (Means, 1933, 1939a, and 1962).

Corporate enterprise

In the administrative sector, Means argued, the most prevalent form of the corporate enterprise was the multi-plant modern industrial corporation, in which ownership and control were separated, while control and management were closely linked. As a consequence, the controllers and high level management, as opposed to the owners, were the centre of policy formation and directed the co-ordination of economic activity – they controlled the destiny of the corporate enterprise. Moreover, because management could continuously reorganize itself so as to make itself efficient at any scale of production, the size (or number of operating plants) of the corporation had no limit. Consequently management, in its drive to have the corporation grow larger, could internalize many former market activities while taking on new ones by employing a bureaucracy to co-ordinate them.

Because of the large size of the corporate enterprise, Means argued that there existed barriers to entry to the markets in which it operated. Consequently management did not have to be primarily concerned with making the maximum amount of profit on each transaction or for the current pricing period (which covered a number of sequential transactions). Moreover, because the managers had no legal claim over corporate profits, they had no reason to try to maximize the corporation's profits in the 'long period'. Rather, as a result, they had the freedom to adopt a policy of obtaining profits over time which would not induce entry or otherwise inhibit the growth of corporate profits or the corporation itself. Given this latitude, management could and did in fact engage in a multitude of competitive activities aimed at maintaining the corporate enterprise as a going concern while meeting dividend and other obligations.

To carry out their growth strategy for the corporation, management adopted, Means argued, an administered price policy. That is, within the current pricing period, management sets its price and administers it to the market for a series of transactions.[4] Thus rather than having the price determined in the process of the transaction itself, as it was for the atomistic enterprise, management determined its price prior to the transaction itself. As a result, it had the freedom to alter its administered price frequently in response to changes in sales or inventories or maintain it for a long period of time covering many sequential transactions. At the same time, corporate management also adopted a production policy, which Means called the flow principle of production, which let the level of market activity regulate the rate of production at the given administered price:

> Once the [corporate] enterprise has determined its prices, it will hold these prices constant and vary the flow of output in the light of the demand at these prices, changing its prices only occasionally as conditions change so greatly as to exceed some threshold.
>
> (Means, 1962, p. 200.)

By uniting administered prices with the flow principle of production, corporate management was explicitly stating, Means argued, that the variations in the cost of producing a unit of output brought about by changes in demand did not affect the administered price at which the output was sold during the pricing period. That is, when producing its output, he noted that the corporate enterprise incurred both pay-out or variable costs, which consisted of such items as raw materials and operating labour costs, and fixed costs, which consisted of supervisory labour, depreciation, interest, and property taxes. Moreover, he noted that average variable costs were constant while average fixed costs were declining with respect to increases in the flow rate of output, with the consequence that average total costs declined with increases in the flow rate of output. Thus, for management to set a cost-based price which did not reflect the cost changes resulting from every variation in the flow rate of output, Means argued, it had to utilize the standard flow rate of output approach to eliminate the problem of cost variability. In utilizing the standard flow rate output, management was able to calculate its standard average total cost (SATC), a cost that, by virtue of the manner in which it was determined, was independent of the actual costs of producing any specific unit of output. Thus, Means noted, any price based on SATC would not reflect the costs of producing a specific unit of output (Means, 1962).

The uniting of administered prices and the flow principle of production also implied that the actual events surrounding any specific transaction or the variation in conditions prevailing during the current pricing period did not effect the margin or mark-up for profit. To do this, Means noted that management selected a target rate of return on equity capital invested in producing the output to determine a total amount of profit needed to be raised during the current pricing period for growth purposes.[5] In deciding upon the specific rate of return, Means argued, management took into account the degree of market competition and the prices of the competitors and thus arrived at a rate of return that would not undermine the corporation's position in the market. Hence the rate of return decided upon by management was designed to maintain a healthy financial condition for the corporate enterprise and to generate enough funds to permit a continued expansion of capacity so as to maintain its desired growth rate. In this manner, according to Means, management would maximize the corporation's value as a going concern. With the rate of return, hence the total expected profits, for the current pricing period determined, management would then calculate the mark-up or margin for profit which, when attached to SATC, would yield the administered price. Because the target rate of return was expected and based on the long-term prospects of the corporation's growth, Means noted that it was not readily altered over time and certainly not altered during the current pricing period. By setting the administered price in this manner, i.e. before production and the current pricing period starts and based on SATC and a long-term growth determined target rate of return, it was, Means concluded, inflexible with respect to sequences of market transactions and variations in the flow rate of output over the current pricing period (Means, 1962).

Means viewed competition among corporate enterprises as consisting of a series of strategic moves and countermoves. Thus the intensity of competition could be measured by the frequency and number of moves made over a specific time period. In this context, he argued that the potential for severe competition existed among corporate enterprises because of the continuous and sequential nature of market activity combined with the desire by the corporations to increase their share of market transactions and volume of market sales. Since simple price competition to obtain such an objective would not work, because all competitive price declines would quickly be met and thus would threaten the corporation's financial health, corporate managers would be driven to adopt competitive tactics that would not be easily matched by strategic countermoves or would directly threaten the corporation's financial integrity. In this context, Means argued that sales promotion designed to create, maintain, or alter goodwill among the buyers while not disturbing prices in the market fitted the bill quite nicely. Thus competition among corporate enterprises emerged as an extension of their internal administrative activities as embodied in the administered prices in the market and the administered sales campaigns designed to alter customer goodwill and hence market share and growth rate. Since the competitive pressure of the sales campaign was felt with each passing transaction in the market, Means concluded that constant and severe competitive pressures confronted all corporate enterprises (Means, 1962; and Clifton, 1987).

ADMINISTERED PRICES, PRODUCTION, EMPLOYMENT, AND INFLATION

Means denoted a continuous and functioning monetary economy in which the continuous flow of economic activity was co-ordinated by market and administered prices, by administrative co-ordination, and rules and goals as a going concern. However, because the mechanisms that co-ordinated and organized economic activity within the market and administered sectors differed in degree and emphasis, Means realized that a good overall co-ordination of activity between the two sectors could not be assumed. In particular, the clash of market and administered prices, of maximizing profits on each transaction and the desire for long-term unmaximized profits, and of market and non-market controls could affect the overall co-ordination of economic activity and with it the full use of the economy's resources.

To explore the impact of the clash of market and administered prices on the operation of the economy, Means utilized the twin concepts of balanced economy and balanced price structure. He defined the former as a going concern in which the utilization rate of productive plant and natural resources and rate of employment remained stable over time; while the latter was defined as a specific set of market and administered prices associated with a given balanced economy, hence with a given rate of employment and of plant and resource utilization. Thus in a balanced economy with a balanced price structure, there would be no business cycle, variations in the economy's growth rate, or large continuous variations in production and employment in specific industries. However, if the price structure became unbalanced, owing to a change in the level of aggregate demand or to administrative action, then, as Means argued, the resulting clash of market and administered prices would directly affect the utilization of all economic resources, including labour, productive plant, and natural resources.

ADMINISTERED PRICES AND THE BUSINESS CYCLE

Means noted that in the market sector market prices behaved pro-cyclically over the business cycle, while production remained relatively unchanged. Specifically, he argued that during the downswing of the cycle, market prices declined significantly (as measured by percentage change in magnitude) and relative to declines in production, while during the upswing of the cycle, they advanced significantly and relative to production. Such behaviour, he felt, could be explained by reference to the economic behaviour of the owners of the atomistic enterprises. As noted above, the owners limited their profit-making activities to the immediate transaction at hand. Thus, using the market price of the previous transaction as a proxy, the owners would produce the amount of output that would maximize their profits at the proxy price. But, when they actually entered the market, they had to obtain the best price possible that was consistent with selling all their output. Hence, over a series of transactions, given the fortuitous nature of demand, the owners would face a sequence of changing market prices and, as a consequence, would constantly be altering the amount produced.

Now in the context of the downswing of the business cycle, Means argued that the owners would discover that the market price in each successive transaction was lower than the preceding market (proxy) price. Because the marginal cost curve of the atomistic enterprise increased slowly, the incremental decline in the market price with each successive transaction would be matched with a much greater incremental decline in production. However, as the downturn lengthened and the market price declined, the owners reluctantly would accept a reduction in their standard of living, hence in their wages of management, thus shifting the enterprise's marginal cost curve downward and therefore limiting the extent to which production must be reduced. The net result of all this, Means concluded, was that over the length of the downturn the owners of the atomistic enterprise would reduce their production relatively little in comparison to the reduction of the market price. Conversely and for the same reasons, the owners would increase their production relatively slightly in comparison to the increase in the market price during the upswing of the business cycle. Thus, in aggregate, the market price of a good would vary frequently and incrementally but significantly and pro-cyclically over the business cycle, while its market production would vary frequently and pro-cyclically but relatively little.

With regard to the behaviour of prices and production in the administered sector, Means argued that administered prices were relatively insensitive to changes in aggregate demand over the course of the business cycle, while production was sensitive and reacted in a pro-cyclical manner. Specifically, he argued that during the downswing of the cycle, administered prices either declined relatively little in comparison to declines in production, not at all, or behaved perversely and increased, while during the upswing, they increased relatively little, not at all, or behaved perversely and declined. Such behaviour, he felt, could be explained by reference to the economic behaviour of the corporate enterprise.

As noted above, the managers of the corporate enterprise administered the price for the length of the pricing period, even though many transactions occurred and the volume of sales associated with each transaction varied greatly. Since both the downturn and the upturn of a business cycle covered a number of pricing periods, they had the option of altering their prices at discrete points over the cycle in the light of existing and future economic conditions. For example, assuming that management decided to maintain its current target rate of return and standard flow rate of output over the cycle, the administered prices of the corporate enterprise would alter from one pricing period to the next, depending on the change in input costs. Thus, if non-labour input costs declined during the downswing, the corporation would reduce its price accordingly and vice-versa. Also if management administratively reduced wage rates, it would also reduce its prices at the same time. Finally, if a new union wage contract resulted in higher standard labour costs per unit of output, then the corporate enterprise would increase its prices accordingly, in spite of the decline in production, i.e. perverse pricing would occur. With particular regard to perverse pricing, Means argued that it would be more likely to occur if management altered the standard flow rate of output from one pricing period to the next in order to reduce the difference between the actual and the predetermined target rate of return for each pricing period as opposed to over the business cycle. In contrast to their administered price policy, which keeps the magnitude of price change small, both absolutely and relative to changes in production, management's production policy permits the flow rate of output to vary directly and sharply with every variation in aggregate demand.

If the market sector dominated the economy, then, Means

argued, variations in aggregate demand over the business cycle would work themselves out primarily through price adjustments and secondarily through output adjustments, hence through variations in the level of employment. On the other hand, if the administered sector dominated the economy, the co-ordination of economic activity would not be worked out through price adjustments so as to ensure full employment; rather, it would be largely in the hands of the managers of the corporate enterprises whose business policy consisted of administering their prices to the market while letting production, hence employment, adjust accordingly. Thus, as noted above, while administered prices do assist in organizing economic activity, they cannot co-ordinate it to maintain full employment in the face of variations in aggregate demand.

However, in the modern corporate economy, as Means noted, both the market and administered sectors exist and are interdependent, thus preventing the co-ordination of the economic activity solely through price adjustments. That is, if a balanced (although not necessarily a fully employed) economy with a balanced structure of market and administered prices suffered a decline in aggregate demand, the immediate result would be an unbalancing of both the economy and the price structure. On the one hand, prices in the market sector would decline or deflate, thus maintaining production and employment, while production and employment in the administered sector would decline in face of relatively stable administered prices. Because of this asymmetrical response, the level of economic activity would decline further, owing to the decline in demand caused by the existence of unemployed workers combined with relatively stable administered prices, resulting in a still further deflation in market prices and hence unbalancing of the price structure, and decline in production in the administered sector. An increase in aggregate demand at this point would, conversely, reflate market prices, thus bringing the price structure back into balance and increase production in the administered sector. Thus with the existence of administered prices, the co-ordination of economic activity so as to maintain a fully employed, balanced economy with a balanced price structure was completely undermined. Instead of the business cycle being solely the 'dance-of-prices', administered prices had made it both a price and a production and employment phenomena (Means, 1939b, 1939–40, 1947b, and 1964).

ADMINISTERED PRICES AND INFLATION

Means identified three types of inflation involving administered prices – monetary inflation, reflation, and administrative inflation. The first type, he argued, was similar to the classical inflation analysed by neoclassical economists. That is, in a fully employed, balanced economy with its associated balanced structure of market and administered prices, an increase in aggregate demand brought about through increasing the money supply would result in a rise in prices comparable to the end result of a classical monetary inflation. However, instead of all prices increasing simultaneously and proportionately, Means argued that the immediate result of an increase in aggregate demand was an unbalanced rise in prices in which market prices increased relative to administered prices. The unbalanced rise in prices would continue until the average of market and administered prices was high enough to raise the demand for money to the level of the increased supply. At this point a readjustment between market and administered prices would take place, with the former declining and the latter increasing until the price structure was in balance again. On the other hand, reflation, as noted previously, pertains to the rise of market prices during the upswing of the business cycle, in spite of the existence of idle labour and other economic resources, so as to restore the initial balance of the structure of market and administered prices (Means, 1962 and 1975a).

In testimony before the Senate Subcommittee on Antitrust and Monopoly, Means argued that most of the rise in the general level of prices in the years 1955–7 was due to the rise in prices in the administered sector of the economy. Since he attributed the increase in prices to the ability of the corporate managers to administer their prices to the market and not to any expansionary forces in the market, Means (1957) denoted this decidedly non-traditional inflation as administrative inflation:

> . . . the area of discretion implicit in administered prices could lead to creeping inflation without an initial impetus from fiscal and monetary expansion while fiscal and monetary expansion might serve to maintain employment only at successively higher price levels. I suggest that we could properly call this type of inflation administrative inflation, in contrast to the traditional monetary inflation which arises from too much money chasing too few goods (p. 84).

Thus, for Means, administrative inflation occurred when price increases in the administered sector took place even though no change in demand occurred or was expected, and hence dominated the general rise in the price level, since the prices in the market sector remained relatively stable because of the absence of demand pressures. Because he attributed administrative inflation to corporate pricing power, Means sought to explain it primarily in terms of administrative actions by corporate management.[6]

Means recognized that if labour increased wage rates faster than productivity gains, the result would be higher administered prices, since the use of target rate of return pricing procedures enabled corporate management to pass along the higher costs in the form of price increases. However, he felt that the historical record showed that labour's contribution to administrative inflation was relatively small in that the quest for higher wage rates was largely a belated attempt to catch up with the increases in the cost of living brought about by management's unilateral action to raise prices. Consequently, Means felt that administrative inflation was primarily due to corporate management widening its margin for profit and adopting perverse, or current period, pricing procedures. Since the management of the corporate enterprise finances much of its capital investment internally, i.e. through the retention of profits, any increase in the cost of investment goods or in the taxes upon corporate revenue or profits would necessitate a widening of the margin for profit and an increase in the target rate of return. In addition, management might also use its pricing power to increase the margin for profit to reduce the rate of capacity utilization at which the corporate enterprise would just break even. Both of these administrative actions would result in management increasing its prices even if demand was not increasing or expected to increase. As noted in the section on the business cycle, perverse pricing occurred during the downturn of the business cycle when management adopted the pricing practice of revising its standard flow rate of output from one pricing period to the next. Consequently, because management was not as quick to make downward price adjustments as in making upward adjustments, Means concluded that perverse pricing would lead to a relatively permanent increase in administered prices and hence in the general price level over the business cycle (Means, 1962, 1975b, and 1975c).

Because administrative inflation caused the structure of market and administered prices to become unbalanced, Means believed that it would likely push the economy into a recession or a prolonged stagnation if not counteracted by an expansion of the money supply. That is, assuming a balanced economy with its associated balanced price structure, an increase in administered prices brought about by, for example, corporate management widening its margin for profit would unbalance the price structure and increase the general price level. As a result, Means argued, the real purchasing power of the money stock held by the consumers and business enterprises would decline, hence reducing the real level of aggregate demand below the level required for the economy to remain in balance. Consequently, if the money supply was not increased so as to raise market prices and restore the price balance, a decline in economic activity and employment would result, although somewhat mediated by the subsequent fall in market prices (Means, 1962 and 1975c).[7]

THE DOCTRINE OF ADMINISTERED PRICES AND THE VISIBLE HAND OF CO-ORDINATION

In conceiving of the corporate economy as a continuous monetary flow of economic activity that was co-ordinated by market and administered prices, by administrative co-ordination, and by rules and goals, Means sought to dispel the notion that the American economy operated as a cybernetic mechanism which automatically tended to eliminate under-utilization of all economic resources, including labour, productive plant, and natural resources. Given the existence of administered prices combined with the investment behaviour of business enterprises and the distribution of consumer income and savings, he argued 'that a serious deficiency of buying is unlikely to be corrected by any of the economic forces inherent in the modern [corporate] economy in such a way as to bring about and maintain reasonably full use of resources' (Means, 1939c, p. 23). He also felt that if unused resources did exist, it was not due to the lack of consumer wants to be filled. Thus he concluded that the under-utilization of economic resources was a problem of social organization which could only be corrected through social or government making of industrial policy:

> . . . the government must exercise a continuing responsibility for the maintenance of buying so as to insure reasonably full use of resources, taking whatever positive steps are essential to this end.
>
> (Means, 1939c, p. 23.)

In a going-concern corporate economy without the benefit of government involvement in the co-ordination of economic activity, Means noted, industrial policy was not made in the market but rather was primarily the result of the interaction of corporate enterprises' administered activities in the market with institutions outside the market who could directly or indirectly affect those activities. One such institution was the corporate community. That is, through interlocking directories, intercorporate minority stockholders, the activities of the larger financial corporations in the use which they make of their investment funds at their disposal, and the interrelationships resulting from the servicing of the large corporations, there existed, he argued, a corporate community in which corporate managers reside. Moreover, within the corporate community there also existed corporate interest groupings which consisted of a core corporate institution(s) and a number of satellite corporate enterprises. As a result of these community relationships, Means felt that 'the controls exercised by this corporate community among the larger corporations are of major importance' (Means, 1939a, p. 163). He also felt that the influence of these controls extended beyond the corporate community and affected the whole corporate economy, including the economic activities in the market sector. Means also noted that private economic interest groups, such as business associations, labour unions, farmer organizations, and consumer organizations, affected the economic activities of all business enterprises, either through direct contact with the enterprises or through influencing government policy, public thinking, and legislation; while federal, state and local government units affected the co-ordination and organization of economic activity by sanctioning or not particular rules and goals that govern market behaviour and by direct participation in the development of industrial policies in regulated industries.

In this context, Means felt that the government could devise an industrial policy which relied solely on the market mechanism to create the full use of resources or one which relied on modifying the existing system of administrative policies and activities of the corporate enterprise in a way so, when combined with the market mechanism, their ensuing interaction would result in full employment. The first policy would require major structural changes, such as the breaking-up of corporate enterprises and the consequent elimination of the corporate community, the elimination of any large size private interest groups and governmental units, and the reintroduction of perfectly flexible prices, which he felt were politically unfeasible, economically impossible, and economically inefficient. Consequently Means advocated the second policy approach because it was in the realm of possibility and sought to make the already highly efficient corporate economy work better.

He believed that the government policy-makers could develop a variety of coherent industrial policies depending on the technique they used to affect financial flows, the rate of capital formation, and the operating policies of industry, especially with regard to the flow of production and the administering of prices. For example, he argued that if the government was to devise an industrial policy in which the key decisions regarding the operating policies of industry were co-operatively determined, as in the case with the codes of fair competition under the National Recovery Administration, then it was necessary to establish a mechanism or technique that would distribute economic power among the various economic interest groups in a manner which would ensure that the policies were made correctly. Similarly, when considering the problem of administrative inflation, he argued that the government should take an active role in affecting the administered price policies of corporate enterprises, such as by establishing price guidelines and a price advisory board, creating an index of administrative inflation, and urging corporate enterprises to adopt a longer-term horizon when administering their prices (Means, 1935, 1940, and 1975b).[8]

SUMMARY AND CONCLUSION

In 1932, Means argued that the rise of the modern corporation required economists to forge new concepts and create a new picture of economic relationships. His doctrine of administered prices was his attempt to do just that. In articulating the picture of economic relationships embodied in the doctrine, such as target rate of return pricing, administered prices, administrative inflation, market power, and non-market control of economic activity, Means emphasized their human and institutional nature and hence their amenability by social action. Thus, since the corporate economy did not automatically tend to full employment, the implication of the doctrine of administered prices was that non-market government involvement in guiding economic activity was both necessary and desirable. Since the visible hand of co-ordination, whether it be advisory, in the form of codes of fair competition, or creating regulatory boards, is both a necessary component as well as a necessary outcome of the doctrine, Means clearly developed the novel and non-neo-classical analysis of the modern corporate economy. Moreover, because the doctrine is intimately concerned with both the market and non-market co-ordination of economic activity, its theoretical development is closely tied to the developments actually occurring in the economy. That Means's doctrine had such an important property was not lost on Eichner; he was always remarking that his model of oligopolistic pricing and theory of the determination of the mark-up were a result of trying to explain the twin evils of inflation and stagnation that afflicted the American economy since the 1950s.

Although Means's work has not found its way into the discussions on post-Keynesian price theory, many of his ideas and arguments have. For example, post-Keynesians have distinguished between cost-determined inflexible prices and demand-determined flexible prices and cited Kalecki as the originator of the idea. However, Means made a very similar distinction when he argued for administered and market prices to be analysed separately, and did so twenty years before Kalecki. Moreover, both post-Keynesians and Means, independently drawing from similar but also different sources, argued that consumers adopted a lexicographic approach when ranking their wants, that the physical flow of produced goods consisted of one way and circular flows, that the distinction between a real and a monetary economy was a false one, that corporate enterprises used target rate of return pricing procedures and did not maximize either short- or long-term profits, and that one of the determinants of the target rate of return was the corporation's need to raise funds for capital investment. Finally, both utilized the target rate of return pricing procedures to explain the twin evils of inflation and stagnation.

In spite of these numerous parallel but largely independent developments, post-Keynesians have missed the core of Means's doctrine of administered prices. That is, whereas post-Keynesian price theorists are primarily concerned with delineating the micro foundations of a macro model which can then be used to discuss the problem of aggregate demand in a capitalist economy, Means's primary concern was delineating the forces which affected the co-ordination of economic activity in a corporate economy, because it was these forces (as opposed to aggregate demand) that largely determined the economy's macro performance. While the primary interests of Means and the post-Keynesians are different, they are not necessarily incompatible – in fact, Eichner attempted to fuse both interests in his *Megacorp and Oligopoly*. If Eichner were alive today, he would certainly argue that if the current discourse on post-Keynesian price theory is to be fruitful, it must draw more directly on Means's work and be more concerned about delineating both the market and non-market forces with the co-ordination of economic activity.

NOTES

Research for this paper was partially funded by a grant from the Franklin D. Roosevelt Foundation.

1. Much of the material in this paragraph was obtained from the late Alfred Eichner in the course of causal conversation and correspondence. However, because his death was unexpected, I never attempted to obtain a complete and consistent picture of his connection with Means. It was always a project for the future.
2. In categorizing the two sectors according to market concentration, Means defined an unconcentrated market as, using Marshall's well known phrase, one of the trees in the forest. Therefore, for example, the market for cotton was unconcentrated in Means's view because, of the 4 850 000 farms producing cotton in 1935, the four largest produced 0.14 per cent of the output. In contrast, in 1935 there existed less than 170 000 separate manufacturing enterprises, and in the least concentrated manufacturing industry (women's, misses' and children's apparel) there existed about 10 000 manufacturing establishments, with the four largest enterprises producing 1.4 per cent of the total

output (or ten times the amount of the four largest cotton farms). Thus for Means all manufacturing markets were relatively concentrated, since it was not possible to have a forest of competing enterprises in each market, as in the case of the cotton market, and thus belonged in the administered sector. More generally, Means felt that retail distribution and consumer services markets and various natural resources and securities markets were relatively concentrated and belonged in the administered sector, while agricultural markets, construction markets, and some natural resources and security markets were relatively unconcentrated and belonged in the market sector. It is also of interest to note that because the scale of production of an efficient manufacturing establishment is large in comparison to the market, Means felt that it was not possible in general to 'atomize' a manufacturing market, even if each establishment was made a manufacturing enterprise (Means, 1933, 1939a, and 1962).

3. Means denoted such a competitive market situation as 'classical competition' rather than perfect competition. The former he defined as simply a competitive situation in which producers and buyers are both numerous and small enough to lack any power to affect the market price.
4. Means defined pricing period as a period of calendar time which covered a series of sequential transactions. Depending on the aims of management and the nature of the market in which the corporate enterprise competed, the pricing period could be as short as a week or as long as three months or a year. And the number of transactions within the pricing period could vary greatly as well. Defined in this manner, the pricing period is neither the same as the short period found in neoclassical economics or congruent with the analytical units of time utilized by economists in general. Although pricing period is a necessary element in Means's definition of administered prices, his first reference to the concept comes in 1947 (see Means, 1947a) and he does not fully integrate it into his definition until 1962.
5. Once in a short note, Means (1938b) argued that corporate enterprise capital expenditure was a function of the current and the preceding year's level of production. Thus, since the corporation desires to generate its investment funds internally, it is possible to conclude that the target rate of return is largely a function of current and lagged production, and hence determined by factors lying outside the current pricing period. However, Means never formally made this connection, although subsequent followers in his footsteps, such as Eichner (1976), did.
6. Means differentiated his notation of hypothesis of administrative inflation from the hypothesis that most economists have substituted in its place, namely that the higher the degree of concentration, the greater the price rise: 'The two hypotheses are not at all the same. If the second hypothesis were valid, the first would necessarily follow. But the second could be far from true when the first was true . . . Or, stating it

another way, to say, "The bulk of the rise in the wholesale price index came where there was substantial pricing power" is not the same as saying, "Where there was substantial pricing power, prices went up most" ' (Means, 1963, p.2).

7. The theoretical underpinnings of this paragraph can be found in Means's monetary theory of employment. His theory was based on his doctrine of administered prices and on his monetary theory of aggregate demand. The former explains why changes in aggregate demand will work themselves out through changes in both prices and employment, while the latter explains the level of aggregate demand in terms of the relation between the demand for money and the stock of money outstanding. Thus, when the price level increases, the real stock of money declines and so do, as a consequence, the propensities to consume and invest which determine the level of aggregate demand. Therefore, in order to restore the real level of aggregate demand, Means argued that the stock of money had to be increased. Because Means saw his monetary theory of employment as opposing Keynes's investment-savings theory of employment, and because his monetary views were so non-Keynesian, Eichner never subscribed to them. In fact, he found them quite unfathomable. Hence this aspect of Means's work has never found its way into the post-Keynesian paradigm (Means, 1947c and 1947d).
8. As supplements to the second policy approach, Means also advocated effective monetary policy in the form of changing the stock of outstanding money and the level of the federal debt, and fiscal policy (Means, 1947e).

REFERENCES

Acs, Z. (1984), *The Changing Structure of the U.S. Economy* (Praeger Publishers: New York).

Clifton, J.A. (1987), 'Competitive Market Process', in J. Eatwell, M. Milgate, and P. Newman (eds), *The New Palgrave: A Dictionary of Economics* (Stockton Press: New York).

Eichner, A.S. (1976), *The Megacorp and Oligopoly* (Cambridge University Press: Cambridge).

Eichner, A.S. (1978), 'Review of *Studies in Pricing* by P.W.S. Andrews and E. Brunner'. *Journal of Economic Literature* (December), pp. 1436–8.

Hodgson, G.M. (1988), *Economics and Institutions* (Polity Press: Cambridge, Mass.).

Kriesler, P. (1987), *Kalecki's Microanalysis* (Cambridge University Press: Cambridge).

Levine, D.P. (1981), *Economic Theory, Volume II: The System of Economics as a Whole* (Routledge & Kegan Paul: London).

Means, G.C. (1933), 'The Corporate Revolution', G.C. Means Papers, Series I, *The Corporate Revolution* (Franklin D. Roosevelt Library, Hyde Park: New York).

Means, G.C. (1935), *Industrial Prices and Their Relative Inflexibility* (Senate Document No. 13, 74th Cong., 1st session, Washington, DC: 17 January).

Means, G.C. (1938a), *Patterns of Resource Use* (Government Printing Office: Washington, DC).

Means, G.C. (1938b), 'Incentives to Capital Creation' (Jerome Frank Papers, Box 33, Folder 472, Yale University).

Means, G.C. (1939a), *The Structure of the American Economy, Part I: Basic Characteristics* (Government Printing Office: Washington, DC).

Means, G.C. (1939b), 'Possibilities and Limitations of Antitrust Policy', G.C. Means Papers, Series III, *Antitrust Policy* (Franklin D. Roosevelt Library, Hyde Park: New York).

Means, G.C. (1939c), 'Chapter X: Conclusion' (National Archives: Central Office Records of the National Resources Planning Board, Record Group 187, 751).

Means, G.C. (1939–40), 'Big Business, Administered Prices, and the Problem of Full Employment', *Journal of Marketing*, Vol. 4, pp. 370–81.

Means, G.C. (1940), 'The Controversy Over the Problem of Full Employment', *The Structure of the American Economy, Part II: Toward Full Use of Resources* (National Resources Planning Board; Government Printing Office: Washington, DC).

Means, G.C. (1947a), 'Insensitive Prices', G.C. Means Papers, Series IV, *A Monetary Theory of Employment – Chapter 6* (Franklin D. Roosevelt Library, Hyde Park: New York).

Means, G.C. (1947b), 'Insensitive Prices and Aggregate Demand', G.C. Means Papers, Series IV, *A Monetary Theory of Employment – Chapter 7* (Franklin D. Roosevelt Library, Hyde Park: New York).

Means, G.C. (1947c), 'The Determinants of Aggregate Demand', G.C. Means Papers, Series IV, *A Monetary Theory of Employment – Chapter 10* (Franklin D. Roosevelt Library, Hyde Park: New York).

Means, G.C. (1947d),'A Monetary Theory of Employment', G.C. Means Papers, Series IV, *A Monetary Theory of Employment – Chapter 11* (Franklin D. Roosevelt Library, Hyde Park: New York).

Means, G.C. (1947e), 'Toward a Positive Program', G.C. Means Papers, Series IV, *A Monetary Theory of Employment – Chapter 18* (Franklin D. Roosevelt Library, Hyde Park: New York).

Means, G.C. (1957), 'Statement', US Congress, Senate, Committee on the Judiciary, *Administered Prices – Part I: Opening Phase – Economists' Views: Hearings before the Subcommittee on Antitrust and Monopoly* (85th Congress, 1st session).

Means, G.C. (1962), *Pricing Power and the Public Interest* (Harper and Brothers: New York).

Means, G.C. (1963), *Letter to Kefauver, Estes* (May 31, John M. Blair Papers, National Archives).

Means, G.C. (1964), *Letter to Cohen, Jerry* (March 20, John M. Blair Papers, National Archives).

Means, G.C. (1975a), 'Simultaneous Inflation and Unemployment: A Challenge to Theory and Policy', in *The Roots of Inflation* (Burt Franklin and Co., Inc.: New York).

Means, G.C. (1975b), 'How to Control Inflation in the United States: An Alternative to "Planned Stagnation" ', *Wage-Price Law and Economic Review*, Vol. 1, pp. 47–74.

Means, G.C. (1975c), 'Prepared Statement of Gardiner C. Means, Economic Consultant', US Congress, House, *Incomes Policy Legislation – 1975, Hearings before the Committee on Banking, Currency and Housing on H.R. 4594, H.R. 6577, H.R. 4214, and H.R. 5142* (94th Congress, 1st session).

Moss, S. (1981), *An Economic Theory of Business Structure* (John Wiley and Sons: New York).

Sawyer, M.C. (1985), *The Economics of Michal Kalecki* (M.E. Sharpe, Inc.: Armonk, New York).

Semmler, W. (1984), *Competition, Monopoly, and Differential Profit Rates* (Columbia University Press: New York).

Sylos-Labini, P. (1984), *The Forces of Economic Growth and Decline* (MIT Press: Cambridge, Mass.).

Ware, C.F. and Means, G.C. (1936), *The Modern Economy In Action* (Harcourt, Brace and Company).

7. Kaleckian and Post-Keynesian Theories of Pricing: Some Extensions and Implications

Peter J. Reynolds

INTRODUCTION

This chapter outlines and compares various approaches to pricing which loosely may be referred to as Kaleckian or post-Keynesian.[1]

Kaleckian and post-Keynesian economists recognize that all markets are not perfectly competitive. Most begin by following Michal Kalecki, who distinguished between goods whose price changes are generally 'cost-determined' and those where they are generally 'demand-determined'.[2] The important consideration, which is common to all Kaleckian and post-Keynesian models, is that the prices of most finished goods – which we are mainly concerned with in this chapter – are determined by a mark-up on some measure of unit costs. The level of output is determined by the level of demand and fluctuations in demand, at least in the short-run, are reflected mainly as output changes rather than as price changes, although it is recognized that demand may influence price via its effect on input costs. If full capacity is reached, then demand may affect prices, but this is thought to be the exception rather than the rule.

A number of writers in the Kaleckian tradition, most notably Steindl (1952), Baran and Sweezy (1967), Asimakopulos (1975a), Cowling (1982) and Sawyer (1982a,b) follow Kalecki's dichotomy very closely.[3] There is also a very important group of post-Keynesian economists who, having accepted Kalecki's distinction between cost-determined and demand-determined prices, have developed a series of models whereby it is assumed that firms seek to maximize their rate of growth. The most important feature of these models is that a link is derived between the pricing and investment decisions.[4]

The next two sections set down the various models and these are followed by a section that discusses some of their crucial similarities and differences. Particularly, it is shown how the degree of monopoly may be lurking in the background to Eichner's analysis and the latter is further extended to incorporate a role for class struggle. Next, we introduce some of the effects of uncertainty followed by a section which is concerned with some of the macroeconomic implications of the different pricing models. Following a discussion of short-term stability, explicit consideration is given to the financing of investment, leading to an elaboration of the effects of changes in industrial structure on investment, income determination and distribution and on long-term employment prospects.

KALECKIAN PRICING MODELS

Kalecki's theory of pricing was developed in a number of versions over many years. In 1940 he considered a 'Model of Pure Imperfect Competition', in which the number of firms is sufficiently large that oligopolistic interdependence can be ignored and in which firms are assumed to know both their demand and marginal cost curves. Kalecki recognized that under these circumstances short-period equilibrium would entail the equality between short-period marginal cost and marginal revenue (Kalecki, 1940, p. 92). However, he believed that once the assumptions of pure imperfect competition are relaxed, then marginal revenue would not be set equal to marginal costs, and in 1954 he was quite explicit that, 'In view of the uncertainties faced in the process of price fixing it will not be assumed that the firm attempts to maximise its profits in any precise sort of manner' (Kalecki, 1954, p. 12; 1971, p. 44).[5]

In Kalecki (1954), firms set their prices by considering both average prime-costs (which are assumed to be constant) and the prices of other firms producing similar products. This leads to the pricing equation,

$$p = mu + n\bar{p} \qquad (1)$$

where

p = firm's price.
$\bar{p}$ = the weighted average price of all firms in the industry.
u = average prime costs.

m,n are parameters, which reflect what Kalecki called 'the degree of monopoly of the firm's position'.

The degree of monopoly is determined by a number of environmental/institutional factors, including the degree of industrial concentration, the extent of sales promotion activities, the influence of trade unions and changes in the level of overheads in relation to prime costs. The influence of overheads is not too clearly specified and Kalecki concluded his discussion of this topic by stating, 'The degree of monopoly *may* but need not necessarily, increase as a result of a rise in overheads in relation to prime-costs' (Kalecki, 1954, p. 18; emphasis in original).

The relationship at the industry level is given by,

$$\bar{p} = \frac{\bar{m}\bar{u}}{1 - \bar{n}} \qquad (2)$$

where $\bar{m}$ and $\bar{n}$ are weighted averaged of the individual firm's coefficients, m and n, and $\bar{u}$ is a weighted average of unit prime-costs.[6] For ease of exposition of what follows, we now define $k = \bar{m}/1 - \bar{n}$ so that the industry pricing equation can be written as,

$$p = ku \qquad (3)$$

Despite various reservations, Kalecki's basic ideas have remained sufficiently appealing to stimulate others either to extend his work or to provide alternative 'Kaleckian' pricing models.

The Asimakopulos model

In Asimakopulos (1975a), Kalecki's distinction between 'manual' and 'non-manual' labour is formalized into a distinction between 'direct' and 'indirect' labour, the former referring to those workers directly concerned with the production process, the latter including not just administrative personnel but also caretakers, security guards, etc. Complete vertical integration in industry is assumed, so that there are no raw-material inputs. Hence, direct labour costs are the only prime costs and Asimakopulos decomposes these into the money-wage rate (w) and the average product of labour (a). His price equation is given by,

$$p = (1 + z)(w/a) \tag{4}$$

where z is the mark-up over unit prime costs. Underlying the equation, however, is a completely different view of how firms actually arrive at their prices, the main features being that a price-leader sets the price, taking particular account of the expected return on capital. Thus, Asimakopulos follows Kalecki in recognizing that the degree of monopoly is *reflected* in the mark-up over unit prime-costs but argues that what it 'makes possible and protects' is the rate of profit on capital earned by existing firms in the industry. 'It is thus the realised rate of return on investment which is a reflection of the degree of monopoly' (*op. cit.* p. 315).

According to Asimakopulos, the mark-up is designed to cover both overhead costs and an expected rate of return, or profit, on capital. This expected rate of profit includes both what is expected to be a 'normal' rate of return on industrial investment and any additional return due to the degree of monopoly.

This interpretation of the degree of monopoly, whereby it is 'reflected in expected rates of return on investment', pervades Asimakopulos's work, and he also argues that it is implied by some of the writings of Joan Robinson.[7] Furthermore, a few years earlier, Riach had argued that:

> But to the extent that monopoly power is exercised we would logically expect that in the long-run this would be directed towards obtaining a higher rate of return on capital rather than a high ratio of profits to sales proceeds.
>
> (Riach, 1971, p. 53.)

Thus, in both the Riach and Asimakopulos analyses the mark-up on prime-costs is set with reference to the expected rate of return on capital. In fact, Asimakopulos is quite explicit that, 'Provision for such returns become formalised in their mark-ups in the guise of some target rate of return' (*op. cit.*, 1975a, p. 320).

There is here a convergence between the analysis of Riach and Asimakopulos and the work of some of the post-Keynesian economists that is considered below.

The Cowling model

Cowling and Waterson (1976) present a model based on an industry consisting of n firms, each pursuing independent profit maximization but taking account of the expected reactions of its rivals. Given the following definitions,

X_i = Output of firm i.
p = Industry price.
C' = Marginal cost.
η = Industry price elasticity of demand.

$$H = \frac{\Sigma_i Xi^2}{X^2}$$

which is the Herfindahl index of concentration.

$$a = aij = \frac{dX_j}{dX_i} \cdot \frac{X_i}{X_j}$$

which measures expected response by firm j to output changes by firm i, assumed to be the same for all i,j.[8]

The model predicts a precise relationship between mark-ups on the one hand and the industry price elasticity of demand, the Herfindahl measure of industrial concentration and the individual firms' reactions coefficient on the other. This is given as equation 5.

$$\frac{\Sigma pX_i - \Sigma C'X_i}{pX} = \frac{a}{-\eta} + \frac{(1-a)H}{-\eta} \tag{5}$$

This provides a microeconomic analysis of individual firms' pricing behaviour, based on short-run profit maximization, which not only filled this possible gap in Kalecki's analysis but also provided an important constituent in Cowling's own analysis of monopoly capitalism and has subsequently been taken up, particularly by Sawyer (1982a,b), as one of the building blocks of a Kaleckian macroeconomics.

In Cowling's model there are just three determinants of margins, viz. H, a and η. Changes in H take a long time to occur and so we would not expect short-term fluctuations in price from this source. On the demand side, if demand changes, then η may still be unaffected; so that again price may remain unchanged.[9] The symbol 'a' can be thought of as a parameter determining the 'rules of the game' for any particular industry and hence also not subject to any short-term fluctuations. The stability of H, a and η means that short-run price changes will be those resulting from cost changes, so that the model is entirely consistent with Kalecki's view that short-run price changes in the manufacturing sector are in general cost-determined rather than demand-determined.

In all three models considered above, the institutional environment in which the firm operates, including particularly the extent of industrial concentration, has a direct and positive effect on firms' mark-ups.

POST-KEYNESIAN MODELS – PRICING AND THE INVESTMENT DECISION

In the early 1970s a number of very similar models were developed, with the declared objective of explaining the 'plus' factor in cost-plus pricing but without the assumption of short-run profit maximization. Instead, it is assumed that firms aim to maximize their rate of growth. To be precise, we will follow Eichner and refer to the rate of growth of profits, though we note that this may be quite consistent with the rate of growth of other variables and indeed with long-run profit maximization. A very similar pricing model was also proposed in the same year by Kregel (1973). However, the focus of Kregel's analysis was essentially macroeconomic, his treatment of pricing serving to demonstrate the existence of a pricing strategy consistent with any particular steady state. Firms would set a price sufficient to generate the funds required to finance the investment necessary to maintain the rate of growth. Similar models were also developed by Wood (1975) and Harcourt and Kenyon (1976), with interesting extensions made by Levine (1981), Shapiro (1981) and Ong (1981) amongst others. For our purposes we choose to focus on the Eichner model.[10]

The Eichner model

Figure 7.1 sets out the cost curves for the individual firm, or megacorp, following Eichner (1976, p. 64). Full-capacity refers to the individual plant and is defined in physical or engineering terms. Eichner uses the expression 'Engineer Rated Capacity' (ERC). 'Standard Operating Ratio' (SOR) refers to that percentage of ERC at which firms typically

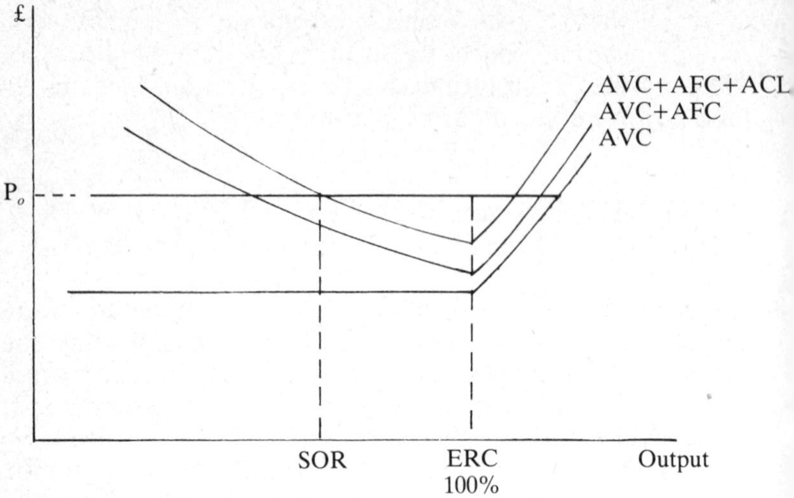

Figure 7.1 *Price determination in Eichner's model.*

expect to operate. Average Variable Costs (AVC) are as conventionally defined and assumed to be constant up to capacity. Eichner's definition of fixed costs is slightly unconventional in that it includes the dividend paid to equity shareholders and excludes those expenditures designed to enhance the megacorp's long-run market position.

The novel feature of Eichner's analysis is the concept of the 'Corporate Levy' (CL), which is defined as 'the amount of funds available to the megacorp from internal sources to finance investment expenditures' (Eichner, 1976, p. 61).

Interdependence between firms in an industry is taken account of by a price-leader, who estimates the standard operating ratio and then adds a mark-up to average variable costs that will be just sufficient to cover fixed costs and the corporate levy if the plant is operated at this expected level. This leads to price P*o* on Figure 7.1.

The corporate levy is determined in terms of the demand curve for additional investment funds, which is represented by the marginal efficiency of investment schedule and the supply curve of such funds. Investment funds can be generated either internally via the corporate levy or externally by borrowing. However, there are certain real costs associated with internally generated funds. The price-leader can increase its net revenue in the short-run by raising the industry price, but in doing so it is limited by three factors: (1) the substitution effect, (2) entry factors, (3) government intervention. The substitution effect refers to the loss of the market to competing products, either from other industries or from imports. The entry factor refers to the potential loss due to new entry and the probability of such entry occurring following any price change. The threat of government intervention could take a number of forms, such as possible nationalization, price-controls or potential prosecution under anti-monopoly legislation. The probable loss of future cash flow resulting from these factors is represented by an implicit interest rate, R, which would have to be paid if the same amount of funds were to be generated by recourse to external financing.

It is assumed that R will be an increasing function of the size of the mark-up so that increasing the mark-up generates more funds, but the cost of these funds increases. Such an analysis implies an upward sloping supply curve of internally generated funds, shown as Sig in Figure 7.2.

It is further assumed that external funds are available at an interest rate i, which for convenience of analysis is assumed to be fixed, implying a perfectly elastic supply of such funds at the going rate, although such an assumption is not critical, and we later examine the possibility of this being upward sloping. Thus, the overall supply curve of additional investment funds is shown by the heavy line, SS′. By introducing the marginal efficiency of investment schedule on to the same diagram, the corporate levy is determined.[11] With MEI schedule D^1, all investment funds are generated internally. With schedule D^2 the firm increases the mark-up to its maximum rate, being where the implicit interest cost, R, is just equal to the cost of externally borrowed funds, i. This generates oa funds internally, leaving an amount, ab, to be financed from external sources. A third possibility is that the MEI schedule may not enter the positive quadrant, implying

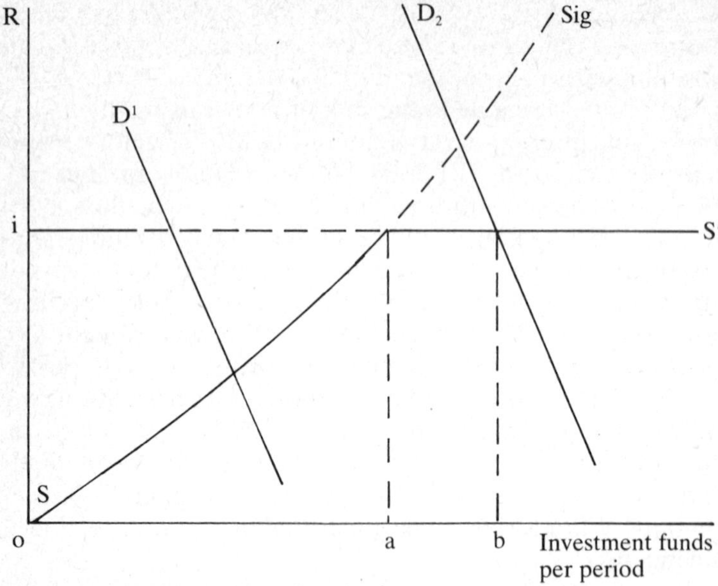

Figure 7.2 Determining the level of investment and the source of funds in Eichner's model.

a reduction in the level of investment. The analysis can be extended to permit firms to lend funds on the finance market but we do not pursue this.[12]

There is a common but ill-conceived objection to Eichner's model, expressed amongst others by Weintraub (1981), which we must address.[13] In essence it is that the link between mark-up pricing and investment relies on an unused residual of unexploited monopoly power and the corollary argument that if investment potential does not exist, firms will forgo potential profit. This argument appears to stem from a failure to appreciate the importance of the link between current mark-ups and *future* profits in Eichner's model. Any increase in current mark-ups will have adverse future effects on profits, which we have argued can be reduced to an implicit interest rate, R. This is reflected in the position of the supply curve for internally generated funds. Further increases in current profits may be possible but at a cost in terms of future profits. If one assumes that firms aim at maximizing current (short-run) profits only, then Weintraub's objection is pertinent. If one adopts a broader time horizon, then it is not. To labour the point; the 'unexploited' monopoly power remains unexploited because to do otherwise is not consistent with the objective of growth or long-run profit maximization.

COMPARING KALECKIAN AND POST-KEYNESIAN MODELS

Measuring costs

Two main issues will be discussed. The first concerns whether or not firms base their mark-ups on historic costs or expected future costs and the second concerns the use of prime-costs by Kalecki and subsequent Kaleckian economists as opposed to the concept of 'normal' costs used in the post-Keynesian literature.

Although it may be more rational for firms to relate their prices to the costs of replacing inputs rather than to historic costs, the way in which firms actually calculate their input prices depends on the particular accounting procedures adopted. Where firms use first-in-first-out (FIFO) methods, inputs are essentially being valued at historic rather than replacement costs. Although evidence is by no means conclusive, the important empirical work by Coutts, Godley and Nordhaus (1978) – CGN for short – suggests that, at least in the UK, many firms value inputs at historic costs, a view supported by Domberger (1983).[14]

In Eichner (1973, 1976), Wood (1975), Harcourt and Kenyon (1976) and the empirical work of CGN just referred to, firms are assumed to set their mark-up on the basis of 'normal' costs. However, in most of these studies, including Eichner's, average prime or variable costs are also assumed to be constant up to the level of capacity. The importance of the 'normal costs' concept is that average fixed costs and the average corporate levy vary with the degree of capacity utilization, so that the normal rate of utilization, or standard operating ratio, becomes important in determining the per unit mark-up. Thus, the per unit mark-up is calculated with reference to the actual level of costs, but computed at the 'normal' level of output rather than the actual level. Fluctuations in the level of demand have no effect on price, since, although they affect actual cost, they do not affect normal costs. In fact, there is a degree of overkill in the Eichner formulation. Invariance of price with respect to demand changes may be achieved *either* by the assumption that a fixed mark-up is added to assumed constant prime-costs *or* that a fixed mark-up is added to prime-costs, calculated at the normal level of output. Eichner needs the notion of normal capacity in order to calculate average fixed costs and the average corporate levy. Average prime-costs are also calculated at this output level. The behaviour of prime-costs either side of this output level is irrelevant as far as the pricing decision is concerned. This point becomes pertinent in view of recent discussions whereby the empirical constancy of average prime-costs has been questioned. Lee (1986) has assimilated evidence from an impressive array of studies which he uses to question the behaviour of average prime-costs. Lee reminds us that although average prime-costs may be constant within plant segments, the average prime-costs for the plant as a whole may be upward rising (consisting of a series of step segments) as plant segments of different levels of efficiency (vintages) are brought in to use as demand fluctuates. Furthermore, since a firm may consist of a number of different plants, the same argument applies at plant level: Successive increases in demand may lead firms to bring in plants of successively lower efficiencies. In fact, Eichner had previously addressed this issue and argued that to ignore these effects 'was not a serious matter' (Eichner, 1976, pp. 34–5). He repeats this response in a comment on Lee's paper.[15]

If we accept that firms make their pricing decisions with respect to actual prime-costs at a normal level of plant utilization, then we can accept or reject Lee's evidence without it substantially affecting either the structure of post-Keynesian pricing theory or its implications for macroeconomics. If, however, we choose to stick with the Kaleckian idea that actual prime-costs are assumed constant and marked up, then the implications of Lee's contribution are more far-reaching.

The general thrust of the foregoing, at least within an Eichnerian treatment, is that mark-ups are not expected to fluctuate over the trade cycle. Kalecki was less rigid than this. In an often quoted passage, he stated, 'aggregate overheads by their very nature fall in depression less than prime costs. As a result there is a tendency for the degree of monopoly to rise in the slump, a tendency which is reversed in the boom'. But then in a footnote he added, 'This is the basic tendency; however, in some instances the opposite process of cut-throat competition may develop in a depression' (Kalecki, 1954, p. 18). Although often quoted, the full implications of this note are rarely recognized. Surely, there is an implication that the degree of collusion may change according to circumstances, which is tantamount to suggesting that the nature of oligopolistic interdependence is not fixed but depends on external influences.

There are lessons to be learned by proponents of all models herein considered. For Cowling and Waterson, the reaction coefficients may be different according to the phase of the trade cycle. For the price-leadership models of Eichner and others, there is a case for relaxing the rigid price-leadership assumption and replacing it with a modified version whereby other firms in the industry may or may not follow the price-leader, depending on the circumstances of the time. This is taken up below. There is also an important point of methodology: Kalecki recognized that sometimes firms may behave in one way, sometimes in another. Taken to extremes, this would lead any model-builder to despair, but recognized as an important feature of the world in which we live, it acts as a caution against the trap of settling for a single general model of oligopoly and believing it to be applicable to all circumstances.

Whether prices in the core sector are related to prime-costs, which are assumed to be constant, or to normal costs, which are constant by definition, the important conclusion follows that short-term fluctuations in demand, *ceteris par-*

ibus, lead to changes in output, leaving prices unchanged, However, the effect on industrial prices of short-term fluctuations in commodity prices, which are neither assumed constant in the prime-costs version nor 'normalized' in the normal cost version, has important macroeconomic implications, to be returned to.

Objectives

We considered two approaches used by Kalecki, (1) where firms aim to maximize short-run profits and (2) where the objective is left rather vague but where the mark-up is determined by the degree of monopoly, of which the level of industrial concentration is an important component. The Cowling model retains the assumption of short-run profit maximization and predicts that mark-ups will be directly related to the Herfindahl measure of industrial concentration and inversely related to the absolute value of the industry price elasticity of demand; it thus provides rigorous foundations of the choice theoretic type for the relationship between industrial concentration and the mark-up through the entire range of market structures from pure imperfect competition, through oligopoly to monopoly, always based on short-run profit maximization.

The post-Keynesian models are all based on the assumption that firms aim to maximize their rate of growth, which implies a different strategy from short-run profit maximization but may be consistent with the assumption that firms aim to maximize the discounted present value of profits into the indefinite future.

Kalecki (1954) was quite clear that, 'In view of the uncertainties faced in the process of price fixing it will not be assumed that the firm attempts to maximise its profits in any precise sort of manner' (*ibid.*, p. 12). Although the negative aspects of this statement are quite clear, the positive implications leave room for speculation. Quite explicitly, uncertainty is stated as the reason why profit maximization is not precisely attempted. Should we take this to mean that in the absence of such uncertainty profit maximization would be pursued? Even if this were the case, would we wish to assume that firms maximize short-run profits or the net present value of future earnings? Since these two strategies are only consistent in the special case where periods are quite independent, the usefulness of models based on short-period profit maximization is to be questioned. Thus, if we choose to assume that firms seek to maximize their long-run profits, then it is quite consistent to argue that in the face of uncertainty this goal will come closest to being achieved by adopting the sort of approach to pricing which Kalecki subsequently outlined. We are making a distinction between choice of objective and the strategy for achieving that objective in the face of uncertainty.

The view of firms' objectives adopted above is not inconsistent with that expressed by Penrose, who argued that, 'in general the financial and investment decisions of firms are controlled by a desire to increase total long-run profits' (Penrose, 1959, p. 29). Indeed, Penrose also recognized that since investment generates profits, firms will wish, 'to expand as fast as they can take advantage of opportunities for expansion that they consider profitable' (*loc. cit.*). This point is important since it led Penrose to the view that, 'it does not matter whether we speak of "growth" or "profits" as the goal of a firm's investment activities' (*op. cit.*, p. 30). Thus, if we take the view that firms invest to grow to make further profits, which themselves are used to finance further growth and investment, then the objective of long-run profit maximization under uncertainty is quite consistent with the approach embodied in Eichner's model, whereby the megacorp expands to the point where the marginal efficiency of investment is equal to the marginal supply cost of the funds required, with the mark-up and thus the price determined accordingly.[16]

One conclusion from the above would appear to be that Eichner's model provides microeconomic underpinnings to Kalecki's analysis which are closer to the spirit of Kalecki's own work than those provided by the Cowling (Cowling and Waterson, 1976) model, which is apparently favoured, for example, by Sawyer (1982a,b). Against this view, it could be argued that a significant advantage of the Cowling model is that it more directly highlights the importance of market structure, thereby providing rigorous underpinnings to the notion of the degree of monopoly. This is taken up in a subsequent section.

Industrial concentration, entry barriers and the mark-up

Although at first sight it may appear that Eichner's model fails to provide an explanation for a link between the degree of monopoly and the mark-up, a closer examination of the model reveals that similar effects to those predicted by the Kalecki and Cowling models might be expected. The relationship between the mark-up and the price elasticity of demand for the industry product appears quite explicitly under the guise of the substitution effect. Although this goes some way to relating the Eichner and Cowling models, it is debatable how we should interpret Kalecki's attitude towards the price elasticity of demand. Certainly, in the 1954 version of his model, there is no mention of elasticity and Kriesler (1987) has argued that too much attention has been paid to elasticity by subsequent commentators on Kalecki.

There is plenty of theoretical and empirical evidence to suggest that there is a positive correlation between industrial concentration and the presence of entry barriers. For example, the higher the degree of concentration, the greater will be the absolute size of any one firm's output, so that both the minimum capital requirement effect and the percentage effect of economies of scale as entry barriers will be enhanced. Thus, where industrial concentration is high, any given mark-up is less likely to attract new entrants, *ceteris paribus*, than where industrial concentration is low. In Eichner's terminology, when concentration is high, the (fear of) entry effect will not be so great, so that the implicit interest rate associated with that mark-up will be lower in circumstances of high concentration. Mark-ups will therefore be higher, causing a higher proportion of investment funds to be generated internally.

Although the net effect on mark-ups of high levels of concentration appears to be similar as between the Cowling and Eichner models, the underlying behavioural analysis is fundamentally different. Eichner's treatment of entry effects as implicit interest rates associated with different levels of mark-up implies the acceptance that firms explicitly consider the threat of entry as one of the factors affecting the price decision and thus, to an extent at least, engage in the process of limit pricing. By comparison, Cowling (1982) is quite explicit that such strategies are not pursued. Instead, in Cowling's analysis, protection against entry is afforded by the degree of excess capacity, following the analysis of Spence (1977).

Class struggle

An important cause of change in the degree of monopoly in Kalecki's analysis is, 'the significance of the power of trade unions' (Kalecki, 1954, p. 17). This is important to the whole Kaleckian vision of economics, since it provides the route whereby (direct) labour may exert power to affect its share of value added. It is also the substance of Kalecki's final published paper, on 'class struggle and distribution of national income', which appeared in *Kyklos* (1971) and was included in the collected papers, Kalecki (1971). In this paper, Kalecki demonstrated that under a variety of assumptions about market structures, changes in money-wage rates would be reflected entirely as changes in the mark-up, so that the arena of class struggle is not the process of money-wage setting but the process of mark-up determination. Indeed, parts of post-Keynesian theory are sometimes summarized by stating that inflation is determined in the labour market and the real-wage is set in the product market.[17] Although this position is a gross oversimplification, it does highlight that, if trade unions are to be effective in increasing the manual wage share, then in the long term at least they must have a constraining affect on firms' mark-ups. From the perspective of the firm, the presence of powerful trade unions may act as a further constraint on raising investment funds via the corporate levy. There may be a point whereby mark-ups beyond a certain level will trigger militant action by trade unions, who may feel that since the firm is achieving high profit rates, the workers deserve a share of the action. Even though firms may be aware that any ensuing wage increases may be subsequently marked up, the higher prices will still entail adverse costs due to the substitution effect. There may also be other costs associated with a situation of tension between management and workforce, such as poor performance due to bad morale, uncertainty about the meeting of production quotas and deadlines, etc. Although there is no role for class struggle to affect the mark-up in Eichner's model as so far formulated, the potential for worker unrest may easily be incorporated as an additional cost associated with increasing the mark-up and converted to an implicit interest rate in exactly the same way as the potential for meaningful government intervention. Thus, we may introduce an explicit role for class struggle in Eichner's model in a similar way to that in which it enters Kalecki's formulation.

Having introduced class struggle in this way, it is important to recognize that this is not the end of the story. There is another very important way in which the struggle for relative income shares manifests itself, but paradoxically this is obscured by the way in which both Kaleckian and post-Keynesian models are usually presented. In the way in which Eichner's model has been presented so far, there has been no discussion of the dynamic process by which cost changes, changes in the MEI or changes in the factors underlying the implicit interest rates become translated into price changes. Under the assumption that prices adjust instantaneously following any change in money-wages, it is entirely in the process of wage setting that inflation is determined and entirely in the product market that the real wage and income distribution are determined. Yet analysis of these issues has gone beyond this. Whether inflation is modelled in terms of conflict or cost push forces, the relative speeds of price and money-wage adjustment will influence not just the rate of inflation but also the path of relative income shares.

UNCERTAINTY

Paradoxically, although the Cowling model yields the 'Kaleckian' relationship between mark-ups and industrial structure, it does so in a short-run, profit-maximizing framework where uncertainty is assumed away. Similar objections can be levelled at the price-leadership approaches of both Asimakopulos and Eichner. Yet, if one of Kalecki's main insights is not to be lost, the problem of uncertainty must be faced up to. As indicated above, Kalecki (1954) cited the existence of uncertainty as a reason for moving away from the more orthodox approach to price determination. Uncertainty is pervasive and we make no pretence at capturing its many manifestations. We focus on just two aspects. The first derives from firms' interdependence and concerns the formation of expectations about the response of other firms in the industry. In the price-leadership approach, the price-leader acts in the certain knowledge that other firms will respond and the followers behave as price takers. The behaviour of other firms is captured in the Cowling model by the reaction coefficients, a_{ij}, which are taken as given. In both cases, although oligopolistic interdependence is assumed, one of its key features, viz. uncertainty, is assumed away.

By introducing uncertainty into the price-leadership hypothesis, within an Eichnerian type model, we derive a more general model with a number of interesting implications. One such implication is to reveal a more direct route by which industrial concentration may affect the mark-up, without relying either on short-period profit maximization or on any notion of limit pricing. A strong motivation for developing our microeconomic analysis along these lines is to reflect the importance of uncertainty in analysis at the macroeconomic level, consistent with the work of both Kalecki and Keynes. As various authors in the post-Keynesian tradition remind us, Keynes was concerned with the analysis of a monetary production economy, in which decisions are taken in the face of an uncertain future.[18]

Under the price-leadership hypothesis as it is usually expressed, there is one price-maker who anticipates that other firms will follow, with a probability of 1.0. Other firms in the industry follow, so that the expectation is fulfilled. Suppose that we modify Eichner's analysis by suggesting that the price-leader may be slightly wary of his position. There may be some degree of risk about whether or not other firms in the industry decide to follow a price change. Thus, faced with an increase in investment plans, or some other reason for reassessing the pricing decision, the additional risk that other firms may not follow will provide an additional constraint on the mark-up. Analytically, this risk may be treated in one of two ways: it may be perceived as an additional, fifth factor constraining the mark-up and also converted to an implicit interest rate. Alternatively, we may slightly redefine the substitution effect to include not just the possibility that the price-leader (and other firms in the industry) will lose sales, owing to customers substituting to other products, but also that the price-leader may lose out to other firms in the industry. Whether we treat this risk as a fifth constraining factor or as part of the substitution effect, its extent will depend on the price-leader's confidence that any price changes will be matched by other firms in the industry. Following from the above, the price-leader must form a subjective estimate of the probability that other firms will exactly follow any price change. For simplicity, we assume either that firms follow in total or that they do not follow at all. If the price-leader has complete faith in its own subjective estimate, then the effect of this fifth factor on the implicit interest rate can be calculated as the monetary loss accruing if followers do not follow multiplied by the probability of them not following. In this treatment, the effect exactly parallels that of the fear of government intervention or of entry.

There is a further dimension to this uncertainty. Since the price-leader is making a subjective estimate of the probability of other firms following, this subjective probability estimate is itself a random variable and thus has a probability distribution attached to it. Suggesting that the price-leader has complete faith in its own subjective estimate of the probability that the others will follow is simply to imply that the variance of the distribution of the probability estimate is zero.

A second area of uncertainty is the effect on future sales revenues of alternative short-run pricing strategies. In models of short-run profit maximization these effects are not considered at all. In the terminology of Eichner's model, the substitution, entry and possible government intervention effects, plus the potential worker unrest effect outlined above, all reflect long-run effects of the pricing decision, but in the face of uncertainty these may not so easily be reduced to an implicit interest rate, in the way set out above. A possible modification to the model, which would go some way towards meeting this objection, would be to suggest that firms think of these effects in terms of subjective probabilities, which would be a way of modelling risk, though not uncertainty, *per se*. The implicit interest rate would then be thought of in terms of an expected value, although of a probability distribution with unknown variance. With appropriate assumptions about the degree of risk preference or averseness, the model could be amended. In fact, Eichner went some way towards recognizing this in his treatment of entry and government intervention effects. However, in the face of true uncertainty, any attempts at estimating the implicit interest rate may be considered quite futile, in which case, even if the firm's objective is long-run profit or growth maximization, it may be reduced to a more simplistic approach to price-setting as a strategy for achieving this objective.

Exactly the same arguments apply to the oligopoly price-leader's estimate of the expected return on any new investment projects, that is to the MEI schedule in Eichner's model. In fact, since long-term expectations are likely to be more volatile than short- or medium-term expectations, uncertainty will be even more pervasive here. This point should not surprise us, since it is the state of long-term expectations which Keynes considered to be the most important factor in determining investment.

So far, both in discussing the fourth constraining factor and in discussing the probability distributions associated with estimates of the implicit interest rate, we have referred to risk rather than uncertainty. This is not to suggest that true uncertainty may not be even more pervasive. However, the broader concept is far less tractable and even conceptually cannot be converted to an implicit interest rate. None the less, firms do have to make decisions in the face of uncertainty and this fifth, additional constraining factor, along with recognition that firms have, at best, an estimate of the implicit interest rate, serve to highlight the importance of Kalecki's assumption that firms do not maximize their profits in any precise sort of way. If we interpret profits in a long-run sense, then we may assume that firms do not aim to maximize their long-run profits or their rate of growth in any precise sort of way either. Although Eichner's model provides a determinate solution for the mark-up, investment and source of finance, consistent with a particular steady-state growth path when expectations are fulfilled in a world of certainty, the insights that it offers into the process of price determination in the face of uncertainty are only slightly less restricted than those from orthodox models.

Changes in industrial concentration under uncertainty

We now consider how these two spheres of uncertainty may influence the way in which changes in industrial concentration affect the mark-up. Firstly, we consider the price-leader's estimate of the probability that any price change will be matched by other firms in the industry, assuming for the moment either that it is risk neutral or that it has complete confidence in its estimate of the probability of being followed. This will depend, at least in part, on the efficiency of information flows within an industry. It will also depend on the price-leader's confidence that other firms in the industry will continue to consider it to be in their advantage to maintain the price-leader-follower situation as it currently stands and to maintain their existing roles in that situation. Both of these factors will depend on the structure of the particular industry, an important dimension of which is the degree of industrial concentration. Information will probably be transmitted between firms more quickly the fewer the number of firms in the industry, and hence for more concentrated industries there is a higher probability that followers will follow, provided that there is no change in the pattern of preferences regarding the leader–follower structure. A more interesting question is whether or not a change in industrial concentration causes any desire to change the leader–follower situation.

Pursuit of this issue is complicated because the notion of industrial concentration is rather ill-defined. However, some insight may be gained by considering a situation with n equal sized firms. For very large n, oligopolistic interdependence is often ignored and firms are assumed to behave as independent units. Conversely, the smaller is n, the more significant does interdependence become. As n becomes very small and oligopolistic interdependence becomes greater, the costs of ignoring one's rivals becomes greater, so we may hypothesize that rivals are less likely to break away as n becomes smaller. Any significant increase in concentration and hence in the degree of monopoly may reduce the risk element associated with any increase in mark-up by the price-leader and hence reduce the associated implicit interest rate.

Now let us address the fact that the probabilities of non-following, entry, intervention, substitution and trade union response are not known but are subjective estimates. If we can argue that the degree of confidence with which such estimates are held is positively related to the degree of concentration, then it will follow that for a risk-averse firm any changes in the mark-up will be further constrained the lower is the degree of industrial concentration. (We are suggesting that the variance of the estimator is negatively correlated with the degree of industrial concentration.) *Prima facie* this seems quite plausible, since the existence of a highly concentrated industry reduces the amount of data that the price-leader needs in order to estimate the relative probabilities.

Notwithstanding the caveats at the end of the previous section, we have indicated how certain, limited dimensions of uncertainty (confining ourselves to some of those which can be treated as risk) can be incorporated into an Eichner-type model and thereby reinforce the conclusion that changes in industrial concentration may be positively associated with changes in the mark-up.

SOME MACROECONOMIC IMPLICATIONS

A foundation for short-run macroeconomics

Based on Kalecki's distinction between demand-determined and cost-determined prices, let us divide the world economy into a core of advanced, industrialized, or 'centre' countries, where prices are largely determined in accordance with the factors discussed above, and a periphery, producing food and raw-materials for use by the centre countries, where prices of goods produced are primarily demand-determined.

Recent work by Kaldor (1983), Beckerman (1983) and Beckerman and Jenkinson (1985), as well as much earlier work, e.g. by A.J. Brown (1965), lends support to the proposition that interaction between the core and the periphery at a global level may be critically important for our understanding of the relationship between unemployment and inflation.[19] As demand expands in the centre countries, output is expanded, with little or no direct or immediate effect on prices. However, the increased demand for the products of the periphery puts upward pressure on raw-materials prices, which, in turn, leads, via the mark-up, to increased prices in the core. Inflationary consequences are reinforced to the extent that the higher import prices affect the target real-wage and a wage–price spiral ensues. Inflation then occurs as a manifestation of conflict over relative income shares, this conflict occurring in various arenas, including the conflict between workers and employers over who bears the reduced real-income following the adverse movements in the terms of trade, which in turn can be seen as a manifestation of the conflict between primary producers and the centre countries at the world level. Following Kaldor (1983), there is then reduced aggregate monetary demand for the products of the core countries, which is reinforced by the restrictive fiscal and monetary policies of the leading industrial nations, leading to a sustained world depression. This has a deflating effect on commodity prices and the rate of inflation is reduced. Beckerman and Jenkinson thereby suggest a form of Phillips curve at the *world* level, though this scenario does not lead us to expect a trade-off for any *individual* country.

To what extent do the alternative Kaleckian and post-Keynesian pricing theories fit such a scenario? If firms mark up *actual* prime-costs, then the model works. Whether the mark-up is applied to actual historic costs or to expected replacement costs will affect the speed with which increased commodity prices are transmitted to the core sector. Similarly, provided that we interpret normal costs as *actual* prime-costs calculated at a normal operating level, then world commodity price increases will lead to increases in the prices of core sector products.

We now note an unpleasant policy implication of this scenario. Those of 'Keynesian' persuasion regularly advocate an expansion of demand to cure unemployment. One of the favoured responses to the question of the balance of payments constraint is to make the case for a co-ordinated expansion of economies on a global scale. The above acts as a warning that such would be the surest way to rekindle inflation and with it the draconian deflationary policies of right-wing governments. The crucial policy implication is that if demand is to be expanded, then there must be measures co-ordinated at the international level whereby commodity prices are stabilized. Keynes was aware of this problem in the 1940s. Discussions preceding Bretton Woods centred on the establishment not just of an IMF and World Bank but also on a third agency, which would be responsible for the regulation of world trade, including the behaviour of commodity prices. Once again, we observe that the apparent inadequacies of 'Keynesian' type policies are not due to any deficiencies in Keynes's analysis but to its translation into over-simplistic recommendations centred on demand management alone.

Income distribution and macrodynamics

The relationship between the pricing decision and income distribution is seen most starkly if we consider a perfectly integrated economy. Materials costs are zero and Kalecki's pricing equation, (3), written at the industry level becomes

$$p = kW/Q \qquad (6)$$

where W represents the aggregate wages bill of direct labour and Q is the volume of output. Multiplying both sides by Q we obtain,

$$pQ = kW \tag{7}$$

The left-hand side represents total sales revenue, which, in the absence of any materials costs, is equal to value added, Y. Thus, labour's share of value added is seen to be the reciprocal of the mark-up, obtained by dividing both sides of (7) by kY.

$$\frac{W}{Y} = \frac{1}{k} \tag{8}$$

Once materials costs are introduced into the analysis, the algebra becomes a little more complicated and the equation for direct (manual) labour's share becomes,

$$\frac{W}{Y} = \frac{1}{1 + (k - 1)(1 + j)} \tag{9}$$

where j represents the ratio of the materials bill to the wages bill.[20] Equation (9) represents Kalecki's famous degree of monopoly theory of income distribution. The theoretical as opposed to tautological nature of this relationship derives from the pricing hypothesis, whereby k depends on a set of institutional and environmental factors.

Unfortunately, the contemporary relevance of this model is weakened by the lack of explicit treatment of indirect labour. Since the latter is an overhead, the total reward of indirect labour is a constant (in the short run) so that indirect labour's share of income varies with the level of demand and output. Thus, the total (direct and indirect) wage share becomes a function both of the mark-up and of the level of output.[21]

Kalecki also had a theory of profits, determined by past investment and capitalists' spending, which can be written as

$$\pi_t = \frac{I_{t-\lambda}}{s_c} \tag{10}$$

where s_c represents the marginal propensity to save out of profits and λ is an unspecified time-lag. Equations (8) and (10), in conjunction with the identity that all income goes as wages or profits, supported by the theory that k is determined by a set of institutional/environmental pressures, serve to determine both the level and distribution of income. The solution for the level of income may be obtained by substituting (8) and (10) into the national accounting identity to give

$$Y_t = (1/k)\ Y_t + (1/s_c)\ I_{t-\lambda} \tag{11}$$

which can be rearranged to give,

$$Y_t = I_{t-\lambda}/s_c[1 - (1/k)] \tag{12}$$

If there is a rise in the degree of monopoly, direct labour's share falls and indeed the level of income falls also. It is the income redistribution effect, in conjunction with the differential savings propensities, which causes the fall in income. This effect is not compensated for because in the above model and – as far as the author is aware – in Kalecki's writings in general, there is no mechanism by which a rise in the degree of monopoly can have a positive effect on investment. Indeed, if we consider the important contributions made by Joseph Steindl, we note that a rise in the degree of monopoly may lead to an increase in the extent of excess capacity, causing investment to fall, adding further force to the general thrust of the monopoly capitalism literature, which is that a rise in the degree of monopoly leads us further towards stagnation.

Retaining a broadly Kaleckian framework but replacing Kalecki's fairly simplified pricing hypothesis with the modified Eichner model enables us to retain the important link between industrial structure and the mark-up, or between the degree of monopoly and income distribution, yet also makes us aware that increases in the degree of monopoly may – under certain circumstances – have a positive effect on investment, as we now show.

Changes in industrial concentration, finance and investment

One way to highlight the importance of the degree of monopoly and to elucidate the potential effects of changes in the degree of monopoly on investment would be to use Eichner's diagram to consider the effect of a dramatic increase in the degree of industrial concentration – such as may be caused by the intense round of merger activity currently taking place throughout much of Europe, ostensibly in preparation for the single European market of 1992. Referring to Figure 7.3, which is Figure 7.2 extended, the arguments above imply that a rise in the level of industrial concentration in a particular industry may cause the cost of internally generated funds to decrease.

The potential decrease comes about for at least three possible sets of reasons. Firstly, the higher concentration, *ceteris paribus*, may be associated with higher entry barriers, so that the threat of new entry associated with any given mark-up is lower. Secondly, the price-leader may be less fearful of the leader–follower relationship being broken. Thirdly, the price-leader may also perceive a lower variance to be associated with its estimate of the implicit interest rate. Although this does not affect the expected value of R *per se*, if the firm suffers from any degree of risk averseness, then the implicit interest rate underlying its calculations will not be the expected value of R but a function of both the expected value and variance. Thus, the increase in concentration may cause a shifting of Sig downwards and to the right, from Sig. 1 to Sig. 2, so that if we are in the segment where all funds are internally generated, the level of investment rises, say from x_1 to x_2. Furthermore, to the extent that increases in the degree of monopoly lead to larger, more powerful firms, this may make it easier or cheaper for them to raise borrowed funds, which would be reflected as a downward movement in the i

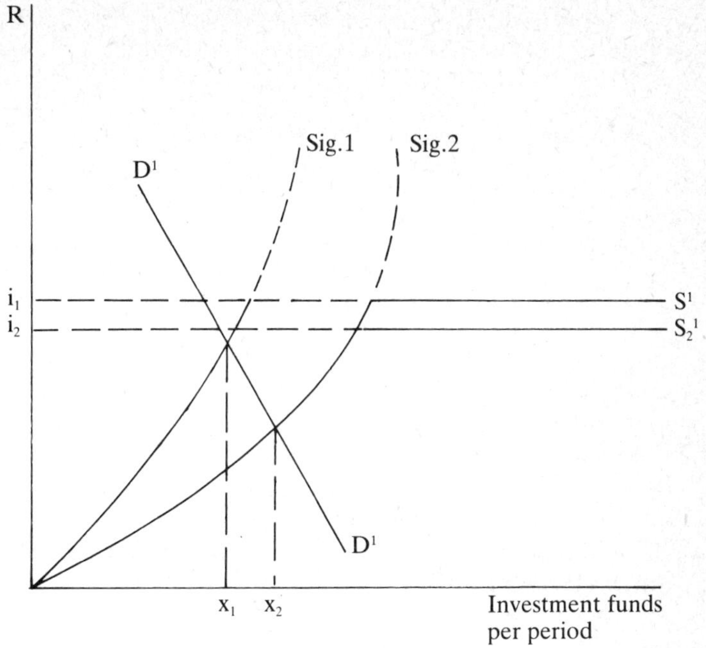

Figure 7.3

line, say from i_1 to i_2. Thus, the entire supply curve of both internally and externally generated funds may shift downwards, affecting the level of investment, the eventual mark-up and the proportion of investment which is internally financed.

The above is still far from the complete story: the cost of borrowed funds may not be independent of either the total level of investment or the proportion of investment which is externally financed or indeed of the nature of the external financing. This point, which is recognized by Mott (1985-6), follows from Kalecki's principle of increasing risk.[22] As the level of investment, the proportion of externally financed investment or the gearing ratio increases, the cost of borrowed funds may rise. Following Eichner, external funds can be obtained either via the issue of fixed interest obligations or by the issue of equity shares. Although there may be an extent to which the two are substitutes in the long run,

> In the more immediate period, they are more likely to be viewed as complements, with the megacorp first determining its optimum debt-equity ratio based on the attendant risks and other relative disadvantages of the two types of securities, then using that optimum debt-equity ratio as a rule of thumb in its subsequent decision making. The cost of external funds will thus be an average of the interest rate that must be paid on fixed-interest obligations and on equity shares, weighted by the current debt-equity ratio. (Eichner, 1976, p. 86)

Eichner appears to be assuming that the gearing ratio will not be changed by the raising of additional finance and that the proportion of fixed interest debt to equity on new funds will be the same as that on existing capital.

As an individual investment project entails an increasing proportion of the firm's total assets, then the perceived risk associated with it will be higher. This would be reflected both in the capital market's assessment of the worth of any new issues and in the cost at which fixed interest loans could be negotiated. Thus, the higher the level of investment, the higher may be the cost of additional externally generated funds, though on *a priori* grounds, there is no apparent reason to expect a change in the relative cost of debt as against equity, so that there is no reason to expect a change in the gearing ratio. However, if for any reason the firm faces constraints on its ability to issue additional shares, then its debt–equity ratio may increase, which may lead to further increases in the cost at which it can obtain further borrowed funds, so that the effects just outlined will be reinforced.

To the extent that higher investment causes an increase in the cost of externally generated funds, whatever the nature of such funds, there is an upward movement in the i line. Thus, the total supply curve of investment funds cannot be drawn independently of the proportion obtained externally. For any given supply curve of internally generated funds, there will be a series of supply curves for total borrowed funds, each corresponding to a different ratio of internal to external finance (which we refer to below as the source ratio, as

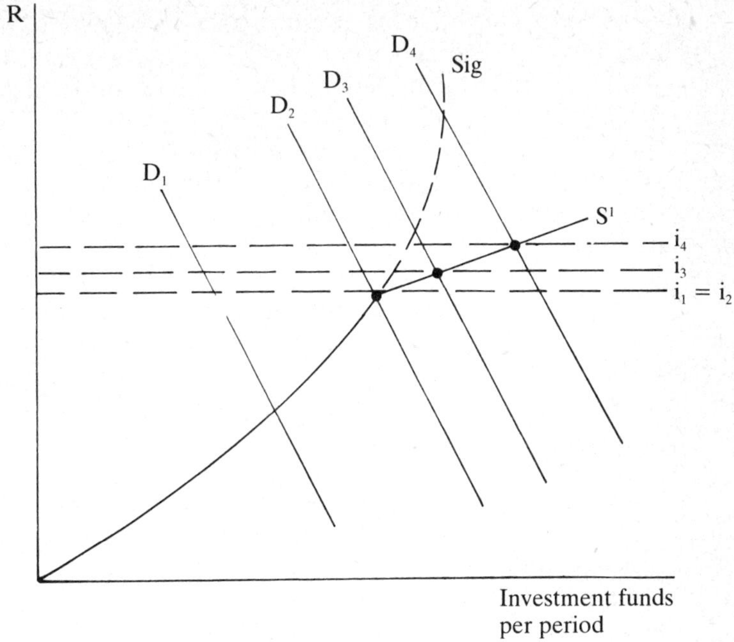

Figure 7.4

distinct from the gearing ratio). This is illustrated in Figure 7.4. For a given Sig, different investment demand functions would result in different source ratios and thereby to differences in the cost of borrowed funds. Thus, successive movements in the D line from D^1 to D^4 result in successive shifts in the i line from i_1 to i_4. By drawing the locus of points whereby each D line intersects the corresponding i line, we construct a total supply curve of investment funds which continues to slope upwards, even in the section where any increments to investment are financed entirely by externally generated funds.

Both the initial change in the degree of monopoly and any subsequent changes in the gearing ratio may have even further implications, via their effects on the demand function for investment funds. Following the analysis of Joseph Steindl

(1979), increases in the level of industrial concentration, by raising the extent of excess capacity, may cause the level of investment to fall. In terms of our Figure 7.4, D would shift to the left. Also, following Steindl (1952), the gearing ratio may enter directly into the investment function, so that if, for example, the gearing ratio rises, there will be a positive effect on investment, causing the D function to shift to the right, with any reduction in the gearing ratio having the opposite effect.

The sum total of the above effects is ambiguous. Following an increase in the level of industrial concentration, an increase in mark-ups is predicted, but the level of investment and the extent to which investment is financed internally may either increase or decrease, depending on the relative effects on the costs of internally as against externally generated funds and on the relative impacts on investment of any changes in the degree of excess capacity following the increase in industrial concentration and of changes in the gearing ratio.

Although these results are ambiguous, the implications are still important. By explicitly considering the financing of investment, within a modified Eichnerian model, we have demonstrated that starting from a situation of price-leadership under limited uncertainty, a rise in the degree of monopoly can, under certain circumstances, actually cause the level of investment to increase. Any effect on aggregate demand will depend on the relative effects of the change in investment and in other components, particularly, the level of consumption, which via the adverse income redistribution effects will be negative.

Even if, in the face of true uncertainty, firms set their prices using fairly simplified procedures, e.g. of the type outlined in Kalecki (1954), some of the additional insights gained from this modified Eichnerian analysis are not entirely lost. In a world of true uncertainty, the extra financial security enjoyed by all firms in the industry following an increase in the degree of monopoly will still reduce the risk and cost of funds for new investment projects, for the various reasons outlined above. The positive effect of increases in the degree of monopoly on investment is retained. In a more faithful 'Kaleckian' approach these effects would be incorporated via the principle of increasing risk.

Income distribution and steady-state models

From the post-Keynesian perspective, once we accept the link between the mark-up and the wage share, the theory of pricing can be interpreted as implying that the wage share is determined by firms' needs to raise funds for investment. In the extreme case where all investment is financed from this source and all savings out of profits are used to finance investment, it follows that,

$$s_c\pi = I \tag{13}$$

which can be used to derive the Kaldor–Pasinetti equation for profit as a share of national income.

$$\frac{\pi}{Y} = \frac{1}{s_c} \cdot \frac{I}{Y} \tag{14}$$

The often quoted but more seldom heeded caution that one should be careful about implying causation from a steady-state relationship now becomes even more pertinent. Looking back at Figure 7.2, if the MEI schedule intersects the supply of funds schedule in the sector for which all funds are internally generated, then the level of investment is affected by the rate at which profits can be generated, which, via the entry effect and the uncertainty or substitution effect, are influenced by the degree of monopoly. The appropriate story is that the degree of monopoly affects both the mark-up and the potential for changing the mark-up, which affects both profits as a share of national income and the potential availability of funds for investment.

Let us consider the case where a rise in the degree of monopoly has caused an increase in the level of investment. I/Y is higher and also π/Y is higher, or conversely W/Y is lower, which is quite consistent with Kalecki. The same story can be told in terms of the Kaldo–Pasinetti equation for the steady-state rate of profit,

$$\frac{\pi}{K} = \frac{1}{s_c} \cdot \frac{I}{K} \tag{15}$$

By our interpretation, the actual and expected rate of profit is affected by the degree of monopoly. A higher degree of monopoly would entail both higher mark-ups and a higher expected rate of profit, simultaneously stimulating the investment decision and generating the funds via the mark-up.

One of the declared objectives of Eichner's analysis was to provide a microeconomic basis for the macroeconomic relationships of the Kaldor–Pasinetti type.[23] To this end, as we have argued above, it yields results consistent with 'post-Keynesian' (steady-state) equations of income distribution in a world of no uncertainty where expectations are fulfilled. What is open to question is the more general usefulness of such steady-state equations, the interpretation typically placed upon them and specifically the claim that they provide a post-Keynesian theory or at least a complete post-Keynesian theory of income distribution. These relationships tell us too little about the economic influences actually underlying the functional distribution of income. Starting from a Kaleckian perspective, where analysis concentrates on the industrial environment and the mark-up, not only focuses attention directly on short-run behaviour but (as others have also shown) enables us to derive the long-run equations as a special case of a short-run model.

Unemployment in the very long run

We now turn to the implications of our modified Kaleckian/post-Keynesian pricing theory for unemployment in the very long run. In the tradition of Kalecki, Steindl, Baran and Sweezy and Cowling, it is recognized that the long-term growth of monopoly brings with it the dangers of a realization crisis and long-run stagnation. The increased industrial concentration may lead to increased mark-ups, a reduction in workers share of value added and the threat of underconsumption. This is reinforced, in Steindl's analysis, by a long-term reduction in investment due to the growth of excess capacity. A Robinsonian leaden age is predicted, whereby the exogenous components of demand are sufficient to maintain full employment. The critical links in this depressing story are (1) the endogenous growth in concentration leading to increases in the degree of monopoly and excess capacity, (2) the link between the degree of monopoly and the mark-up, (3) the effects of increased mark-ups on income distribution and hence, via differential savings propensities, on consumption and (4) the negative effect on investment of the growth in excess capacity.

As we have seen, the second link is also lurking in Eichner's model, disguised under the name of substitution and entry effects but given potential additional bite if uncertainty is introduced into the price-leadership model. However, an important difference between the Kaleckian model and the Eichner or modified Eichner models is that in the latter case the degree of monopoly will only be translated into a higher mark-up if investment is planned. In other words, the mark-up acts as a mechanism for reallocating resources from consumption to investment if the investment demand exists, but avoid the dangers of underconsumption if it does not. The analysis of previous sections leads us to question or modify the fourth link in the stagnationists' story. In a world pervaded by uncertainty, the increase in industrial concentration may have positive effects on the level of investment. These effects would be manifested via the reduced risk and cost associated both with the internal generation of funds and with those obtained externally. The increase in investment may possibly (but certainly not necessarily) reverse any stagnationist tendencies resulting from possible increases in excess capacity.

CONCLUSIONS

Despite their declared origins in the work of Michal Kalecki, the various mark-up pricing models considered have some important and critical differences, both from each other and from the original work of Kalecki. Most notably, all models other than Kalecki's fail to take account of that very uncertainty which was responsible for Kalecki abandoning orthodox price theory in the first place.

We have argued that the objective of long-run profit maximization may form an appropriate basis on which to build a Kaleckian/post-Keynesian analysis and we have shown how both a role for class struggle and a limited degree of uncertainty may be incorporated into post-Keynesian models of the Eichnerian type. The link between the degree of monopoly – interpreted to mean the environmental/institutional influences on the firm – and the mark-up, which is crucial to Kaleckian macroeconomic and macrodistribution analysis, may to an extent also be derived from post-Keynesian models, particularly when extended along the above lines. However, although such pricing models are useful for demonstrating how mark-up relationships which are consistent with steady-state equations for income distribution may be derived in a world in which expectations are continuously fulfilled, the short-run behaviour of individual firms in the face of true uncertainty may, for most purposes, be more usefully modelled by relating mark-ups directly to the institutional environment in which the firm operates. Although the traditional long-run equations of post-Keynesian theory are quite consistent with a Kaleckian formulation, they are more usefully seen as special cases derived by abstracting from the dynamic content of a more complete model.

The macroeconomic implications of Kaleckian type pricing models are far-reaching. The implications for short-run stabilization policy are clear, particularly highlighting the need for international co-operation on the stabilization of commodity prices. Changes in industrial structure are seen to have effects on the levels of both investment and income, which can be either positive or negative, so that various long-run paths are possible, with tendency towards stagnation a possible but fortunately not an assured outcome.

NOTES

1. Parts of this chapter draw extensively from Reynolds (1987), with permission from Wheatsheaf Books. Previous versions of parts of this paper were presented at the Association of Polytechnic Teachers in Economics annual conference in Coventry, 1987, and at the International Workshop on Income Distribution, Tennessee, 1988. I am grateful to many of the participants at both conferences, particularly to Tom Asimakopulos, Jan Kregel and Toshio Ogata and to Philip Arestis, Jerzy Osiatynski and an anonymous referee for useful comments and discussion. The usual disclaimer applies.
2. This distinction, in its starkest form, first appeared in Kalecki (1954), chapter 1, which is a revised version of chapter 1 of Kalecki (1943).
3. Joseph Steindl (1952) built on some of Kalecki's early work by – amongst other contributions – examining the relationships between profit margins, excess capacity, investment and industrial concentration. Particularly, he provides an explanation for the existence of both industrial concentration and excess capacity as *outcomes* of the process of competition between capitalists (of which investment is one aspect). Although his work is of considerable importance in the wider Kaleckian tradition, it falls outside the specific objectives of this chapter. See Reynolds (1987) for a summary of Steindl's contributions and further references.
4. There are also many other models where prices are determined as a mark-up but for our purposes it suffices to confine our attention to the two sub-classes referred to.
5. The model set out in *Theory of Economic Dynamics* (1954) was a substantially altered and amended version of a paper that first appeared in *Studies in Economic Dynamics* (1943). It was subsequently included in *Selected Essays . . .* (1971), although a slightly modified version, originally published in *Kyklos* (1971), was also included in the same volume. For very thorough discussions of the development of Kalecki's pricing theory, see Basile and Salvadori (1984–5) and Kriesler (1987).
6. For derivation and discussion of the industry relationship, see Kalecki (1954), Reynolds (1983), Sawyer (1985).
7. Asimakopulos (1975b) p. 261.
8. Following Cowling, if ai differs as between firms, or if aij differs as between different rivals, then we may think of a as some form of weighted average of the individual aij's.
9. These points are made and elaborated by Domberger (1983), pp. 48–9.

10. For a summary of the other models, see Reynolds (1987).
11. In Eichner's analysis the MEI schedule is slightly unconventionally defined in that it includes investment spending on research and development, promotion, etc.
12. See the interchange between Hazeldine and Eichner in the *Economic Journal*, 1974, for a further discussion and see these and other papers in the same issue for other critiques of the Eichner model.
13. This and other criticisms and extensions are discussed in Reynolds (1987).
14. By contrast, Frantzen (1986, p. 393) suggests that in Belgium the accounting profession has been less reluctant to adopt replacement cost accounting techniques. See Lee (1985) for further discussion of some of the implications of the different accounting conventions.
15. See Eichner (1986).
16. The identification of growth maximization with the maximization of profits over the long run was, of course, recognized by Eichner (1976, p. 54). For a rigorous analysis and comparison of the implications of different objectives see J. Williamson (1966).
17. See, e.g., the papers in Eichner (1979), especially the paper by Kenyon.
18. See, e.g., Davidson (1978), Chick (1983).
19. Kaldor (1983) also refers to unpublished work by Sylos Labini on the relationship between industrial sector output and commodity prices.
20. See Kalecki (1954) p. 18 or Reynolds (1987) for derivation and discussion.
21. For explicit treatment of a Kaleckian model which includes both direct and indirect labour, see Asimakopulos (1975a).
22. Eichner recognized that, 'If at some point further reliance on external funds is likely to lead to an increase in i, the supply curve will from that point on have an upward slope', but he does not pursue the point (Eichner, 1986, p. 87).
23. Eichner (1980), Kaldor (1955/6) and Pasinetti (1962).

REFERENCES

Asimakopulos, A. (1975a), 'A Kaleckian Theory of Income Distribution', *Canadian Journal of Economics*, Vol. 8, no. 3 (August).

Asimakopulos, A. (1975b), 'The Price Policy of Firms, Employment and Distribution: A Comment', *Australian Economic Papers*, Vol. 14 (December).

Baran, P. and Sweezy, P. (1967), *Monopoly Capital* (Penguin: Harmondsworth).

Basile, L. and Salvadori, N. (1984–5), 'Kalecki's Pricing Theory', *Journal of Post Keynesian Economics*, Vol. 7, no. 2 (Winter).

Beckerman, W. (1985), 'How the Battle Against Inflation was Really Won', *Lloyds Bank Review*, no. 155 (Jan.).

Beckerman, W. and Jenkinson, T. (1986), 'What Stopped the Inflation? Unemployment or Commodity Prices?', *Economic Journal*, Vol. 96 (March).

Brown, A.J. (1965), *Introduction to the World Economy*, second edition (Macmillan: London).

Chick, V. (1983), *Macroeconomics After Keynes* (Philip Allan: Oxford).

Coutts, K., Godley, W. and Nordhaus, W. (1978), *Industrial Pricing in the United Kingdom* (Cambridge University Press: Cambridge).

Cowling, K. (1982), *Monopoly Capitalism* (Macmillan: London).

Cowling, K. and Waterson, M. (1976), 'Price-cost Margins and Market Structure', *Economica*, Vol. 43 (August).

Davidson, P. (1978), *Money and the Real World*, second edition (Macmillan: London).

Domberger, S. (1983), *Industrial Structure, Pricing and Inflation* (Martin Robertson: Oxford).

Eichner, A.S. (1973), 'A Theory of the Determination of the Mark-up Under Oligopoly', *Economic Journal*, Vol. 83, no. 332 (December).

Eichner, A.S. (1974), 'Determination of the Mark-up Under Oligopoly: A Reply', *Economic Journal*, Vol. 84 (December).

Eichner, A.S. (1976), *The Megacorp and Oligopoly* (Cambridge University Press: Cambridge).

Eichner, A.S. (1979), *A Guide to Post-Keynesian Economics* (Macmillan: London).

Eichner, A.S. (1980), 'A General Model of Investment and Pricing', in Nell (1980).

Eichner, A.S. (1986), 'A Comment on "A Post-Keynesian View of Average Direct Costs" '. *Journal of Post Keynesian Economics*, Vol. 8, no. 3 (Spring).

Frantzen, D.J. (1986), 'The Cyclical Behaviour of Manufacturing Prices in a Small Open Economy', *Journal of Industrial Economics*, Vol. 34, no. 4 (June).

Harcourt, G.C. and Kenyon, P. (1976), 'Pricing and the Investment Decision', *Kyklos*, Vol. 29.

Hazledine, T. (1974). 'Determination of the Mark-up Under

Oligopoly: A Comment', *Economic Journal*, Vol. 84 (December).

Kaldor, N. (1955–6), 'Alternative Theories of Distribution', *Review of Economic Studies*, Vol. 23.

Kaldor, N. (1983), 'The Role of Commodity Prices in Economic Recovery', *Lloyds Bank Review*, No. 149 (July).

Kalecki, M. (1940), 'The Supply Curve of an Industry Under Imperfect Competition', *The Review of Economic Studies* (February).

Kalecki, M. (1943), *Studies in Economic Dynamics* (Aberdeen University Press).

Kalecki, M. (1954), *Theory of Economic Dynamics* (Unwin University Books: London).

Kalecki, M. (1971), *Selected Essays on the Dynamics of the Capitalist Economy* (Cambridge University Press: Cambridge).

Kregel, J.A. (1973), *The Reconstruction of Political Economy*, second edition, 1975 (Macmillan: London).

Kriesler, P. (1987), *Kalecki's Microanalysis* (Cambridge University Press: Cambridge).

Lee, F.S. (1985), 'Full-cost' Prices, Classical Price Theory and Long Period Method Analysis: A Critical Evaluation', *Metroeconomica*, Vol. 37, no. 2 (June).

Lee, F.S. (1986), 'A Post-Keynesian View of Average Direct Costs: A Critical Evaluation of the Theory and the Empirical Evidence', *Journal of Post Keynesian Economics*, Vol. 8, no. 3 (Spring).

Levine, D.P. (1981), *Economic Theory*, Vol. II (Routledge and Kegan Paul: London).

Marris, R. (1964), *The Economic Theory of Managerial Capitalism* (Macmillan: London).

Mott, T. (1985–6), 'Kalecki's Principle of Increasing Risk and the Relation among Mark-up Pricing, Investment Fluctuations, and Liquidity Preference', *Economic Forum*, Vol. 15 (Winter).

Nell, E.J. (ed.) (1980), *Growth, Profits and Property* (Cambridge University Press: Cambridge).

Ong, N. (1981), 'Target Pricing, Competition and Growth', *Journal of Post Keynesian Economics*, Vol. 4, no. 1 (Fall).

Pasinetti, L.L. (1962), 'Rate of Profit and Income Distribution in Relation to the Rate of Economic Growth', *Review of Economic Studies*, Vol. 29 (October).

Penrose, E.T. (1959), *The Theory of the Growth of the Firm* (Basil Blackwell: Oxford).

Reynolds, P.J. (1983), 'Kalecki's Degree of Monopoly', *Journal of Post Keynesian Economics*, Vol. 5, no. 3 (Spring).

Reynolds, P.J. (1987), *Political Economy: A Synthesis of Kaleckian and Post Keynesian Economics* (Wheatsheaf: Brighton).

Riach, P. (1971), 'Kalecki's Degree of Monopoly', *Australian Economic Papers*, Vol. 10.

Sawyer, M.C. (1982a), *Macroeconomics in Question. The Keynesian-Monetarist Orthodoxies and the Kaleckian Alternative* (Wheatsheaf: Brighton).

Sawyer, M.C. (1982b), 'Towards a post-Kaleckian Macroeconomics', *Thames Papers in Political Economy* (Autumn).

Sawyer, M.C. (1985), *The Economics of Michal Kalecki* (Macmillan: London).

Shapiro, N. (1981), 'Pricing and the Growth of Firms', *Journal of Post Keynesian Economics*, Vol. 4, no. 1 (Fall).

Spence, M. (1977), 'Entry, Investment and Oligopolistic Pricing', *Bell Journal of Economics* (Autumn).

Steindl, J. (1952), *Maturity and Stagnation in American Capitalism* (page refs to second edition, 1976) (Oxford University Press: Oxford).

Steindl, J. (1979), 'Stagnation Theory and Stagnation Policy', *Cambridge Journal of Economics*, no. 3.

Weintraub, S. (1981), 'An Eclectic Theory of Income Shares', *Journal of Post Keynesian Economics*, Vol. 4, no. 1 (Fall).

Williamson, J. (1966), 'Profit, Growth and Sales Maximization', *Economica*, Vol. 33, no. 129 (February).

Wood, A. (1975), *A Theory of Profits* (Cambridge University Press: Cambridge).

8. Vicious Circles and Cumulative Causation

Peter Skott

INTRODUCTION

Orthodox neoclassical models of growth and international trade would tend to suggest a gradual equalization of factor incomes between different regions and countries. The stylized facts of economic development do not, however, support this hypothesis (see, for instance, Kuznets, 1971). One may choose to ascribe the lack of convergence to the effects of exogenous shocks, but it would seem more promising to examine the possibility that there exists endogenous economic forces which tend to cause income levels to diverge between regions and countries.

The Kaldor–Myrdal principle of circular and cumulative causation offers an alternative to the neoclassical vision. The principle of cumulative causation emphasizes the existence of dual characteristics in the economy – the co-existence of advanced and backward sectors – as well as the importance of increasing returns. The combination of dual characteristics and increasing returns will entail endogenous tendencies for growth rates to diverge between different countries, and it implies that economic activity cannot be regarded as resource-constrained in any meaningful sense.

It is the purpose of this chapter to relate the Kaldor–Myrdal principle of cumulative causation to both neoclassical and Keynesian theory, and to explore some general implications of the Kaldor–Myrdal view. The chapter is in five sections. The Kaldor–Myrdal critique of neoclassical theory is outlined in the first section. The second section describes three different model-economies: a simple exchange economy, a Keynesian production economy and a Kaldor–Myrdal economy. The distinguishing properties of the Kaldor–Myrdal economy are discussed in the third section. The notion of vicious and virtuous circles is discussed in the penultimate section with the final section presenting a few concluding remarks.

THE KALDOR–MYRDAL CRITIQUE OF NEOCLASSICAL THEORY

Myrdal has been a long-standing critic of orthodox economic theory. In Myrdal (1957) he focuses on the large economic inequalities between countries and on the tendency for these inequalities to grow rather than diminish. He argues that orthodox theory is unable to account for these phenomena and that this is due to deep-seated problems in the dominant approach to economics: the dominant approach needs to be replaced by an alternative vision based on the 'principle of circular and cumulative causation'.

Myrdal's critique could be seen as a narrow critique of international trade theory of the Heckscher–Ohlin–Samuelson variety. The heart of the critique would be simply that neoclassical trade theory had proved inadequate to explain actual events. This narrow critique would hardly be terribly contentious. Most economists would probably express misgivings regarding the direct applicability of Heckscher–Ohlin–Samuelson theory to real world problems. That the conclusions derived from the simple models still govern many policy recommendations is another matter and one well deserving of attention. But from a theoretical point of view, the significance of the critique would be limited.

International trade theory is not, however, completely separate from general economic theory. On the contrary, the central idea of international trade theory is that of general equilibrium, and the work on trade theory contributed to the development of the general equilibrium research programme in its early phases. As a matter of fact, the close links between Heckscher–Ohlin–Samuelson trade theory and the general equilibrium research programme provides, according to de Marchi (1976), a major part of the explanation for the resilience of the former in the face of what appeared to be decisive empirical refutation.[1] Myrdal insisted that his critique had wide ramifications and in view of the close connection[2] between international trade theory and the research programme which has dominated theoretical economics over the last forty years, it seems worthwhile to examine a wider interpretation of the critique.

Myrdal's central empirical proposition concerns the existence of large and in many cases growing inequalities. One might ask whether large and increasing regional inequalities are logically incompatible with the predictions of full-fledged general equilibrium models. The answer is no. Increasing inequalities are even compatible with the classical Arrow–Debreu model of intertemporal equilibrium. The specific conclusions in international trade theory regarding tendencies to equalization are predicated on very special assumptions, and the general neoclassical model does not stand and fall with these assumptions. A general neoclassical model is perfectly compatible with a widening gap in living standards.

The generality of the full-fledged general equilibrium model, its ability to generate a wide variety of scenarios, obviously does not in itself imply that it is a useful framework. The generality may signify nothing but vacuity. Any finite set of observations will be consistent with an infinite number of theories, and the choice between these theories cannot be based on the observations with which they are all equally consistent. Similarly, a theory or a framework which is so general that it yields no operational predictions cannot be judged on the basis of its (non-existent) predictions. The very generality of general equilibrium theory means that an assessment of the framework must be based on the plausibility of its basic assumptions and of the mode of explanation of observed phenomena which it offers.

Myrdal actually presents numerous criticisms of basic neoclassical assumptions. It is to these criticisms that one must look in order to assess the validity of his critique. The criticisms also provide the clue to a proper understanding of the principle of circular and cumulative causation. Myrdal's presentation, however, suffers from a lack of precision on crucial issues. It will therefore be helpful at this stage to draw also on Kaldor's later criticism of neoclassical theory and his formulation of the alternative vision.[3]

The main points which Kaldor and Myrdal raise can be summarized under four headings:

1. Any long run development must be seen as a sequence of short run events and it can only be understood and analysed if due recognition is given to the factors which determine the constraints and behaviour of 'agents' in the short period. Particular attention should be paid to the short and ultra-short run sequential patterns which are vital for the specification both of the constraints faced by agents and of their perceptions regarding the optimal course of action within these constraints.
2. The equilibrium notion associated with general equilibrium theory embodies a 'harmony predilection'. Conflict over the allocation of limited resources between competing ends is, of course, at the centre of general equilibrium theory. But in the static notion of simultaneous equilibrium, conflicts have been completely tamed; the preoccupation of neoclassical theory with questions of Pareto optimality is symptomatic of this. In place of a static theory of simultaneous equilibrium one needs a dynamic theory where the non-fulfilment of static equilibrium conditions acts as an impulse to change and where the induced changes will themselves alter the position of the (unattained) short period equilibrium in the ensuing period. The focus of economic theory should shift from questions of 'allocation' to questions of 'creation'.
3. Abstract mathematical generality and elegance must be relinquished as criteria for judging developments in economic theory. There is a need for abstract theory, but

even abstract theories must be judged on their relevance and adequacy with respect to the specific problems and facts which they purport to illuminate.

4. Neoclassical theory is built on a number of 'unrealistic assumptions'. The following stylized facts – neglected by neoclassical theory – are of particular importance:

   (a) The world economy (as well as most if not all national economies) has the characteristics of a dual economy. Advanced and dynamic sectors coexist with backward sectors. The exact delineation of 'advanced' and 'backward' sectors is a matter of judgement and will depend on the purpose of the analysis. In many cases, however, it is useful to identify the advanced sector with industry and the backward sector with agriculture. The service sector is rather a mixed bag, some parts of it being definitely advanced but others backward.
   (b) Production in manufacturing industry is subject to increasing returns. Three different forms of increasing returns are distinguished: the classical case of static increasing returns which are internal to the individual firm; external increasing returns associated with Adam Smith's and Allyn Young's recognition of the interdependence between the division of labour and the extent of the market; and, finally, dynamic increasing returns denoting endogenous changes in the production possibility set. Although often conceived of in a narrow sense as 'endogenous technical progress' or 'learning by doing', dynamic increasing returns could also encompass wider social aspects such as endogenous changes in industrial relations or in attitudes to work and risk-taking.
   (c) Apart from supplying industry with necessary raw materials, the primary sector and parts of the service sector also play an important role as a repository of hidden unemployment; the marginal contribution of additional workers to output in traditional agriculture and in some small scale services is zero or negligible.

(d) The notion that exogenously given factor endowments and production possibility sets act as binding constraints on economic outcomes is false except in the very short run – this is almost a corollary of (b) and (c) above.

The four criticisms raised under 1–4 above are closely related. The charge of a 'harmony predilection' in neoclassical theory is reinforced by the simultaneity of the equilibrium concept in general equilibrium models. The term conflict is inherently dynamic. It is in the nature of a conflict that the conflict is played out in actual time and that the actions of one party to the conflict will affect the (future) opportunity set of other parties. In the terminal states of simultaneous general equilibrium the focus is on (logically possible) final outcomes, and a final outcome can only be a *final* outcome if it is akin to a compromise accepted by all parties; in a final outcome the conflict has been resolved. A – perhaps rather silly – metaphor may help to clarify. A football match is a simple example of a limited and well-defined conflict. In order to understand and analyse this conflict one will have to pay careful attention to the 'sequential patterns' of events on the field. Split seconds can make all the difference on the effect of an otherwise beautiful pass down the middle. The possible final outcomes, however, can be described in simple static terms: either one of the two sides will win or it will be a draw. The rules of football stipulate that the final outcome will be found after 90 minutes of play. In the economic 'game' there is no such time limit; a terminal state for an economy is therefore more like a football match which is interrupted before full time by the two sides resolving their conflict and agreeing on a suitable compromise, a draw for instance.

There is also a link between the need for on the one hand sequential analysis and, on the other, a relevance criterion to assess abstract theory. One of the main reasons why many economists regard general equilibrium theory as the appropriate general framework of analysis, is the way the framework can accommodate an arbitrary number of commodities and agents. The theory, in other words, seems to offer true generality in the commodity and agent spaces. In practical applications one may need and want to aggregate and to introduce specific assumptions, but the general framework, it is held, eschews the need for any such 'ad hoc' restrictions.[4] In fact, the generality of general equilibrium theory is somewhat illusory even as regards the commodity and agent spaces but, more importantly, disaggregation in the commodity and agent spaces is achieved at the expense of extreme aggregation in the time dimension: the simultaneous equilibrium of general equilibrium theory is fundamentally static. The research strategy of general equilibrium is that of a corner solution: (almost) complete disaggregation in the agent and commodity sphere goes hand in hand with (almost) complete aggregation in the time dimension.[5] It is the alleged 'generality' of the general equilibrium framework which supposedly leaves the framework immune to questions of relevance and realism, and the illusory character of this generality is most clearly seen in the treatment of time in general equilibrium theory. All theories must be 'partial theories'; there are no truly 'general theories', and the common view that 'partial theory' (or partial equilibrium analysis) is 'bad' and 'general theory' (or general equilibrium analysis) is 'good' is either wrong or based on an identification of partial with 'leaving out relevant factors' and general with 'including all the factors which I consider relevant'. Down to earth questions of 'realism' and 'relevance' are, in other words, pertinent even with respect to abstract theory.

'Realism', obviously, should not be taken in the sense of detailed, accurate, descriptive realism, but in a weaker sense: if one has reason to believe that factors which are omitted by a given theory exert a significant and systematic influence on the problems which the theory addresses or if the theory includes assumptions which are known to be at variance with the properties of the real world counterparts which the assumptions refer to, and if one has reason to believe that this discrepancy is of material importance for the conclusions derived from the theory, then the theory has failed the test of realism. The wording here may be thought so vague that the statement verges on the meaningless. The wording, however, reflects the simple fact that 'good judgement' will always be involved in the test for realism; economics and pure mathematics are very different ball games.

If it is agreed that general equilibrium theory neglects sequential patterns and adopts an extreme aggregation in time, then the next question becomes whether this is acceptable. Does the neglect of the time dimension have a material effect on the relevance of the model. The answer to this question will depend crucially on the characteristics of the economy and this is where Kaldor's and Myrdal's fourth point – the unrealistic assumptions of neoclassical theory – becomes important. Broadly speaking, the more static are the underlying 'real factors' of the economy the less important are the sequential patterns likely to be. The next section presents three examples which illustrate this point.

THREE MODEL ECONOMIES

Consider first a pure exchange economy. At the beginning of each period individual agents receive endowments in the form of fixed bundles of (perishable) goods.[6] The endowments may differ between individuals but the endowment of any given individual is the same in all periods. An agent may either consume his/her endowment or try to alter the composition of the consumption bundle through trade.

In the absence of an omniscient auctioneer or recontracting facilities it is highly unlikely that all acts of trading in the first period will reflect the same relative valuation of the commodities. The relative prices of commodities will change within the period and if different bilateral acts of trade take place simultaneously, then the ratio in which one good is exchanged for another may not even be uniform at a given moment in time. 'False trading' and 'false consumption'[7] will be pervasive. In subsequent periods, however, agents will be influenced by their past experience. They will have gathered some information on the preferences of other agents and on the trading possibilities which they face. Although it may be extremely difficult to set up a formal (and interesting) analytical model and establish the result rigorously, it seems reasonable to suppose that the continuous learning experience of agents will make the economy approach a 'terminal state'; i.e. the trading and consumption pattern of agents will asymptotically be constant.[8] In the analysis of the long run properties of an economy like this it would therefore be justified to focus on the properties of possible terminal states. The set of Walrasian general equilibrium states will only be a subset of the set of possible terminal states[9] and, furthermore, the actual pattern of 'false trading' and 'false consumption' in the early periods will in general play a part in determining which particular terminal state will emerge. Nevertheless, even the simple Walrasian model would probably not be grossly misleading if one were concerned merely with the asymptotic outcome in an exchange economy of this sort.[10]

If production is introduced, matters become a little more complicated. The extent of the complications will depend on the precise assumptions. In the simplest case where production takes place wholly within each unit period and where there is no possibility of augmenting production possibilities in one period by the transfer (investment) of resources from the previous period, the introduction of production makes no material difference. Each period will in this case remain completely self-contained with given exogenous constraints which are independent of events in previous periods. But this type of production economy is a far cry from actual modern production economies.

To be interesting, the model of a production economy must allow for the possibility of investment, i.e. for the existence of produced inputs to production and the possibility of tranferring produced inputs from one period to the next. The implication of this is that the individual periods cease to be self-contained. Intertemporal consideration, expectations concerning trading possibilities in future periods, will now play a part in determining the outcome in any given period. Furthermore, past mistakes in the form of false trading, false consumption and false investment will directly affect current trading possibilities and current constraints on consumption and investment. *A priori* one would expect this to diminish the chances of the economy settling down to a terminal state or at least to slow down the speed of convergence to a terminal state. But without more specific assumptions regarding the structure of the production economy it is impossible to say much more.

One theory of a production economy which has at least some claim to relevance in relation to advanced capitalist countries is the Keynes–Kalecki theory of effective demand (Keynes, 1936; Kalecki, 1971). The theory of effective demand, however, is a short run theory. The unemployment equilibrium described by Keynes is at most a temporary terminal state. The accumulation of physical and financial assets will gradually change some of the parameters determining the behaviour of agents and thus induce changes in the short run equilibrium configuration. The possibility (or likelihood) of persistent involuntary unemployment is thus put into question. As a matter of fact, it is difficult to see how *large* and *persistent* rates of unemployment could be directly attributed to Keynesian involuntary unemployment. Involuntary unemployment involves the coexistence of extra capital capacity and unemployment. Endogenous investment and scrapping decisions of firms will, however, ensure that the long run average rate of utilization of capital will be close to the desired rate of utilization. The long run average rate of involuntary unemployment is thus limited by the desired degree of excess capacity. But, of course, demand shifts which affect the current level of output and capacity utilization could have a long term effect on the rate of growth of capital capacity: the investment decisions, which help determine the position of the short run equilibrium, will also imply a certain rate of growth of capital capacity, and the rate of growth of capacity in conjunction with the rate of growth of labour augmenting technical progress sets an upper limit to the potential rate of growth of employment.[11] If this upper limit falls below the rate of growth of the labour supply then 'Marxian' unemployment may result. The appearance of Keynesian involuntary unemployment in any given short period may therefore have long run repercussions in the form of subsequent Marxian unemployment.

Empirical evidence, however, shows that registered rates

of unemployment fluctuate within relatively narrow limits. If one were to accept, as Keynes apparently did, that the allocation of employed resources is always optimal in the sense that the marginal value product – at the ruling prices – of any input is at least as high in the line of production where it is actually used as in any other line and if, furthermore, one assumes – as most modern growth models do – that technical progress and the growth of the labour force are exogenous, then the conclusion seems inescapable: the long run growth rate is determined by exogenous supply constraints. Keynes's theory of employment may explain short run variations of actual from potential production, and the average level of production (as a proportion of potential output) may be affected by trade cycle fluctuations, but the long run growth rates of output and productivity remain anchored to exogenous and real supply constraints. With some qualifications, neoclassical theory may therefore provide an acceptable stylized description of how the economy works in the long run. The qualifications relate to the *level* effects of the average degree of underutilization of resources associated with fluctuations in effective demand.

The existence of underutilized resources is of course no unimportant matter. If in this sort of economy the careful demand management policies of a central government could succeed in raising permanently the average degree of utilization by, say, 1 per cent then this would certainly be an achievement of great importance. The point therefore is not that government intervention is unnecessary in a 'Keynesian production economy' but merely that neoclassical theories of simultaneous general equilibrium may provide a useful account of average long run outcomes (the one proviso being that the level of the average actual activity will be below the potential level predicted by neoclassical theory). The scene is then set for a division of economic theory into short run Keynesian theories of market failure and of the determination of the level of economic activity relative to the potential given by exogenous resources, and on the other hand long run neoclassical theories of market success in the efficient allocation of all employed resources, the average rate of employment of resources being constant. The Keynesian analysis of the short run behaviour of the economy may rely on explicit considerations of sequential patterns (cf. Skott, 1983a), but empirical evidence of relatively narrow limits on fluctuations in registered unemployment in conjunction with Keynes's acceptance of all but one of the neoclassical postulates implies that exogenous supply constraints reassert themselves in the long run, and the average long run behaviour of the economy can therefore be understood without reference to socio-economic factors and the sequential patterns of the socio-economic system.

As the third example consider a simple model economy which departs more radically from orthodox neoclassical models and which embodies some of the Kaldor–Myrdal assumptions described in the previous section. The model economy is divided into two main sectors, A and M. Sector M may be thought of as a 'modern', capitalistic, industrial sector (producing 'machines') and sector A as a 'backward' agricultural sector (producing 'corn').

The A sector supplies consumption goods to workers in the M sector and raw material inputs to the M sector. It also serves as a repository of surplus labour: employment in the M sector is determined by the demand for labour in that sector leaving employment in sector A as the residual. There is no overt unemployment but the marginal contribution of labour to output in sector A is zero.

It is assumed that production of machines takes place at two different production centres, Birmingham and Essen, which are, as it were, isolated M sector islands in a sea of agricultural production.[12] Output from the two centres is indistinguishable and, since there are no costs of transportation, will be sold at the same price, p_m. The capital output ratio is the same in the two centres and constant over time, and both centres have an infinitely elastic supply of labour (from the surrounding A sector) at the ruling wage rates, w_b and w_e respectively.

The production of machines is subject to dynamic increasing returns to scale. The rate of growth of labour productivity in Birmingham (Essen) is positively related to the rate of capital accumulation in Birmingham (Essen) and, ignoring for the moment production lags and variations in the utilization rate of capital, the rate of accumulation is equal to the rate of growth of production. Algebraically this is expressed by

$$\hat{q}_b = f(\hat{M}_b) \tag{1a}$$

$$\hat{q}_e = f(\hat{M}_e) \tag{1b}$$

where $\hat{q}_b$ ($\hat{q}_e$) and $\hat{M}_b$ ($\hat{M}_b$) denote the proportionate rates of growth of labour productivity and output in Birmingham (Essen).

The rates of growth of production, in turn, are determined by profitability conditions,

$$\hat{M}_b = g(\pi_b, \pi_e) \ ; \ g_1 > O, g_2 < O \tag{2a}$$

$$\hat{M}_e = g(\pi_e, \pi_b) \ ; \ g_1 > O, g_2 < O \tag{2b}$$

where π_b and π_e are the profit shares (which are proportional to profit rates) in the two centres),

$$\pi_b = 1 - \lambda \, p_a/p_m - w_b/(p_m \, q_b) \tag{3a}$$

$$\pi_e = 1 - \lambda \, p_a/p_m - w_e/(p_m \, q_e) \tag{3b}$$

where λ is the agricultural raw material input per unit of industrial output.

Equations (2a)–(3b) reflect the hypothesis that the desired rate of growth of production in, say, Birmingham depends on the absolute level of profitability in Birmingham as well as on the relative profitabilities in the two production centres; there is some degree of international (money) capital mobility and firms are induced to invest in the country offering the highest prospective return. Current profitability acts as an indicator of future prospects.[13]

Substituting (2a)–(3b) in (1a) and (1b) appropriately, one gets

$$\hat{q}_b = f(g(\pi_b\ ,\ \pi_e)) = h(1 - \lambda p_a/p_m\ ,\ w_b/(p_m q_b),\ w_e/(p_m q_e)) \quad (4a)$$

$$\hat{q}_e = f(g(\pi_e\ ,\ \pi_b)) = h(1 - \lambda p_a/p_m\ ,\ w_e/(p_m q_e),\ w_b/(p_m q_b)) \quad (4b)$$

where $h_2 < O$, $h_3 > O$

If it is assumed that efficiency wages in the two industrial centres are equal initially and that nominal wages grow at the same proportional rate in the two centres, it is readily seen that the two centres will have identical profit shares and hence the same rates of growth of output and labour productivity. It is also easy to see, however, that if for some reason firms take a pessimistic view of future prospects in, say, Birmingham and therefore initially expand production in Birmingham less than indicated by equation (2a), then this pessimistic view will be vindicated by actual events: the slower rate of expansion will lead to slower rates of productivity growth, profitability in Birmingham will suffer relative to profitability in Essen and even if 'animal spirits' revive and expansion starts following equation (2a), the rates of growth of output and productivity in the two centres will diverge. A similar process of divergence would result if, say, 'false trading' in the initial period led to Essen machines fetching on average a higher price than Birmingham machines. In this model short run events may set in motion a cumulative process; 'false trading' or 'false investment' at any given moment in time may have dramatic effects on the long run outcome. The long run outcome is not determined by exogenous constraints.[14]

It may be noticed that divergence does not depend on the absence of catching-up effects of the sort that have played an important role in the debate following Kaldor's inaugural lecture.[15] Even if equations (1a) and (1b) were replaced by

$$\hat{q}_b = f(\hat{M}_b) + \phi(q_b/q_e)\ ;\ \phi' < O \quad (1a)'$$

$$\hat{q}_e = f(\hat{M}_e) + \phi(q_e/q_b)\ ;\ \phi' < O \quad (1b)'$$

there would be no tendency to equality in the growth rates of output or in the levels of productivity.

PROPERTIES OF THE KALDOR–MYRDAL MODEL

In the preceding section the Kaldor–Myrdal model was described in a rather simultaneous way: we paid only limited attention to the short run sequential patterns, and these patterns are of vital importance. Consider the problems facing the centre which for some reason has become the slow growing region. As it stands, the model suggests that a lowering of money wages in the region would improve profitability instantaneously and boost the rate of growth of output and productivity. If the cut in money wages is sufficiently large – and if money wages in the fast growing centre are unaffected by changes in the slow growing centre – then profitability in the initially slow growing centre will come to exceed profitability in the initially fast growing centre and the relative ranking of the centres in terms of growth will be reversed. Even if the money wage change is insufficient to reverse the growth ranking it will still lead to an improvement in the relative growth performance of the slow growing centre. The growth rate of the slow growing region will be enhanced and the growth performance of the fast growing centre will deteriorate. On close examination this clearcut conclusion may, however, become suspect.

Notice first that there are no obvious reasons why money wages in the slow growing region should fall relative to money wages in the fast growing region. Both centres have, by assumption, an infinitely elastic supply of labour at the ruling wage rates.[16] If the reserve army of hidden unemployment exerts downward pressure on money wages then it should do so in both centres. Declining levels of employment in the slow growing region – and thus a threat of redundancy to already employed workers – could be a factor making for adjustments in relative wage rates, but industrial employment may be increasing even in the slow growing region. Indeed, if wage adjustments do not come into operation unless the employment level is decreasing, then they can at most arrest the speed of decline of the slow growing centre. Finally, firms are likely to prefer workers with previous industrial job experience so the possibility of migration of workers as well as general pressures for wage comparability may limit the extent to which wage rates can diverge, between regions.

The model, however, does indicate that *if* changes in relative money wages can be effected then these changes will have immediate and powerful effects on growth. A Keynesian policy of increasing the demand for industrial output by fiscal measures on the other hand will improve profitability in both centres and may not enhance the relative performance of the slow growing centre.[17] A stimulus to industrial demand does not correct the underlying cause of relatively slow growth, namely the relatively low profitability in the centre. Money wage policies or devaluation would thus – from the point of view of the slow growing region – seem preferable to demand management policies.

These conclusions depend on the postulated short run behaviour of the economy. The model ignores factors such as product differentiation, information lags and (short run) consumer loyalties. It was assumed that output from the two industrial centres is indistinguishable even in the short run and that a common price of machines is therefore established.[18] Variations in capital utilization rates, production lags and lags in firms' responses to different stimuli were also neglected. If these factors are allowed for, the conclusions may not hold: strong short run consumer loyalties and competitive advantages on the home market would greatly improve the chances of success for a policy of domestic demand expansion; the benefits of increased productivity may occur before the factors limiting competition in the short run wear out.

The simple remedy of lowering money wages or devaluing the currency, on the other hand, becomes more suspect in these circumstances. Product differentiation implies that a larger cut in money wages will be required to ensure the same effect on profitability and growth;[19] the almost immediate effects of wage cuts on (nominal) domestic demand in conjunction with a semi-protected home market also weaken the effects of a given wage cut on profitability. The danger of wage cuts as a remedy against slow growth are thereby aggravated: cuts in money wages will almost certainly upset relative wage differentials within the industrial centre (at least temporarily) with likely adverse short run effects on industrial relations and productivity. And in so far as reductions in the price of output lead to lower levels of money profits, the financial position of firms may also be put under stress and bankruptcies may add their weight to the adverse affects. The larger the average wage cut required to ensure significant positive effects, the more severe are the adverse effects likely to be.

A policy of devaluation would have a better chance of reducing all wages simultaneously without upsetting wage differentials within the centre, but devaluation carries with it its own dangers. Inflationary tendencies may have implications for business confidence and industrial relations. Secondly, and perhaps more important, the fast growing region will probably not just sit back and allow its competitiveness and growth to be undermined by an undesired revaluation of its currency. The outcome of an attempted devaluation by the slow growing region could therefore well be a whole series of exchange rate adjustments with little or no effect on the relative profitability and growth rates of the two regions but with inflationary consequences. Beggar-thy-neighbour policies of wage reductions or devaluations thus offer little hope of success in improving the overall growth of industrial production, and retaliation may even make the prospect of success for any individual centre doubtful.[20]

We may conclude that short run sequential patterns will be of crucial importance in the Kaldor–Myrdal economy. *The sequential patterns will influence the short run effects of 'exogenous shocks'* – be they policy interventions, stochastic changes in agricultural prices or sudden changes in workers' money wage demand – and *the short run outcome may have cumulative long run effects*. This indeed is one of the main points of the example. The vital importance of sequential patterns is one of three important characteristics which distinguishes the Kaldor–Myrdal economy from the general equilibrium vision of the world.

The second distinguishing characteristic concerns the relationship between economic and non-economic factors. The model predicts inherent tendencies to divergence between regions. The prediction of the long run winners in the growth game is however extremely hazardous if, initially, industrial regions experience similar rates of profit and growth; a small shock may turn what looked like a winner into a loser. If, on the other hand, large disparities in profitability and growth rates have developed, then this will almost certainly provoke strong attempts at direct intervention. If the regions belong to the same political entity, the intervention will probably take the form of centrally financed schemes to counteract the relative decline of slow growing regions and to rejuvenate industry in these regions. If the regions are in fact sovereign states, then pressures for government intervention are likely to mount in the slow-growing countries. In the first instance the intervention could be measures to stimulate demand. If this created balance of payments problems then import controls or exchange rate policies might follow. But if differences in growth rates persist and lead to significant shifts in relative economic power between countries, then political and institutional upheavals can be expected. The breakdown of the Bretton Woods agreement following two decades of relative decline of the US economy is a case in point. The rise of German strength (in particular vis-à-vis England) and the outbreak of the first world war is another example. The general idea, that political and social institutions are adapted to a particular economic situation and that changes in the economic sphere lead to (possibly abrupt and violent) changes in the superstructure, is of course straight out of Marx.

The implication of the above is not that balanced growth of the industrial regions will be established as the result of direct intervention. The outcome of any such intervention may not be that desired by the party who instigated the change and even if a 'loser' had complete knowledge of the causes of uneven development it may not be within the powers of the 'loser' to effect changes which will remedy the situation. The important conclusion therefore is quite different. It is that a narrow economic analysis which takes institutions and socio-political factors as given is likely to be misleading. A free market laissez-faire game will create winners and losers and this will cause pressures for revisions of the 'rules of the game' to be built up. The model points to latent conflicts and the uneven development predicted by the model will exacerbate these conflicts and bring them out into the open. The conclusion of the model is that it may be very difficult for Birmingham to arrest a relative decline but that attempts to do so by direct intervention (changing the rules) are to be expected. The outcome will depend both on the economic and political strength of Birmingham (which defines the range of feasible interventions) and on the skill and wisdom exercised 'by Birmingham' in the choice and implementation of intervention measures. Both of these factors will in turn be influenced by the extent of social conflict within Birmingham and by the balance of forces in those internal conflicts – Birmingham is no homogeneous decision unit.

The third major difference between a neoclassical vision and the Kaldor–Myrdal view concerns the nature of the effective constraints on the economy. The economy described by neoclassical models (and to some extent by the Keynesian model discussed in the previous section) is constrained by exogenous and real supply factors. The same cannot be said about the Kaldor–Myrdal economy. To be sure, all real world economies are faced with some exogenous constraints. Land and other natural resources, the size of the population and the inherited capital equipment, technical knowledge as well as the socio-economic set-up are predetermined at any given moment in time, and there are no doubt upper limits to the possible rate of change in these factors. But *it is difficult to ascertain what those limits are*.

Even the available quantity of land and natural resources which would seem the most promising candidate for a truly exogenous constraint, may change over time. New mineral deposits may be discovered. Hitherto unused and barren land may be turned into fertile farm land following the invention of new farming techniques. Whether one wants to classify these changes as advances in knowledge rather than as changes in the available natural resources makes little difference. The point is that the discovery of mineral deposits or the introduction of new farming techniques are the results of human activity, and human activity – including all economic activity – will always and everywhere take place in a social context. Social factors and exogenous physical and physiological constraints are inextricably mixed in the outcome. Exogenous physical and physiological production possibility sets are unknown and unknowable, but even if they were known this would not be very helpful in explaining the actual development of an economy: the relevant 'possibility sets' are constrained also by the social and institutional organization of economic activity. And we do know that social factors can play an important part. It is not contentious, for instance, to argue that feudal societies differed from capitalism with respect to innovative dynamism. Debates in industrial economics about the effects of X-efficiency and dynamic efficiency of different market structures also reflect an awareness even within orthodox economics of the impact of the social environment on technical efficiency and dynamism.

The fact that exogenous production possibility sets are unknown and unknowable implies that notions of Pareo-*optimality* and intertemporal *efficiency* become meaningless. Recognition of the social character of economic activity and of the interaction between the economic sphere and wider social factors means that questions of 'efficiency' and 'optimality' in an absolute sense become ill-defined and irrelevant. The social framework may constitute the effective constraint on the growth path of the economy.

In the simple Kaldor–Myrdal economy, for instance, the 'animal spirits' of industrial firms have a decisive influence on the growth rate of the whole economy. An upward shift in the g-functions describing the production and investment decisions in industry would take the economy to a new growth path with a higher rate of growth. A shift in the g-functions could be the result of, say, changes in the financial sphere which for given rates of expansion and profitability diminish the risk of bankruptcy and takeover for individual firms; the position of the g-functions is not determined by exogenous supply constraints. The increase in growth rates following the shift in the g-functions may of course entail a temporary drop in real wages, but since the supply of labour is infinitely elastic at the given money wage rates this does not imply an effective constraint on growth. The constant capital output ratio does set an upper limit to the potential rate of expansion of industrial production, but this constraint is hardly likely to be binding. The surplus of agricultural production which is made available for workers' consumption and as raw material input in industry could also constrain industrial production. The agricultural production and its growth rate cannot, however, be regarded as exogenously given. The social and institutional framework plays a prominent part in determining the agricultural surplus, and a cursory look at the world economy today suggests that social and institutional factors rather than constraints of technical feasibility present the more important limits on primary production and its rate of expansion.

We may summarize this section as follows: the Kaldor–Myrdal vision breaks with neoclassical orthodoxy on three fundamental issues: (i) the nature of the relevant constraints on the economy, (ii) the relation between the economic sphere in a narrow sense and wider social developments, and (iii) the importance of short run sequential patterns and adjustments speeds for the long run evolution of an economy. It is the difference in these areas which more than anything else separate Kaldor and Myrdal from neoclassical economics. Where neoclassical economists see intertemporal equilibria constrained by exogenous possibility sets, Kaldor and Myrdal see economies which are not effectively constrained by exogenous factors but by social and institutional factors, and they predict that (under capitalism) inherent tendencies to unequal development across regions and sectors will generate irresistible pressures for changes in the social and institutional set-up. It should be apparent that although it is cast in different terms, the Kaldor–Myrdal position has in fact many affinities with traditional Marxian views.

VICIOUS AND VIRTUOUS CIRCLES

The section on 'Three model economies' presented three simple models. Assumptions of private property and the pursuit of self-interest were common to the three models, but they differed with respect to the specification of exogenous and socio-economic constraints. Perhaps not surprisingly, these differences had dramatic effects on the behaviour of the economies as well as on the appropriate framework for analysing the economies.

It seemed plausible that the simple exchange economy could be described and analysed within a timeless general equilibrium framework. The Keynesian one sector production economy allowed for the occurrence of involuntary unemployment but when the secular development of advanced Western economies were looked at through the glasses of the Keynesian one sector model, then long run growth rates appeared to be determined by exogenous supply constraints and a modified neoclassical framework seemed adequate for the analysis of the long run properties of these economies.

The Kaldor–Myrdal economy differed from the Keynesian economy in three respects: dynamic increasing returns were introduced along with some dual economy features and some spatial disaggregation. This meant that there would be a tendency for growth rates in different industrial centres to diverge and that socio-economic constraints – as opposed to exogenous, 'technical' constraints – came to the forefront also as regards long run development.

As far as medium to long run questions are concerned, the main division is between the Kaldor–Myrdal economy on the one hand and the resource constrained exchange economy and Keynesian production economy on the other. By abandoning the idea that exogenous resources are the effective constraints on the long run development of actual economies, a new vision is opened up. One enters a world of circular and cumulative causation where success breeds success and failure only failure. Some regions will find themselves in a virtuous circle of rapid and self-sustained growth and other regions will be thrown into a vicious circle of relative decline, and the reasons for success in one region and failure in another have more to do with historical accident than with exogenous resource endowments.

The notion of vicious/virtuous circles can be viewed as a dynamic long run analogue to Keynes's notion of involuntary unemployment. The existence of involuntary unemployment implies that the level of production is not constrained by available resources. More workers would be willing to work even at a reduced real wage rate and firms would employ more workers if the real wage rate were lower. But the specific social organization of economic activity under capitalism makes it impossible for workers to engineer a decline in real wages and thus to increase employment. Workers may accept a cut in money wages but this will not in itself cause a change in real wages and declining money wages may even destabilize the whole system and aggravate the employment situation. The effective constraints on the levels of production and employment are social and institutional; the social organization of production prevents the full utilization of available resources.

The notion of vicious circles generalizes this Keynesian notion: a regional economy is in a vicious circle if the endogenously generated forces of the socio-economic system depress the economic growth and development of the region relative to the development of other regions. Similarly, a regional economy experiences a virtuous circle if endogenous forces of socio-economic system favour the economic development of the region relative to the development of other regions.

These definitions do not really have the clarity and precision that ideally one would desire. For a start, vicious/virtuous circles have been defined in purely relative terms. The focus is on the differential impact of the socio-economic system on the development opportunities of different regions, and if one were interested in more than two regions – as in most cases one would be – then some regions may experience a vicious circle if the most favoured region is used as a yardstick and a virtuous circle if comparison is made with the least favoured regions. This ambiguity is closely related to the absence of an absolute measure of 'neutral development' or 'potential development'.

By accepting most of the neoclassical postulates and limiting himself to short run issues where the size and composition of the capital stock and the labour force as well as the skills, attitudes and values of all 'agents' could be taken as given, Keynes was able to devise a measure of actual achievement relative to the short run resource constrained potential of the economy. It was argued above, however, that the set of potential development paths of an economy which is constrained only by initial conditions and physical and physiological resources, is unknown and unknowable. There is no way therefore – even in principle – of measuring the performance of an economy over some period of time relative to its 'potential'. One may try to estimate the likely effects of some specified change in the social organization of the economy on the time path of the economy; i.e. one may compare the predicted 'no change path' with the predicted path following the specified change.[21] But the larger the change, the more uncertain the conclusions, and changes in social organization will in general entail changes in attitudes and preferences which further complicate the comparison.

With respect to an open regional/national economy there is an additional reason for the impossibility of devising an absolute measure of potential development. The development path of an open economy must inevitably be influenced by what goes on in the rest of the economic system which it is part of. This 'complication', however, also creates the possibility of comparing the development paths of different regions and investigating whether endogenous forces of the prevailing socio-economic structure lead to a concentration of economic growth and development on some regions and (relative) decline in other regions, or whether they tend to produce a uniform level of development in all regions. The definition of regional vicious and virtuous circles given above relates to this kind of evaluation of the extent to which the world-wide economic system is conducive to economic development in different regions. The notions of regional vicious/virtuous circles, thus, are based on inter-regional comparisons within a given socio-economic structure.

An assessment of the effects of the socio-economic structure on regional development must be based on a theory which separates basic socio-economic causes from the influence of 'other factors' (e.g. natural resources, stochastic disturbances and political interventions). Endogenous socio-economic factors and 'other factors' will interact in their effects on development. The separation therefore cannot take the simple form of allocating, say, 50 per cent of a region's economic growth over some time period to socio-economic factors and the remainder to 'other factors'. The separation must consist in a theoretical explanation of the dynamic interaction between different factors which produced the outcome. It is therefore only in the context of a fully articulated theoretical model that the notion of vicious circles can be given a precise meaning.[22]

Consider for instance the simple Kaldor–Myrdal model. The industrial centre which initially happened to have the lowest profitability would subsequently experience the effects of a vicious circle. The precise meaning of vicious circle is quite clear here: the vicious circle consists in (i) the tendency for investment and growth to take place where profitability is high and (ii) the fact that investment and output growth determine the growth of labour productivity with the implication that initial difference in profitability will be exacerbated. Uniformity in the movement of money wages in different regions, profit induced investment, interregional mobility of money capital for investment, and dynamic increasing returns to scale are the socio-economic factors behind the vicious circle.

Some degree of vagueness is inherent in all terms which attempt to capture and describe the content of a general outlook (or vision, paradigm, research programme). The notions of 'general equilibrium approach' or 'monetarism', for instance suffer from a similar lack of precision. And the vagueness of 'vicious circle' does not imply that the term will not be useful. Giving a name to something may be a necessary first step: the name, the conceptualization, may guide and stimulate further research.[23]

SUMMARY AND CONCLUSIONS

The Kaldor–Myrdal approach asserts the central importance of factors which are ruled out *a priori* in orthodox theory. Prominent among these factors are (i) the existence of hidden unemployment and (ii) increasing returns to scale in industry. In this paper I have tried to argue that these factors may have implications not just for specific neoclassical models but for the appropriate general theoretical framework of analysis.

Where neoclassical economics see only exogenous constraints and given preferences, Kaldor–Myrdal see socio-economic factors interacting with truly exogenous constraints of nature. Where neoclassical theorists see questions of allocation of given resources between competing ends, Kaldor–Myrdal see questions of the creation of resources: the economic system constantly transmits impulses to change and the changes are not just movements along some exogenously given frontier. The behaviour of agents changes as a result of the signals they receive; the signals cause revision of perceived constraints as well as of general attitudes and preferences. And changes in the behaviour of agents have effects on the socio-economic factors which influence (or 'constrain') the path of the economy. The absence of well-defined and binding exogenous constraints implies that sequential patterns become vitally important.[24] If the economy were always at or near some well-defined exogenous constraints then the socio-economic factors could 'only' influence the exact position of the economy along the exogenous constraint boundary. Nature or God-given physical constraints can be expected to have permanence (relative to the time scale of human activity). These constraints can therefore be stated in static or timeless form, and if they exert a powerful influence on economic outcomes then economic theory might also be cast in static simultaneous form.

Without binding exogenous constraints (and with an unknown position of the exogenous constraints), the 'relevant constraints' will be socio-economic in character. And the constraints imposed by the manner in which the social interaction of agents takes place, cannot be understood without regard for the time dimension. The law of gravity may be equally valid in 1066 and 1985, but the outcome of an industrial dispute cannot be understood on the basis of a simple listing of 'events' which have taken place; the time ordering of the sequence of events is crucial.

The essence of the Kaldor–Myrdal approach was put succinctly by Young (1928), very early on, indeed! Modifying Smith's famous dictum, he stated that 'the division of labour depends in large part upon the division of labour' (p. 533). This as Young argued, is more than a tautology. It means that economic activity is not in general constrained by exogenous resources. The division of labour is both cause and effect in a dynamic process, a chain reaction, where the socio-economic system transmits signals and the responses of agents produce new signals which induce new responses. The chain reaction may sometimes (or in some regions) proceed at a fast pace and at other times (or in other regions) at a slow pace. The absence of known and well-defined exogenous constraints on economic activity implies that the emphasis in economic theory must be on the socio-economic factors which shape the chain reaction of economic development. This is the central message of the Kaldor–Myrdal approach.

NOTES

I wish to thank Philip Arestis, Paul Auerbach, Victoria Chick and Peter Swann for helpful comments on an earlier draft.

1. Cf. the celebrated Leontief paradox. The debate which followed the publication of Leontief's original paper, Leontief (1953), is surveyed in Chipman (1966) and Bhagwati (1965).
2. Blaug (1980) goes as far as to argue that 'the assessment of the Ohlin–Samuelson research program thus cannot be separated from the assessment of the wider Hicks–Samuelson–Arrow–Debreu general equilibrium research program of which it forms an integral part' (p. 213).
3. In particular Kaldor (1972); but see also Kaldor (1970, 1978).
4. Tobin (1960) expressed this in a rather extreme form. Defending neoclassical distribution theory, he argued that 'For all the flaws that Mr Kaldor detects in it, neoclassical theory is general; it will divide up the national product among 3 or 101 factors as well or as badly as between 2. Mr Kaldor's substitute should not do less' (p. 191).

5. This argument is developed in greater detail in Skott (1986).
6. The beloved textbook example of red cross parcels to inmates in a prison camp may serve as a case in point.
7. I.e. acts of consumption which in the light of subsequent information on trading possibilities are seen to be suboptimal.
8. A mathematical literature on learning does exist but whether it is interesting is perhaps an open question. It seems to me that agents are usually assumed to possess far too high a degree of rationality and computational powers while on the other hand important sources of information (e.g. direct communication with other agents and publicly available information in newspapers etc.) are neglected. Furthermore, analytical difficulties make the formal modelling of learning processes virtually impossible except in the very simplest of cases, and the relevance of the very simple cases to more interesting learning problems is not obvious.
9. 'Possible states' in the sense that they cannot be ruled out given the information presented above.
10. Assuming that one had reason to believe that the effects of direct personal domination of some agents over others or of theft and other violations of the rules of private property were insignificant.
11. Assuming that the scope for capital labour substitution is very limited once 'capital' has taken the specific forms decided as part of the investment decision, i.e. assuming that capital is of the putty-clay or clay-clay variety.
12. The analysis could easily be generalized to allow for more than two centres of production.
13. A more rigorous justification for the link between growth and profitability is given in Skott (1989a), (1989b).
14. The determination of p_m/p_a need not concern us here. See Skott (1983b) for a more complete specification of the Kaldor–Myrdal model.
15. Among others, Kaldor (1966), Rowthorn (1975), Gomulka (1971, 1982), Cornwall (1977), Parikh (1978).
16. This assumption implicitly restricts the applicability of the model to situations where the real wage rate (in terms of consumption goods) is above a certain minimum level.
17. Whether in fact it does will depend on the chosen measure of relative performance and on the exact specification of the output expansion functions, (2a) and (2b).
18. For the long run the indistinguishability assumption is less objectionable. A Citroen Visa may be different from a Mini Metro and in the short run demand may not be very sensitive to variations in the relative price. But the long run price elasticities of demand are likely to be high, and even if they are not and if, say, the production of Metro in the low productivity (high cost) country yielded higher profits then the Citroen designers would surely be able to come up with a new modified Metro look-alike. The possibility of changes in

the composition of output makes the specification of long run demand functions without perfect substitutability of goods from different regions very dubious. The problem therefore is not so much whether the (long run) demand function should stipulate perfect substitutability but whether it is at all reasonable to specify a stable long run demand function defined over regional 'goods' whose composition will change endogenously over time.

19. If firms do not adjust their production decisions then the impact effect on profitability of a cut in money wages will be the same as in the absence of product differentiation. Increased growth and a relative expansion of market shares, however, will require that firms lower their prices relative to the prices of firms in the other region.
20. This should not be taken to mean that substantial changes in efficiency wages and competitiveness cannot be effected. But where large economies are involved, extraordinary circumstances may be required in order to make the increase in competitiveness acceptable to other countries, and to make the concomitant decline in living standards acceptable to workers. The gross undervaluation of the German and Japanese currencies after the Second World War may be a case in point. This undervaluation may provide part of the explanation for the post-war economic 'miracle' in the two countries. It is unlikely that other countries would have accepted the undervaluation if circumstances had not been extraordinary, and only the effects of fascism and war on the strength of the working class made the large squeeze in living standards possible.
21. The change in question may be a relatively minor adjustment of an orthodox policy instrument or it may be more fundamental changes, e.g. land reforms or the nationalization of all major financial institutions. Ellman *et al* (1974) give an interesting attempt at quantifying the likely economic effects of some fundamental changes in the socio-economic structure.
22. An analogue may be the use of the term multiplier in short run Keynesian theory. Given a fully specified model of the economy, it is possible to work out exactly the effects on all variables of the model of an autonomous change in some variable. In general, a change in one variable will have effects on many, if not all, variables. The effects will be drawn out over time and the magnitude of the effects may not be a simple linear function of the size of the original change. Yet it may sometimes be convenient to refer to 'the multiplier'. Should this give rise to confusion, one may always go back to the fully specified model.
23. Kuhn's notion of 'paradigms' may illustrate this in more ways than one. Paradigm is one of the central concepts in Kuhn's work on the evolution of science. But the concept is not precisely defined. Masterman (1970) identified 21 different and partly contradictory uses of the term in Kuhn (1962). In spite of the lack of precision, the term paradigm and the various descriptions and analogies used by Kuhn to

give it content, conjured up something which many researchers (and non-researchers) felt they could recognize. It gave a name to 'something' and thereby facilitated further work on the way research is and should be carried out.

24. It is no accident that Keynes's theory departs from Walrasian general equilibrium theory with respect to both the appearance of socio-economic constraints on output and employment and the explicit attention to sequential patterns, cf. Skott (1983a).

REFERENCES

Bhagwati, J. (1965), 'The Pure Theory of International Trade: A Survey', in Royal Economic Society and American Economic Association, *Surveys of Economic Theory Vol. II* (Macmillan: London and Basingstoke).

Blaug, M. (1980), *The Methodology of Economics* (Cambridge University Press: Cambridge).

Chipman, J.S. (1966). 'A Survey of the Theory of International Trade: Part 3, the Modern Theory', *Econometrica*, Vol. 34 (January).

Cornwall, J. (1977), *Modern Capitalism* (Martin Robertson, Oxford).

Ellman, M., Rowthorn, R.E., Smith, R. and Wilkinson, F. (1974), *Britain's Economic Crisis* (Spokesman Pamphlets no 44: Nottingham).

Gomulka, S. (1971), *Inventive Activity, Diffusion and the Stages of Economic Growth* (Institute of Economics, University of Aarhus: Aarhus).

Gomulka, S. (1982), 'Kaldor's Stylized Facts, Dynamic Economies of Scale and Diffusional Effect in Productivity Growth' (Mimeo).

Kaldor, N. (1966), *Causes of the Slow Rate of Economic Growth in the UK* (Cambridge University Press: Cambridge).

Kaldor, N. (1970), 'The Case for Regional Policies', *Scottish Journal of Political Economy* (November).

Kaldor, N. (1972), 'The Irrelevance of Equilibrium Economics', *Economic Journal* (December).

Kaldor, N. (1978), 'Introduction', in N. Kaldor, *Further Essays on Economic Theory* (Duckworth: London).

Kalecki, M. (1971), *Selected Essays on the Dynamics of the Capitalist Economy* (Cambridge University Press: Cambridge).

Keynes, J.M. (1936), *The General Theory of Employment, Interest and Money* (Macmillan, Royal Economic Society edition, 1973: London and Basingstoke).

Kuhn, T.S. (1962), *The Structure of Scientific Revolutions* (University of Chicago Press: Chicago).

Kuznets, S. (1971), *Economic Growth of Nations* (Harvard University Press: Cambridge, Mass.).

Leontief, W. (1953), 'Domestic Production and Foreign Trade: The American Capital Position Re-examined', *Proceedings of the American Philosophical Society*, Vol. 97 (September).

de Marchi, N. (1976), 'Anomaly and the development of economics: the case of the Leontief paradox', in S. Latsis (ed), *Method and Appraisal in Economics* (Cambridge University Press: Cambridge).

Masterman, M. (1970), 'The Nature of a Paradigm', in I. Lakatos and A. Musgrave (eds), *Criticism and the Growth of Knowledge* (Cambridge University Press: Cambridge).

Myrdal, G. (1957), *Economic Theory and Underdeveloped Regions* (Duckworth: London).

Parikh, A. (1978), 'Differences in Growth Rates and Kaldor's Laws', *Economica*, Vol. 45 (February).

Rowthorn, R.E. (1975), 'What Remains of Kaldor's Law', *Economic Journal* (March).

Skott, P. (1983a), 'An Essay on Keynes and General Equilibrium Theory', *Thames Papers in Political Economy* (Summer).

Skott, P. (1983b), 'The Principle of Circular and Cumulative Causation' (Mimeo).

Skott, P. (1986), 'On General Equilibrium Theory, Rationality and the Costs of Spurious Generality', *British Review of Economic Issues*, Vol. 18.

Skott, P. (1989a), 'Effective Demand, Class Struggle and Cyclical Growth', *International Economic Review* (February).

Skott, P. (1989b), *Conflict and Effective Demand in Economic Growth* (Cambridge University Press: Cambridge).

Tobin, J. (1960), 'Towards a *General* Kaldorian Theory of Distribution', *Review of Economic Studies*, Vol. 27 (February).

Young, A.A. (1928), 'Increasing Returns and Economic Progress', *Economic Journal* (December).

Index

abstract theory (relevance), 273–4, 275, 276
accelerator effect, 71
Ackley, G., 111
Acs, Z., 200
adjustment costs, 70, 71
adjustment mechanism, 104, 107, 108, 113
administered prices doctrine, 8–10
  business cycle and, 213–17
  business enterprise and, 207–12
  economic activities and, 202–206
  inflation and, 212–13, 217
  influence and relevance, 199–202
  production and, 212–13
  summary and conclusion, 222–4
  visible hand of co-ordination, 220–22
administrative co-ordination, 204–5, 212–13
administrative inflation, 217, 218–19, 222
advanced sector, 270, 274
agent spaces, 275–6
aggregate concentration, 205–206
aggregate consumption, 66
aggregate demand, 171, 214–17, 219, 224, 252, 253, 260
  curve, 112
  function, 20–22, 33, 57–8, 110, 163
aggregate employment, 33
aggregate investment, 67–8
aggregate overheads, 241
aggregate supply
  curve, 112
  function, 20–22, 33, 57–8
  price, 66, 67
agriculture. 274, 288, 290
Alchian, A., 147, 148–9
Andrews, P.W.S., 199
'animal spirits', 26, 75, 283, 289
Arrow, K.J., 46, 47–8, 52
Arrow–Debreu model, 44, 50, 52, 272
Asimakopulos, A., 19, 32, 34, 229
Asimakopulos model, 232–3, 247
atomistic agents, 165, 166, 168
atomistic enterprise, 205–6, 207–8, 213–14
auctioneer, 49, 121, 165, 277
Auerbach, P., 131, 133, 175
average variable costs, 236, 239–40

backward sector, 270, 274, 281
Bade, R., 113
Bain, J., 141, 145–6
balance of payments, 287
balanced economy, 213, 216–17, 219
balanced price structure, 213, 216–17, 219
banking system, 29, 30, 31

Baran, P., 157, 172, 229
Barro, R.J., 49
'basic signals', 78
Baumol, W.J., 112
Beckerman, W., 252
Begg, D., 110, 111, 112
behavioural investment functions, 180
Benassy, J.P., 49
Blinder, A.S., 112
bonds, 53, 54
Branson, W., 110, 112
Bretton Woods agreement, 253, 287
Brown, A.J., 102, 252
Bukharin, N., 168
business cycle, 107
  administered prices and, 213–17
business enterprise, pricing and, 207–12
buyers and sellers, 158–9, 165

capacity utilization, 112, 171, 179–80, 182–4, 279
capital
  accumulation, 26, 35, 167–8
  centralization, 157, 158, 163, 167, 174, 184, 189
  concentration, 157, 158, 163, 167, 169, 173, 174, 184, 189
  goods, 21
  –labour ratio, 71, 148
  marginal efficiency of, 23, 24, 27
  mobility, 160–62, 164, 166–7, 173–4, 180, 183
  –output ratio, 175, 187
Capital and Growth (Hicks), 51, 52
capitalism (competition in), 157–8, 160–62, 164, 167–71, 173, 176, 189
cartels, 167
cash, 26, 30, 31
causa causans, 24, 29
Central Statistical Office, 12, 144
ceteris paribus clauses, 56
Chamberlain, E., 168
circular causation, 270, 271, 273, 291–4
circular flows, 203–5
Clarke, R., 132, 144
class struggle, 69, 169, 179, 245–6, 264
classical theory, 14–15, 25, 26
  of competition, 157–8, 164, 166, 173–6, 184–5, 189
Clifton, J., 174–5, 186, 187, 212
Clower, R.W., 48, 51, 55, 63, 72
co-ordination of economic activity, 202–6, 220–22
cobweb analysis, 82
Coddington, A., 50
collective bargaining, 120
collusion, 167, 172, 173–4, 241
commodities
  agent spaces and, 275–6
  competition and, 159, 160, 161, 162
  market delineation, 135, 137
  pricing, 199, 242, 253, 264, 277
communication networks, 174–5
comparative statics, 21–2, 36
competition, 7–8
  classical, 173–6
  concept evolution, 158–66
  corporate enterprise, 209, 211–12
  market structure and, 132–3, 139, 145, 147–9, 152
  monopoly power, 157–8, 166–73
  multi-sector model, 176–84
  multi-sector model (implications), 184–9
  perfect, 130–31, 137–8, 147, 150–51, 165, 168, 174
  Phillips curve, 120–21
concentration, *see* capital; industrial concentration; market concentration
conflict, 273, 275, 288
conjectural equilibrium, 45, 49–50, 51, 52
Conklin, M., 144, 145
consistent delineation, 133—4

consumer wants, 202–4, 220, 223
consumption, 263, 277–8
  expenditure, 33, 68–9, 77
  function, 66–7
  industries, 21
  levels, 70–71, 77, 79–80
contracts, 25
core-periphery relationship, 252–3
corporate community, 220–21
corporate enterprise, 205–6, 209–12, 215–16
corporate levy, 236–7, 239, 246
Corporate Revolution, The (Means), 199
cost-determined prices, 229, 230, 234, 252
cost-plus pricing, 235
costs
  adjustment, 70, 71
  average variable, 236, 239–40
  measurement, 239–42
  normal, 239–40, 241–2
  prime, 187, 231, 232–3, 239–42
  transport, 147–8, 149, 150
Coutts, K., 239
Cowling, K., 229, 241, 243–4, 245
Cowling model, 233–5, 244, 245, 247
crisis, 163, 171, 263
cross-elasticity of demand, 138–41
cumulative causation, 12–13
  introduction, 270–71
  Kaldor-Myrdal critique, 271–7
  Kaldor-Myrdal model, 284–90
  summary and conclusion, 295–6
  three model economies, 277–83
  vicious/virtuous circles, 291–4
current prices, 72–3

debt-equity ratio, 258
debts, 27
decision-making, 135
demand, 26
  –determined prices, 229, 230, 234, 252
  effective, 48, 57, 61, 62, 64, 279
  elasticity of, 138–41
  excess, 64, 107, 108, 113, 121, 123, 165
  management, 280, 285
  see also aggregate demand
Desai, M., 118
devaluation, 285, 286
disequilibrium, 46–7, 55, 60, 63, 64, 105–6, 161
division of labour, 274, 296
Dmitriev, V., 163
Domberger, S., 239
Dornbusch, R., 110, 111, 112
'double competition', 159
Drèze, J., 49
Dutt, A.K., 188
dynamic efficiency, 289
dynamic increasing returns, 274, 291

economic activity, 116
  co-ordination, 201–2, 220–22
  inflation and, 107
  structure, 202–6
economic theory, uncertainty and, 146–9
economies of scale, 167, 244
effective demand, 48, 57, 61, 62, 279
effective excess demand, 64
efficiency, 289
Eichner, Alfred, 199, 239, 240, 241
Eichner model, 8–9, 11, 235–9, 244–50, 255–8, 260, 262, 263
elasticity of demand, 138–41
employment
  administered prices and, 212–13
  full, 14, 19, 22, 47, 48, 82, 101, 216, 221–3, 263
  Keynes's general theory, 18–22, 33–4
  see also labour; labour market; unemployment
endogenous
  economic forces, 270, 274, 290
  technical progress, 274, 280
Engels, Friedrich, 167

engineering rated capacity, 235–6
entry barriers, 135, 145–6, 161, 164, 244–5, 256
entry effect, 237, 248, 249, 261, 263
equalization (rates of profit), 160, 163–5, 175, 177, 180, 183, 185–7
equilibrium (in General Theory), 32–5
ex ante, 59, 60
  delineation, 135, 136, 137, 149–50
  investment, 24, 27
ex post, 59, 60
  delineation, 135, 136, 149–50
  investment, 24, 27, 30, 31
excess capacity, 68, 110, 145–6, 167, 179, 181–3, 189, 260, 263, 279
excess demand, 64, 107, 108, 113, 121, 123, 165
excess supply, 112, 165
exchange
  economy (pure), 277–8, 291
  process, 55
  rate adjustment policies, 286, 287
  value, 162
exit barriers (capital), 161
exogenous
  constraints, 278, 283, 288–9, 291, 295–6
  resources, 275, 280–81, 291–2
  shocks, 12, 270, 286
expectations, 70, 250
  –augmented Phillips curve, 114–16, 121–2
  long-term, 18, 22–4, 34, 75–6, 249
  of proceeds, 20, 82
  short-term, 17–19, 21, 34, 59–61, 75–6, 249
expected future costs, 239
expected rates of return, 232–3
external increasing returns, 274

factor endowments, 275, 291–2
false consumption, 277
false investments, 283
false trading, 277, 283
fast growing centre, 284, 286
finance
  Keynes's General Theory, 25–32
  Kaleckian model, 256–61
firms
  behaviour, market structure and, 145–51
  short-period equilibrium, 32–3
first-in-first-out methods, 239
Fischer, S., 110, 111
Fisher, I., 103, 109, 112
fix-price models, 45, 47–50, 52, 64
fix-wage equilibrium, 63, 73, 74
fixed-interest securities, 27
flex-price equilibria, 47–8, 50, 52
flow principle of production, 210–11
forward markets, 64–5
'free lunch', 121–2
free market, 288
Friedman, M., 105, 106, 121, 148
full employment, 14, 19, 22, 47–8, 82, 101, 216, 221–3, 263
full equilibrium, 56
fundamental theory, 2, 15

g-functions, 289–90
gearing ratio, 257–8, 259–60
general equilibrium theory, 272–3, 275–7, 294
  GE–Keynesianism, 46–50
  GE–Keynesianism (origins), 51–4
  introduction, 43–5
  Keynes and Marshall, 55–9
  money wages (changes), 63–74
  short-run equilibrium, 74–83
  short-run unemployment equilibrium, 59–63
General Theory (Keynes)
  employment theory, 18–22
  introduction, 14–16

investment determination, 22–4
money and finance, 25–32
setting of analysis, 2–3, 17–18
time and equilibrium, 32–5, 36
generality (general equilibrium theory), 276
Glick, 176, 186
goals, 204, 205, 212
Godley, W., 239
Goldstein, H., 144, 145
Gordon, R.J., 110
government intervention, 237, 248–9, 287
government policy, 169
Great Depression, 201
Grossman, H.E., 49
growth
g-functions, 289–90
Kaldorian model, 76, 173

Hahn, F.H., 45, 46, 47–52
hand–waving, 112
Harcourt, G.C., 235, 239
'harmony predilection', 273, 275
Harrod, R.F., 34, 119
Hart, P., 132, 144–5
Hayek, F., 130
Heckscher–Ohlin–Samuelson theory, 271–2
Henry, S.G.B., 114
Herfindahl index, 234, 242
Hicks, J.R., 21, 23, 24, 29, 56, 73
GE–Keynesianism, 51–4
Hilferding, R., 157, 167, 185
Hines, A.G., 104
historic costs, 239
historical time, *see* time
Hodgson, G.M., 200
homogeneous product, 165, 166, 168

IMF, 253
import controls, 287
imports, 150
income distribution
Kaldorian model, 76
macrodynamics and, 253–6
steady–state models and, 261–2
incomes policy, 111
increasing returns, 274, 291
independent specification, 134
Industrial Census, 142–5
industrial concentration, 179, 244–5
changes in, 256–61
Herfindahl index, 234, 242
under uncertainty, 247, 250–51, 263
industrial policy, 220–22
industrial pricing, 199
industrial reserve army, 108
industry, 281
defence of, 141–5
homogeneity, 144
see also market structure
inflation, 32
administered prices and, 199, 212–13, 217–19, 223
economic activity and, 107
non–accelerating inflation rate of unemployment, 101, 112–16
Phillips curve, 100–104, 109–12, 118–19, 121–2
information, perfect, 166
input–output ratios, 178, 185
interest groups, 221
interest rate, 24, 25, 26–7, 28, 29, 31
implicit, 244–5, 246, 248–50, 256
'intermediate' theory, 151
international trade
markets and, 149–51
theory, 271–2
intertemporal efficiency, 289
intertemporal equilibrium, 272, 290
intrinsic value, 158
investment
–demand schedule, 23, 24, 27, 36
general equilibrium theory, 66, 68, 70, 71, 76–9

Kaleckian theory, 168, 170–72, 230, 232–3, 235–9, 256–63
Keynes's General Theory, 20–24, 26, 29–33, 36
marginal efficiency of, 237, 246, 249, 261
'invisible hand' process, 133
IS–LM model, 53–4, 73–4, 118

Jenkinson, T., 252
joint stock companies, 167

Kaldor, N., 31–2, 45, 139–40, 252
short-run equilibrium, 74–83
Kaldor–Myrdal model, 12–13, 270, 281–3, 294, 295–6
critique of neoclassical theory, 271–7
Kaldor–Pasinetti equation, 12, 261–2
Kalecki, M., 24, 75, 157–8, 168, 170–71, 176, 179–180, 187, 199, 223, 279
Kaleckian pricing theory, 229–35
comparison with post-Keynesian, 10–11, 239–46
macroeconomic implications, 252–63
uncertainty in, 247–51
Kenyon, P., 235, 239
Keynes, J.M., 279–80, 281,293
General Theory, see General Theory (Keynes)
Treatise on Money, 14, 27, 60–61
Keynes, J.M. and General Equilibrium theory, 3–4, 43–5
GE–Keynesianism, 46–50
GE–Keynesianism, (origins), 51–4
Kaldor and, 74–83
Marshall and, 55–9
kinked demand curve, 122
Knight, F., 165
Kregel, J.A., 235
Kriesler, P., 200
Kuznets, S., 270

labour
contracts, 64–5
direct, 232, 245
division of, 274, 296
indirect, 232, 254
mobility, 159–60
supply, 47, 65
labour market, 62, 64–5
disequilibrium, 105–6, 108
equilibrium, 33, 69
Law of Demand, 118
Lee, F.S., 240–41
Leijonhufvud, A., 48, 55, 66
Lenin, V., 157, 168, 173–4
Levine, D.P., 200, 235
limit pricing, 247
Lipsey, R.G., 102, 104–5, 112, 118–20, 122, 124
liquidity, 26, 28
lack of, 30
preference function, 25–6, 29
loanable funds, 29
long-period, 31, 56
equilibrium, 33–4
expectations, 18, 22–3, 24, 34, 75–6, 249
'losers', 287–8
Lucas, R.E., 63, 109
Lucas critique, 107

McCloskey, D.N., 117–18
McNulty, P., 158
macrodynamics, 253–6
macreoconomic implications (pricing models), 252–63
mainstream theory, 130, 131, 151–2
market delineation and, 133–8
Malinvaud, E., 49
Mann, H.M., 146
manufacturing industry, 132, 142–4, 274
Marchi, N. de, 272
marginal efficiency of capital, 23, 24, 27
marginal efficiency of investment, 237, 246, 249, 261

marginal productivity principle, 201
marginal propensity to consume, 21
marginalism, 164–5
mark-up, 1–2, 229, 232–42, 244–8, 250–54, 256–7, 261–4
market analysis, 136–7, 151–2
  attack and defence, 138–45
market concentration, 131–3, 135, 150–51, 205–6, 207
market delineation, 131–2, 149–50, 151
  alternative approaches, 134–8
  problem of, 133–4
market failure, 4, 138, 280
market mechanism, 204, 206, 221
market structure, 6–7
  introduction, 130–32
  market analysis, 138–45, 151–2
  market delineation, 133–8, 151, 152
  structure-behaviour interaction, 145–51
markets, international trade and, 149–51
Marshall, Alfred, 206
  Keynes and, 2, 3, 16, 17, 32, 33, 55–9, 81–2
Marx, Karl, 108, 158, 160–64, 167, 171, 176
Means, G.C., 8–10
  influence/relevance, 199–202
  see also administered prices doctrine
megacorp, 199–200, 224, 236, 243, 258
Megacorp and Oligopoly, the (Eichner), 199–200, 224
mergers, 166, 167
middlemen, 52, 55
Millstein, J., 151
minimalism, 148, 149
modernism, 117
monetarism, 294
monetary inflation, 217, 218
money
  circular flow, 203–5
  competition and, 162–3
  illusion, 68
  Keynes's General Theory, 25–32
  supply, 28, 30, 31
monopolistic competition, 139, 158, 159, 163
monopoly, degree of, 1, 169, 230–33, 241–2, 244–5, 251, 254–6, 259–64
monopoly capitalism, 132, 157
monopoly power, 157–8, 166–72, 238–9
  classical competition and, 173–6
  multi-sector model, 176–84
  multi-sector model (implications), 184–9
monopoly price, 160
Morgan, E., 150
Moss, S., 200
Mott, T., 257
multiplier effect 3, 20–21, 24, 29, 30, 34, 122
Mulvey, C., 117, 123
Myrdal, G., 271–3
  see also Kaldor–Myrdal model

National Recovery Administration, 222
'near-monies', 25
'neo-classical synthesis', 2, 48
neoclassical theory, 36
  of competition, 164–6, 168–9, 173–4
  Kaldor–Myrdal critique, 271–7
'neutral development', 293
'new monies', 28
Nordhaus, W., 239
normal costs, 239–40, 241–2
notional demand, 48

objectives (Kaleckian/post-Keynesian models), 242–4
Ohlin, B., 29
oligopolistic interdependence, 230, 241, 247, 251

oligopoly, 120, 122–3, 145–6, 173–4, 223, 249
Ong, N., 235
open economy, 293
'orthodox theory', 14, 15, 16, 36
  Kaldor–Myrdal critique, 271–7
outcomes, 148–9, 275
output, 34–5, 66, 68, 69
  Kaleckian theory, 170–71, 172, 173
overheads, 231, 232, 241
overproduction, 163
Oxford Economists' Research Group, 199

Pareto optimality, 165, 273, 289
Parkin, J.M. 113
partial equilibrium analysis, 4, 57–8, 168, 276
Penrose, E.T., 243
period analysis, 55–6, 59, 83
  see also long-period; short-period; ultra-short period
perverse pricing, 215, 219
Philips, L., 132
Phillips, A., 145–6
Phillips critique, 145–6
Phillips curve (political economy of), 5–6
  alternative concepts, 105–9
  introduction, 100-101
  natural rate of unemployment, 113–16
  origins, 101–4
  popularity/influence, 117–24
  summary and conclusions, 124–5
  textbook treatment, 109–13
Pigou, A.C., 15
Pigou effect, 66, 68
political economy of Phillips curve,
  see Phillips curve (political economy of)
positivist methodology, 117
post-Keynesian pricing theories, 1
  comparison with Kaleckian model, 10–11, 239–30
  introduction, 229–30
  macreoconomic implications, 252–63
  models, 235–9
  uncertainty in, 247–51
'potential development', 293
power relations, 157, 168, 172, 176, 177, 183, 185
Prais, S., 152
price(s)
  administered, 175, 188–9
  determination, 176–7, 185–9
  interest rate as, 26, 29
  Keynes's General Theory, 19–22, 26, 29
  –leadership hypothesis, 247–51, 256, 263
  market delineation and, 137–8, 141
  mechanism, 46, 62
  monopoly, 168–9, 173, 175–6
  Phillips curve, 101–3, 106–7, 109, 112–13, 118, 120–21, 123
  of production model, 157–8, 161–4, 173, 175, 177–89
  –takers, 165, 166, 168, 183
  theory (competition role), 158–66
  see also administered prices doctrine; fix-price models; flex-price equilibria
pricing, business enterprise and, 207–12
Pricing Power and the Public Interest (Means), 199
pricing theories, 10–12
  comparison, 239–46
  conclusion, 264–5
  Kaleckian models, 230–35
  macroeconomic implications, 252–63
  post-Keynesian models, 235–9
  uncertainty, 247–51
primary sector, 274
prime costs, 187, 231, 232–3, 239–42

proceeds, 19–20
product
categories, 143–4
differentiation, 130, 145, 146, 285–6
homogeneous, 165, 166, 168
production
administered prices and, 212–13
cycles, 77
economy, 278–81, 291
flow principle, 210–11
possibility sets, 275, 289
prices of, 157–8, 161–4, 173, 175, 177–89
structure, 203–4
productive capacity, 34–5
productivity, 201
growth, 107, 112, 116
profits, 24, 131, 132, 147
competition and, 158–61, 163–6
equalization and, 160, 163–5, 175, 177, 180, 183, 185–7
mark-up *see* mark-up
in pricing theory , 229, 232–47, 254–5
propensity to consume, 20,21
propensity to save, 24
proxy price, 214
Pulling, K., 175

qualitative delineation, 133
quantity constraints, 49–50, 62, 64
Quesnay, F., 158

Rapping, L.A., 109
rate of return, 27
target, 1, 222, 223, 233
rationing schemes, 49
realism, 276–7
recontracting, 277
reflation, 217
regional growth, 272, 291–4
regression analysis, 122, 124
rents, 158, 159
'resolving fund', 31
resource(s)
allocation, 273
constrained exchange economy, 291–3
exogenous, 275, 280–81, 291–2
natural, 288–9
structure, 203
use of, 220, 221, 280–81
restricted equilibrium, 56
Riach, P., 233
Ricardo, D., 160–61, 162, 164, 201
risk, 27, 248–51, 256–7, 260–61, 263
Robertson, D.H., 29
Robinson, J., 17, 27, 35, 55, 75, 168, 233
Routh, G., 103, 123
rules, 204, 205, 212
'rules of the game', 288

sales revenue, 249
Samuelson, P., 15, 107, 110, 111
saving, 24, 26, 29–32, 76
Kaleckian model, 168, 170, 172
Sawyer, M., 100, 105, 109, 114, 117, 144, 200, 229, 234, 243
Say's Law, 26, 48, 162, 171
Scherer, F., 148
Schwartz, J., 163
self-expansion, 173
self-interest, 291
'self-liquidating' finance, 30
self-regulation, 201
self-seeking behaviour, 148–9
sellers and buyers, 158–9, 165
Semmler, W., 173, 174, 175–6, 186–7, 200
sequential patterns
Kaldor–Myrdal model, 273, 275, 284, 286, 290
Keynes's analysis, 3–4, 44–5, 72–4, 76, 79–84, 281
service sector, 274
Shaikh, A., 174
Shapiro, N., 235
Sherman, H., 175, 186
short-period
equilibrium, 31, 45, 74–83

expectations, 17–19, 21, 34, 59–61, 75–6, 249
Keynes's analysis, 17–19, 21, 23–4, 32–4, 36, 55–6, 62, 67, 73
macroeconomics, 252–3
unemployment equilibrium, 44–5, 59–63
simultaneous equilibrium, 273, 280
Skott, P., 131, 175, 281
slow growing regions, 284–5, 286, 287
Smith, Adam, 158, 159, 160–61, 162, 164, 201, 274
Smith, P., 114
Social Darwinism, 147
social factors, 289
social welfare function, 117, 121, 122
socio-economic structure, 13, 294, 295
Solow, R., 107
source ratio, 258–9
'speculators', 31
Spence, A., 146
Spence, M., 245
spillover effects, 48, 64
Sraffa, P., 163–4
Sraffian model, 178, 182, 189
stability analysis, 63, 64, 70–71
stabilization policy, 264
stagnation, 167, 172, 173, 223, 263, 265
standard average total cost, 210–11
standard operating ration, 235–6, 239
static equilibrium, 3
static increasing returns, 274
steady-state models, 12, 250, 261–2, 264
Steindl, J., 157, 158, 171, 176, 179, 180, 199, 229, 255, 259–60, 263
Steiner, P., 137
Steuart, J., 158
Stigler, G., 122, 131
structuralism, *see* market structure
substitutability, 28, 47, 141
substitution effect, 237, 244, 246, 248, 261, 263
Sumner, M.T., 102, 117, 119, 123
supply
constraints, 280–81, 288, 289, 291
excess, 112, 165
see also aggregate supply
surprise supply function, 103, 109
Sweezy, P., 122, 157, 172, 177, 229
Sylos–Labini, P., 172, 200

target rate of return, 1, 222, 223, 233
tatonnement process, 46–7, 49–50, 55, 64
Taylor, J., 123
technical efficiency, 289
technical progress, 274, 279, 280
temporary equilibrium, 4, 45, 46, 47–8, 51–2, 64, 73–4, 81
'terminal state', 278–9
Thirlwall, A., 102
time, 2–3, 134
consistent delineation, 133–4
Keynes's General Theory, 15–16, 26, 27, 32–5, 36
see also period analysis
trade cycle, 120, 241, 280
trade unions, 102, 108, 119, 120, 231, 245–6
transactions model, 133, 136
transport costs, 147–8, 149, 150
Treatise on Money (Keynes), 14, 27, 60–61
Trevithick, J.A., 117, 123
trust, 167
Turgot, A., 158
Turnovsky, S., 107

ultra-short period, 55, 56, 60–61, 75, 76
uncertainty, 25–6, 27

in market, 146–9
pricing theories, 242–3, 247–51, 260–61, 263–4
underconsumption, 167, 263
unemployment, 19, 167, 216, 280
equilibrium, 47–8, 58–63, 69–73, 279
hidden, 284, 295
involuntary, 4, 44, 59–63, 83, 279, 291, 292
natural rate, 101, 106, 111, 113–16
Phillips curve, 101, 105–6, 108, 110–16, 118–23
voluntary, 61, 62, 63
very long run, 262–3
wages and, 69, 107, 113–16
Utton, M., 145, 150

Value and Capital (Hicks), 51–3, 54
value theory, 162
Varga, E., 173–4
Veblen, T., 167
Vicarelli, F., 26
vicious circles, 12–13, 291–4
virtuous circles, 291–4

wages, 19, 22, 25
change (Phillips curve), 101–6, 108, 112, 113, 118–23 *passim*
competition and, 159, 160, 163
Kaldor–Myrdal model, 284–6, 292
mark-up and, 2, 245–6, 261
money, 47, 49, 58, 61–2
money (changes), 63–74
sticky, 61, 62, 73
unemployment and, 69, 107, 113–16
Walras' Law, 48, 54
Walrasian auctioneer, 49, 121, 165, 277
Walrasian equilibrium, 4, 64, 278
Walshe, G., 145
Ward, R., 123
Ware, C.F., 206
Waterson, M., 131, 233, 241, 243
wealth, 25, 26, 69, 70
Weeks, J., 174
Weintraub, E.R., 43, 238–9
Weiss, L., 149
Wiles, P., 119
Williamson, O., 146
'winners', 287–8
Wood, A., 235, 239
working class, 69, 169
World Bank, 253
world economy, 274
Worswick, D., 115

x–efficiency, 289

Young, Allyn, 274, 296

Printed and bound in Great Britain at
The Camelot Press Ltd, Southampton